Globalizing the Soybean

Globalizing the Soybean asks how the soybean conquered the West and analyzes why and how the crop gained entry into agriculture and industry in regions beyond Asia in the first half of the twentieth century.

Historian Ines Prodöhl describes the soybean's journey centered on three hubs: Northeast China, as the crop's main growing area up to the Second World War; Germany, to where most of the beans in the interwar period were shipped; and the United States, which became the leading cultivator of soy worldwide during the 1940s. This book explores the German and U.S. adoption of the soybean being closely tied to global economic and political changes, such as the two world wars and the Great Depression. The attraction of the soybean to stakeholders on both sides of the Atlantic was linked to a need for cheap alternatives to butter and lard and a desire for greater quantities of meat, which led to the soybean becoming a cheap resource for fat and fodder. Only occasionally was it also used as food.

This volume is useful for anyone who is studying or interested in economic history and commodity trading in the twentieth century. It is also connected to the histories of capitalism, globalization, imperialism, and materiality.

Ines Prodöhl is associate professor in history at the University of Bergen, Norway. She specializes in modern economic and global history and has published many works on the history of soybeans and fat.

Routledge Studies in Modern History

Narratives of Dictatorship in the Age of Revolution
Emotions, Power and Legitimacy in the Atlantic Space
Moisés Prieto

Political Power and Colonial Development in British Central Africa 1938-1960s
Alan H. Cousins

How the Church Under Pius XII Addressed Decolonization
The Issue of Algerian Independence
Marialuisa Lucia Sergio

Overseas Economic Relations and Statehood in Europe, 1860s–1970s
Shaping the World, Making the Nation
Gerold Krozewski

Khoesan and Imperial Citizenship in Nineteenth Century South Africa
Jared McDonald

Antisemitism Before the Holocaust
Re-Evaluating Antisemitic Exceptionalism in Germany and the United States, 1880-1945
Richard E. Frankel

Labour in the Suburbs
Political Change in Croydon During the Twentieth Century
Michael Tichelar

Globalizing the Soybean
Fat, Feed, and Sometimes Food, c. 1900–1950
Ines Prodöhl

For more information about this series, please visit: www.routledge.com/Routledge-Research-in-Modern-History/book-series/MODHIST

Globalizing the Soybean

Fat, Feed, and Sometimes Food, c. 1900–1950

Ines Prodöhl

Routledge
Taylor & Francis Group
LONDON AND NEW YORK

First published 2023
by Routledge
4 Park Square, Milton Park, Abingdon, Oxon OX14 4RN

and by Routledge
605 Third Avenue, New York, NY 10158

Routledge is an imprint of the Taylor & Francis Group, an informa business

British Library Cataloguing-in-Publication Data
A catalogue record for this book is available from the British Library

Library of Congress Cataloging-in-Publication Data
Names: Prodöhl, Ines, author.
Title: Globalizing the soybean : fat, feed, and sometimes food, c. 1900-1950 / Ines Prodöhl.
Description: Abingdon, Oxon ; New York, NY : Routledge, 2023. | Series: Routledge studies in modern history | Includes bibliographical references and index.
Identifiers: LCCN 2022056576 (print) | LCCN 2022056577 (ebook) | ISBN 9781032185767 (hardback) | ISBN 9781032185798 (paperback) | ISBN 9781003255222 (ebook)
Subjects: LCSH: Soybean industry--History--20th century. | Soybean--History--20th century. | Soybean as feed--History--20th century. | Soyfoods--History--20th century.
Classification: LCC HD9235.S6 P76 2023 (print) | LCC HD9235.S6 (ebook) | DDC 338.1/7334--dc23/eng/20221208
LC record available at https://lccn.loc.gov/2022056576
LC ebook record available at https://lccn.loc.gov/2022056577

ISBN: 978-1-032-18576-7 (hbk)
ISBN: 978-1-032-18579-8 (pbk)
ISBN: 978-1-003-25522-2 (ebk)

DOI: 10.4324/9781003255222

Typeset in Times New Roman
by KnowledgeWorks Global Ltd.

Contents

Illustrations

Map

Figures

A Note on Measuring Units, Currencies, and Romanization

In the past and the present, the quantity of soybeans has been indicated either by weight or by volume, although historically units of weight were more common. Most statistics I worked with measured soybeans in metric tons (one metric ton equals 36.74 bushels soybeans). Thus, I have decided to convert all indications of quantities, including those for other commodities, to the metric system. Distances and areas are given in miles and acres. I kept currencies according to the source. Names, places, and terms appear in Western spelling only. Places that over time have changed national affiliations, and with that their name or spelling, are referred to in their present forms unless quoted or part of a reference. I chose the Russian names for the rivers which form the Russian–Chinese border, Amur and Ussuri.

Acknowledgments

Several years ago, I joined forces with colleague Frank Grüner to test research ideas and scholarly concepts regarding the history of Northeast China. While I worked on European business and knowledge history, Frank was specialized on Eastern European history, and we were both eager to extend our fields of expertise. The Cluster of Excellence "Asia and Europe in a Global Context" at the University of Heidelberg provided us with the means to do so and allowed us to bring together a set of international scholars working on the history of Northeast China. I am grateful for the cluster's support and the encouraging discussions with Frank, and also those with Dan Ben-Canaan, Madeleine Herren-Oesch, and Heinz-Dietrich Löwe, among other colleagues.

It was in this stimulating environment that I for the first time considered the transfer of goods between Europe and Asia as a research topic. However, I finally decided to work on the history of the soybean in the years to come for rather private reasons. I cherished the unspoken wish to bring my rural upbringing in northern Germany to terms with my urban, academic life, and the soybean seemed to provide me with such an opportunity. For sure, the beans were never grown in Vorpommern when I was a child; nevertheless, they enabled me to combine my profession as a historian with my interest in agriculture, gardening, and botany that my parents had once nurtured. I am thankful to them not only for opening my eyes to the manifoldness and beauty of nature but also for providing me with an understanding of what it means to work the land and make a living from it.

Most of the research for this book was conducted at the German Historical Institute in Washington, D.C. I am thankful to directors Hartmut Berghoff and Simone Lässig for supporting my work. Each work of research thrives when it is discussed with other scholars, and the members of the institute's scientific advisory board as well as my former colleagues have provided exactly the right kind of intellectual exchange that allowed me to develop my ideas further. Special thanks to Uta A. Balbier, Clelia Caruso, Philipp Gassert, Mischa Honeck, Dirk Hoerder, Stephan Hördler, David Lazar, Friedrich Lenger, Jan Logemann, Christina Lubinsky, Alexander Nützenadel, Anke Ortlepp, Mark Stoneman, Patricia Casey Sutcliffe, Corinna Unger, and

Richard Wetzell. In addition, I am indebted to the institute's librarians and many interns who assisted me in finding literature and collecting data.

At the University of Munich, my thanks go to Roland Wenzlhuemer for getting me on board a research project funded by the German Research Foundation. I very much enjoyed the stimulating intellectual environment and the open atmosphere I encountered there. During the years in D.C. and Munich, I was able to publish several articles on the history of the soybean. In this monograph, I engage with these earlier texts, but none of them are replicated here. In fact, this book was written not least because Robert Langham from Routledge reached out. Thanks for doing so and for attending to the entire publishing process. I would also like to thank Adam King, who tirelessly dealt with my language quirks.

The University of Bergen provided me with the funding to publish this book open access. The manuscript has in large parts been written at the university's Department of Archeology, History, Cultural Studies, and Religion. Thanks to my colleagues for providing me with the time that has made it possible to complete this project. I had the chance to discuss earlier versions of some chapters with the members of the research group "Transnational History and Cultural Encounters," and I am thankful for their careful readings and considerate comments. Likewise, thanks to the Department of Modern History and Society at NTNU Trondheim for inviting me to discuss my work.

Writing a scholarly monograph is, just as all other work, hardly possible without the backing of colleagues and friends. Besides those already mentioned, I would like to thank Ruth Ammann, Camilla Brautaset, Yngve Flo, Berit Gehrke, Christhard Hoffmann, Elisabeth Mait, Pål Thonstad Sandvik, and Frode Ulvund for their generous private and professional support in recent years. Last but not least, I am deeply indebted to Christoph Bottin and our boys Jasper and Paul. Thanks for patiently being there with me through all the ups and downs of this project.

List of Abbreviations

ADM	Archer Daniels Midland
ASA	American Soybean Association
BPI	Bureau of Plant Industry
CER	Chinese Eastern Railway
CFB	Combined Food Board
FAO	Food and Agricultural Organization of the United Nations
FAOSTAT	Food and Agricultural Organization Statistics
IIA	International Institute of Agriculture
OPA	Office of Price Administration
PL480	Public Law 480
NSDAP	National Socialist German Workers' Party
SMR	South Manchurian Railway
USDA	United States Department of Agriculture
WFA	War Food Administration
WPB	War Production Board

Introduction

Soybeans have been consumed by humans since the Neolithic period. Biologists trace present-day varieties back to a wild soybean plant that was domesticated in East Asia about 6,000–9,000 years ago.[1] Yet, it took most of this exceptionally long period before the crop found its way to other continents, either by accident or by design. Up until the early twentieth century, soybean cultivation, trade, and consumption largely remained within its Asian origins. Back in ancient times, human migration occurred more slowly and to a lesser extent, but once people encountered different parts of the world in the modern period, they took crops, animals, and diseases along with them. Rice has been a staple all over the world for centuries. The Columbian exchange brought sugar, horses, and syphilis from the Old World to the New and shipped potatoes and tobacco, among many other living organisms, in the opposite direction.[2] In modern times also East Asia gained the attention of European sea voyagers in their search for new trading routes and business opportunities. In the sixteenth century, Portuguese and later Spanish and Dutch merchants brought spices, tea, and silk to European customers, but none considered the soybean a valuable commodity for trade. To be sure, they—as well as missionaries, diplomats, and migrants—also introduced the soybean and foods derived from it, but the scope of this transfer remained rather marginal. Outside Asia, soy did not become a commodity of any significant economic value until the early decades of the twentieth century.

This book sets out to analyze why, then, in the first half of the twentieth century, the soybean suddenly became attractive to the Western world, and what its uses were. In addition to emerging at a comparatively late stage, the Western interest in soybeans was also very sudden. Once the crop left its Asian homeland it unexpectedly became a valuable commodity, and contemporary observers were astonished at the nascent trade. A 1911 report from the Chinese Maritime Customs in Shanghai emphasized:

> It is only in the last three years that soya beans have become important in intercontinental commerce, and their rapid emergence from obscurity has, indeed, been one of the most remarkable commercial events of recent times.[3]

DOI: 10.4324/9781003255222-1

The bean's new economic power was compared to that of the once-thriving trade in tea from China and it was predicted that its importance would soon equal that of the contemporary trade in silk. In the same year, the U.S. ambassador in Beijing reported to the U.S. State Department that until recently the world had known next to nothing about possible trade deals with a certain region called Manchuria, from where the beans destined for global trade were coming. Now, the ambassador wrote, economic developments in Northeast China were being closely watched in New York, London, Hamburg, Seattle, and elsewhere. According to him, this was thanks solely to soybeans, the surging demand for which had been "phenomenal in trade annals."[4]

The unexpected appreciation of soy had nothing to do with a sudden esteem for Asian foods. Instead, from roughly the 1910s onward, the soybean was reduced into its two main constituent parts: oil and protein. Soy turned into an ordinary—yet invisible—ingredient in daily life, a process that was completed by the 1950s. By then the "miracle bean," as it was once called in Europe and the United States, had become a veritable industrial crop, and its components could be found in products as diverse as margarine, soap, paint, mayonnaise, wallpaper, glue, and dynamite, to mention just a few. In addition, the soybean had become a key element in factory farming and with that part of human nutrition, albeit rather indirectly. Now, nearly all meats, from beef steaks to pork loins, chicken wings to salmon are produced from concentrate feed made of soybeans. By way of contrast, it is only since the 1990s that the space regular supermarkets devote to supposedly typical soy products, such as tofu and soy milk, have grown as well.[5]

Global Commodities

What was it that led the beans to suddenly become a global commodity? How did the soybean achieve global economic power in the space of only 50 years? What were the incentives for using it? Who had an interest in soybeans, and why? In finding answers to these questions, I focus on the bean's origins and its principal destinations in the Western world—that is, chiefly Germany and the United States. The term "Western world" or simply "the West" is neither new nor undisputed in modern historiography; nevertheless, for reasons of pragmatism I decided to use it as an umbrella term to describe developments in Europe and North America.[6] The adventure of the soybean outside Asia began on these two continents simultaneously, and, while the initial interest was different, the result remained the same. Shipments of soybeans from Asia reached various European harbors in the first decade of the twentieth century, and while the First World War interrupted this trade, it flourished all the more thereafter. Around the same time, Americans also discovered the soybean; however, they would hardly import, and rather cultivate, the crop. The attraction of soybeans to people on both sides of the Atlantic was tied to a desire for meat and cheap alternatives to butter, in addition to cosmetics and products based on chemical syntheses such as plastics. In result, the soybean mainly became a cheap resource for fat and fodder in the West.

The soybean's global journey began in the aftermath of the Russo-Japanese War (1904–1905) and can be centered on three particular hubs: Northeast China, also known as Manchuria, as the starting point; Germany, where most of the beans in the interwar period were shipped; and the United States, which became the worldwide leading cultivator of soy during the 1940s. Thus, the story told in this book deals with developments on three different continents, thereby encompassing quite distinct economies and national particularities. Regarding Manchuria, the main aspects of trade will be emphasized, while for Germany processing industries are at the heart of the matter, and in the United States, agricultural developments. In light of these differences, the question arises of whether it makes sense to bring these diverse historical developments together. The challenge grows even greater considering the many products made of soy. Chemical research in the interwar period led to many different uses for the crop and thus rather wide-ranging consumer groups. Agricultural scientists, politicians, economists, and entrepreneurs in Europe and Northern America were enthusiastic about the versatile uses of this Asian stranger.[7] While the crop remained rather homogeneous, the products containing traces of it were spectacularly heterogeneous. In result, this book encompasses historical aspects reaching far beyond the crop itself and opens for questions related to agricultural, technological, environmental, economic, and business history in addition to those on soybeans as a commodity. When it comes to historical analyses, dealing with soy implies thus not only crossing a number of geographic boundaries but also breaching the borderlines between a variety of historical subdisciplines.

I agree with other historians in arguing that it is precisely through following a global commodity that a coherent narrative about diverse but interconnected places and phenomena becomes visible.[8] The soybean story is as much about Han Chinese peasants working the soil with the help of an ox as it is about technological innovation in the city of Hamburg. It is about American farmers chugging along their fields in a Fordson and about ammunition for guns in the Second World War. This book contributes to discussions about global economic connections by focusing on how a specific commodity was produced, exchanged, and processed along a supply chain. In tracing the commodification of the soybean, I show how a producing part of the world was linked commercially to financiers, industrialists, and consumers in another area. In the 1920s and 1930s, for example, the industry and agriculture of a developed economy such as that of Germany depended on the ongoing exploitation of a very distant environment, namely Manchuria. The trade evolving in this context, however, was neither controlled by German nor Chinese traders but by Japanese and Danish ones. Following the cultivation, trade, processing, and use of the soybean illuminates the workings of the contemporary world economy. In addition, it allows us to connect people who were not in direct contact at the time, in order to shed light on interactions in global systems otherwise considered as freestanding and unrelated.

There is research on the history of the soybean in various spatial and national contexts, but their transnational linkages have so far largely been undetected. Matthew Roth has written on the rise of the soybean in the United States, thereby pointing out the many uses of the crop and the work of the U.S. engineers and agriculturalists who tirelessly promoted the various industrial uses of the plant. Jürgen Drews has analyzed Nazi Germany's attempts at growing soybeans in southeastern Europe in order to serve war-related needs for fats and proteins on the one hand, and to seek an outlet for the products of the chemical and pharmaceutical conglomerate I.G. Farben on the other. Robert G. Fahs has also focused on Nazi Germany, but paid attention to the regime's trade deals with Japan and Manchukuo, the puppet state Japan had founded in 1932 after the invasion of Manchuria. The deals came about for similar reasons, the acquisition of soybeans and the trade in heavy industrial goods. Together with Hiromi Mizuno, I have worked on the Manchurian soybean trade in the 1910s and 1920s and the role of Japanese imperialism in facilitating it. Other scholars such as Ernst Langthaler and David Wolff have made the first attempts in linking parts of the places and people related to the spread of soy in global agriculture, trade, and nutrition. Christine Du Bois made the most comprehensive effort to date to trace the history of the soybean in different parts of the world and its value for different purposes. Globalizing the Soybean is an attempt at bringing these branches of the story together and interpreting their findings as part of one development, namely the making of soy as a global and ubiquitous commodity.[9]

Recent works on global commodities have described the history of capitalist activity at various times in inspiring ways, taking into account not only economic aspects but also social, cultural, and political factors. They shed light on elaborate systems of local and global connections that lay behind the supply and demand of resources, their processing, trade, and consumption. Giorgio Riello's work on cotton has been particularly inspiring because he told a story of how cotton changed the way in which economies around the world worked by linking what happened in one location to what happened in another.[10] The evolution of cotton as a global fabric was the fruit of complex interactions, and I argue that the emergence of the soybean as global fodder and fat resource was exactly the same—the result of human interactions in different parts of the world.

In addition to being about connections in history, this book is also about historical change. People involved in the business of soybeans had diverse values and interests, but they all played a part in the soybean becoming both an agricultural crop and an industrial commodity on a global scale. Thus, just as John Soluri has done with the example of the banana or Anna Tsing with the matsutake mushroom, I use the soybean as an opening to broader social, economic, and historical processes. Both scholars reveal not only global and transnational connections but also the power relations embedded within them. Soluri points to how the demand for bananas in the United States reshaped local spaces in Honduras, while Tsing works out conditions of capitalism when following the supply chain of a mushroom that grows, among other places, in northern California and is considered a luxury item in Japan.[11] What I try to show is the network of actors which led to a Western dependence on soy as a cheap resource and in turn the evolution of modern consumer societies. Nowadays, soybeans are globally valued as a resource for fat and fodder precisely because societies started this process about one hundred years ago. Who were these people, which businesses were involved, and which role did political institutions play for this process? Placing the soybean at the center of this story helps us understand this process of worldwide historical change.

In global economic history, most of the period under consideration here has been characterized as rather disconnected compared to the globalized world before the First World War. The years before the war, from roughly the mid-nineteenth century onward, had brought spectacular change to the worldwide economic system. Led by Great Britain and other European powers, it was characterized by a laissez-faire market economy and free trade, resulting, among other things, in a broad process of economic integration. That system received a shock both during the war and the challenges arising from it in the 1920s. Now, European states turned to protectionist measures and regulated their markets. Through state interventionism, countries adopted economic nationalism and sought self-sufficiency, with the result that world trade stagnated. The international economic system was then even more shaken during the Great Depression, which led to a significant decline in worldwide output and trade. The volume of European trade, for example, fell from 58 billion U.S. dollars to 21 billion U.S. dollars between 1929 and 1935. Thus, it has become textbook knowledge that the years until the 1950s were a period of distinct economic de-globalization.[12]

Interestingly, the history of the soybean points in the opposite direction. The crop went global in the economically challenging years of the 1920s, 1930s, and 1940s. Hermann Bollmann, a Hamburg-based oil miller, became a leading entrepreneur in processing soybeans after the First World War and was known far beyond German borders. He secured his company, the Hansa-Mühle, progressive innovations in processing soybeans, thereby opening outlets for even more soybean-based products, namely lecithin. This fatty substance was sought after for smoothening food textures, emulsifying and homogenizing liquids, and repelling sticky materials, but was until then rather costly as it was principally obtained from egg yolk. Extracting it from soybeans resulted in lower prices and a general increase in its sheer availability. Since then, lecithin has been used to smoothen margarine and chocolate, make leather soft to the touch, and hold candy bars together, among many other uses. In addition, Bollmann and other oil millers constantly promoted soybean meal as concentrate feed. Thanks to the trifold value of the soybean as a resource for obtaining oil, lecithin, and fodder the trade in soybeans with Germany reached its peak in the early 1930s. Oils mills, such as Hansa-Mühle, were among the companies that thrived in times that were otherwise challenging

Around the same time, the soybean also entered the United States, although as a crop plant, not a commodity. Farmers in the Midwest initially grew them for reasons of soil management, making hay, and seed production. Then, in the aftermath of the Great Depression and in the course of the Second World War, the plant's presence in U.S. farming grew bigger and Americans eventually began to make greater use of the crop. Experts from the U.S. Department of Agriculture (USDA) and state colleges as well as few entrepreneurs convinced farmers to harvest their beans and have them processed into fat and fodder. The chemurgy movement, in which mainly private companies worked on preparing industrial products from domestic raw materials, chimed in and fostered a growing interest in them. Henry Ford was one of the movement's most prominent advocates, his enthusiasm for soy going so far that in the early 1940s he presented a car whose body was made of soybean-based plastics.

There are several reasons for the advancement of the soybean in the challenging years between the First and Second World Wars, and they vary for Germany and the United States. In the early twentieth century, Germany depended heavily on the import of fatty raw materials to secure food supplies, but in the 1920s the country's economic and financial situation was particularly tough. The beans' low price was decisive for why oil millers in Germany preferred soybeans over the import of other resources to serve the demand for cheap fats. In addition, German oil millers were keen to process soybeans because they offered them a notion of independence from other European powers. Soybeans were not the only cheap resource for fat available on the world market; prices for cottonseed and linseed were comparatively low, and their oils' chemical characteristics were similar to that of the soybean. Germany, however, had no direct access to these or any other overseas oilseeds and fruits, as it had lost its colonies after the First World War. Simultaneously, world trade in resources for vegetable oils and fats remained within the imperial structures established before the war. While British companies preferred cottonseed and linseed from Egypt, French oil millers settled on peanuts from French colonies in West Africa. German oil millers could obtain these resources as well, also for a low price, but preferred the soybean in the assumption that its trade was less controlled, or at least not by a competing great power. The soybean trade was in fact heavily controlled by Japanese and Danish trading companies, but the notion of independence led to the soybean becoming a crucial commodity in agriculture and industry in the Weimar Republic. Processing companies channeled soybean oil into the production of margarine, soap, and various industries, and the protein-rich byproduct to farmers. It was during this period that soybean meal for the first time became a key element in livestock breeding to increase meat production.

Americans did not to the same degree depend on the import of fatty raw materials, at least not in the aftermath of the First World War, when the beans took root on farms in the United States. Nevertheless, also in this case, a crisis-ridden economy was the determining factor for why the soybean found entry into the country's agriculture at that time. After the First World War, farmers in the Midwest and South struggled to grow the crops—wheat, corn, and cotton—they had specialized in for decades. In order to service demand, they had not followed crop rotations during wartime and were now suffering from the effects of mismanagement and monoculture. Besides ruined soils, the consequences were overproduction and plagues of insects such as the boll weevil in the South or the corn borer in the Midwest. In this situation, farmers discovered the soybean's ability to enrich their farmlands with nitrogen and thus help to rejuvenate depleted and acidic soils. They were attracted by the idea of simply letting the crop grow and having the plant's root nodules fertilize the soil. Healthier soils meant getting back on track with well-established cash crops. At first, many farmers did not intend to harvest the beans at all but would let their livestock graze the land, thereby providing the animals with protein-rich fodder.

Their hopes were aptly expressed at the founding of the American Soybean Association (ASA) in Indiana in 1920. The program included field trips to examine cultivation trials and the use of harvesters in yielding soybeans and processing them into hay or silage. Lectures were held and experiences exchanged. Farmers' wives offered soy-based dishes that they had brought along or prepared on site, even though none seriously considered growing soybeans as food. To break up the program, a quartet of local soy farmers sang an ode to the bean. Its title, "Growing Soybeans to Get Along," is telling regarding the expectations, and the desperation, of farmers at the time.[13]

Although developments in the United States coincided with those in Germany, sources hardly point to transnational networks between experts or businesses from the two countries. It rather seems that most farmers were unaware of the possibility of making a profit from the beans. These disconnections notwithstanding, the result was the same: Germans and Americans discovered the soybean in economically challenging times.

When the history of the soybean in the Western world is understood as one global historical process, the marked influence of governmental actors and political decisions on its spread comes to light. In addition to becoming a commodity in times of general decline and de-globalization, the soybean was also actively pushed by actors beyond businessmen and farmers. Its spread was enabled by institutional structures and political decisions. In the 1910s and 1920s, the soybean became a commodity of economic value in Europe because the Japanese trading company Mitsui & Co. facilitated its transfer from Northeast China. However, the company's activities were not only backed but also requested by the Japanese government. At that time, Japan was attempting to further its imperialist ambitions on the Asian mainland. This effort was followed by a modernization policy that supported industrialization and international trade. As a result, Mitsui & Co. became one of the strongest Japanese actors in Manchuria besides the South Manchurian Railway (SMR) and the Bank of Chosen. The interplay between these three was enabled, requested, and supported by Japanese imperialism and the policies resulting from it. In Germany, political decisions were equally important. Thanks to trade policies in the Weimar Republic, Germany became the largest soybean-importing country in the late 1920s, and it was through trade agreements with Japan and Manchukuo that Nazi Germany maintained its supply of soybeans until 1941. In the United States, the soybean eventually became a crop not because farmers discovered its manifold benefits but because the government enacted policies that fostered its cultivation during the Great Depression and into the Second World War. In all these cases, the state and other regulatory actors were deeply involved in creating the conditions for the commodification and marketization of the soybean.[14]

The question of human agency in nature, or rather human power over material objects, has recently been challenged in historical writing. In *The Matter of History*, Timothy LeCain writes on the historical significance of nonhuman objects and develops a neo-materialist theory, giving agency to the objects themselves. He argues *inter alia* that the material environment has "creative powers" and is of "independent nature."[15] His approach helped me to imagine that soybeans have power over humans insofar as they now provide us with plentiful amounts of cheap meat and fat. As such, they influence not only the shape of human bodies and the quality of human health but also contribute to an increase in carbon dioxide emissions—from cattle belching methane, for example. On the other hand, was it the soybean that brought itself into this position, or human action? I agree that humans should be viewed as part of nature, but struggle to understand how to weave a coherent story without identifying actors and their intentions. Thus, I rather tend to see things as Raj Patel and Jason W. Moore, who also frame our modern world as a material one but argue that humans organize and control things.[16] In this book, the global spread of the soybean is seen as the result of human agency. People with various interests and values turned it into the almost invisible yet ubiquitous material that it is today.

Of course, soy production and consumption have shifted since the end of the Second World War. The most obvious example is the expansion of soybean cultivation into Latin America since the 1970s and the accompanying devastation of the rainforest in order to gain more arable land. This and other more recent transitions are excluded from this book for two reasons. First, by the time Brazil and Argentina became major soybean-growing regions, the crop was already fully established in the Western world. I am most interested in how the beans became so widely used in Western industry and agriculture in the first place, and see Latin American soy production more as an expansion of developments, the foundations of which were laid earlier. Second, most Latin American soy (as well as much of today's U.S.

soy) has been exported to Asia, where it is used to fatten animals. China currently accounts for three-quarters of Brazil's soy exports. Also, in the United States soybeans are among the top American exports to China. The trade has declined in recent years but was nevertheless worth 14 billion U.S. dollars in 2020 and in 2021, constituting about 40 percent of all agricultural exports from the United States to China.[17] This transfer undoubtedly leads to a number of important questions about global capitalism, trade wars, and not least human exploitation of nature in the twentieth and twenty-first centuries. Nevertheless, the soybean trade to Asia, mainly China, is diametrical to my question about soy's journey in the other direction.

Fertilizer, Fat, Fodder (and Food)

With soybeans essentially containing oil and protein, they hold two of the three macronutrients important for human nutrition. The body needs larger amounts of carbohydrates, proteins, and fats than of other nutrients because these are required for energy supplies and to maintain the body's structure and systems. In theory, soybeans are thus ideal for human consumption; in practice, things are more complex. Soybeans are hard to digest, making it difficult to access their nutrients. They contain a variety of proteins, with one—called a trypsin inhibitor—indeed suppressing the breakdown of the others in the human digestive system. What seems a clever survival strategy for the plant, at least theoretically, results in pain in the upper abdomen in humans, unless the beans are thoroughly cooked. Likewise, certain components cannot be degraded by the human digestive enzymes and pass into the colon, where they are metabolized by anaerobic bacteria, leading to the generation of gas and flatulence. Considering these challenges, humans have had to be inventive since ancient times in order to incorporate soybeans into daily meals, developing methods of processing through which they have become easier to digest. Tofu, soy sauce, and soy milk are merely the best-known examples of a variety of foods which no longer cause digestive problems and are, instead, considered healthy.[18] In addition to the bean's benefits as a food, other uses have been known in Asia since ancient times too. Its oil was highly versatile, as it could both be consumed and used in oil lamps or as a lubricant. The residue from oil extraction, known as soybean cake or meal, was suitable as animal feed and fertilizer. It provided the soil with nitrogen and was shipped to sugar plantations in southern China and paddy fields in Japan, among others.[19]

By the late nineteenth century at the latest, Northeast China came to depend heavily on the soybean trade with Japan. Contemporary Western observers often intoned that the crop was Manchuria's "wealth," "gold," and "fortune," but failed to take into account that it was also the region's fate. In fact, the increased soybean cultivation was not only triggered by the rising demand for fertilizer, as will be analyzed in Chapter 1. That Manchuria could offer soybeans to Japanese rice farmers in the first place was enabled and later accompanied by the geopolitical and imperial disputes between China, Japan, and Russia which played out in this region. While Japan and Russia claimed ownership of this remote region, the Chinese empire opened the provinces for settlement and development in order to push back the colonial interests of other powers. The new Han Chinese migrants worked the fields to make a living from soybeans, thereby ushering in Manchuria's agricultural transformation.[20]

In a global perspective, the late nineteenth and early twentieth centuries are described as the age of New Imperialism. Characteristic to the period were colonial expansions by European powers, the United States, and Japan. In Chapter 2, I show that the soybean was also entangled in this global phenomenon. A prerequisite for the soybean trade with Europe was the Russo-Japanese War, as a result of which Japan expanded its role on the Asian mainland and became the master of the trade routes and trade goods of southern Manchuria. From 1908, thanks to the resourceful action of the Japanese trading company Mitsui & Co., soy appeared in the English port of Hull and since then has been a cheap source of oil for margarine, soap, paints, and many more products. The interplay between imperialism and globalization became a key starting point for the commodification of the soybean in Europe.

Equally important, of course, was strong demand. This was triggered by new technological advances and developments in the processing of fat. When the soybean eventually gained attention as a commodity in Europe, industries paid most attention to it as a resource for cheap and versatile fat. While fats and their liquid equivalent, oils, are despised as a thickener today, they were essential for a variety of foods and nonfood items back in the late nineteenth and early twentieth centuries. Fat was mainly used in foodstuffs such as margarine, but it had industrial uses as well. Machines such as trains or, later, cars, motorcycles, and airplanes not only needed to be lubricated but also painted and varnished; houses and fences also needed to be given a protective coating; people washed themselves and their clothes with soaps; the beauty industry was making advances with numerous products; waterproof fabrics were just as suitable as oilcloth on the table as they were as clothing for the military; candles were to be found everywhere; and finally, dynamite could be made from the glycerin of fats and oils. For all these and many other products, anything that lubricated and was cheap was in demand. Petroleum, which today is mostly used for these more industrial purposes, was far from ubiquitous then, making resources from animal and vegetable origins essential.[21] And soybean oil is still highly valued up to this day. The soybean counts as one of the most important sources of vegetable oil worldwide, which is why the Food and Agriculture Organization of the United Nations classifies it as an oil crop.

In Chapter 3, I will show that Germany depended continuously on fat resources in the Weimar Republic and the Nazi period and that soybeans contributed to addressing the problem. By the late 1920s, no other country in Europe, Asia, or any other part of the world imported more whole and unprocessed soybeans than Germany. The amount of oil in soybeans is low compared to that of other oilseeds and fruits. Copra, the dried flesh of the coconut, contains about 60–75 percent oil; and poppy and peanuts around 50 percent. Contemporary soybean varieties, on the other hand, contained only between 13 and 21 percent in oil, which was quite similar to that of cottonseed and linseed. Besides oil, contemporary soybean varieties contained about 40 percent protein, 12 percent water, and 30 percent other substances.[22] Thus, soybean processing yielded large amounts of residue, and a solution for what to do with it had to be found rather quickly. The Hamburg-based Hansa-Mühle was most inventive when it came to making use of the residue. While the company channeled most of the soybean oil it obtained into the production of margarine, a competitor to butter and lard, it marketed soybean meal to hog and cattle farmers. The feeding instructions the company published along with other pamphlets about soybeans usually made no mention of soybean oil so as not to disturb the margarine business, but highlighted the benefits of cheap soybean meal for increasing milk production and for fattening pigs instead. In fact, soybean meal provided an effective concentrated feed—rich in proteins, it would feed animals to produce more of what the beans contained anyway: fats and proteins.

German agriculturalists in the Nazi period would also have liked for the beans to be grown closer to the Reich. The problem was that growing conditions did not match those in Manchuria. There, the latitude lay roughly between 35 and 45 degrees north, which in Europe equates to the Mediterranean and southeastern Europe. Prevalent varieties thrived best in regions with continuous temperatures between 70 and 95 Fahrenheit and full sun during the growing season, in addition to sufficient water in the summer and days of roughly equal length. Such conditions were hardly likely to be found in Germany. In order to become more independent of overseas supplies, especially in the event of war, powerful figures in Nazi Germany, not least from IG Farben, thus tried to grow them in southeastern Europe. The endeavor never met with much success. Instead, the German foreign ministry negotiated trade deals with Japan and its puppet-state Manchukuo to ensure the beans' supply.

In the period under consideration in this book, the soybean only occasionally received attention as a food in regions outside Asia. Its nutritional benefits were frequently pointed out, not least by physicians, but usually only Asian immigrants, diabetics, and groups promoting a vegetarian lifestyle—often for religious reasons—promoted the benefits of eating soybeans. From the mid-1930s onward, however, German officials in the Nazi era focused more on soybeans as a resource for nutrients which they were struggling to provide the *Volk* in sufficient amounts—that is, fats and proteins. Until the early 1940s, when supplies diminished due to the war, their fostering of the consumption of soybeans was not only vocal. They calculated that feeding soybean proteins to livestock was a costly and wasteful use of nutrients, and distributed soybean flour more directly to the public. It was only after the failure of the general public's enthusiasm for the flour that the majority of it was channeled to the many factory canteens, with Germans then eating soybean flour rather unwittingly as protein bread or soup.

Climates in the South and Midwest of the United States were better suited for growing soybeans, but it nevertheless took until the 1920s for farmers to incorporate them into their crop rotation to the extent that the acreage was also recorded in agricultural statistics. With the help of specialists from the USDA, farmers initially discovered soybeans as an emergency crop, which was supposed to help with depleted soils. As shown in Chapter 4, regional businesses such as railway companies and oil mills teamed up with agricultural experts at state colleges and officials in the USDA to get the Midwestern farmers to adopt the crop in their agricultural practices. What started as an attempt to repair soils soon began producing a crop that was highly valued for fat and fodder.

In fact, shortages in fats led to the breakthrough of the soybean in American farming. It is well known that certain raw materials such as petroleum or rubber were in short supply in every warring nation, albeit to varying degrees and at different times. What is less well known is that fats and oils were also in short supply among the Allies and the Axis powers. Like rubber, which was used primarily to make tires, palm oil and coconut oil arrived in large volumes from the tropical regions of the Pacific. While rubber came almost exclusively from plantations in Malaysia, Southeast Asia supplied the world with about 50 percent of the raw materials used to produce vegetable oils and fats.[23] Accordingly, a shortfall in the event of war resulted in severe cutbacks worldwide. Government attention was now given over to domestically produced oil crops such as cotton, peanuts, and soybeans. Since cotton had already ruined farmland in the southern states, programs for increasing fat production were mainly aimed at raising the production of peanuts and soybeans, and it was through these developments that American farmers eventually fully engaged with the soybean as a crop.

Notes

1 In plant taxonomy, the soybean is called *Glycine max* (L.) Merr. The ancient variety is called *Glycine soya.* Eric J. Sedivy, Faqiang Wu, and Yoshie Hanzawa, "Soybean Domestication: The Origin, Genetic Architecture and Molecular Bases," *New Phytologist* 214 (2017): 539–53, https://doi.org/10.1111/nph.14418; Theodore Hymowitz, "On the Domestication of the Soybean," *Economic Botany* 24 (1970), 408–21, seems outdated but nevertheless provides useful information on the global history of the soybean.

2 See Francesca Bray et al., eds., *Rice: Global Networks and New Histories* (Cambridge, UK: Cambridge University Press, 2015); Alfred W. Crosby, *The Columbian Exchange: Biological and Cultural Consequences of 1492* (Westport, CT: Praeger Publishers, 2003).

3 Norman Shaw, *The Soya Bean of Manchuria* (Shanghai: Inspector General of Customs, 1911), 1.

4 American Legation in Peking to the U.S. Secretary of State in Washington, DC, June 17, 1911, NARA RG 59 Department of State Relating to Internal Affairs of China, 1910–1929, M 329, Roll 183, File 893.61345.

5 Lucy Long, "Culinary Tourism: A Folkloristic Perspective on Eating and Otherness," *Southern Folklore* 55, no. 3 (1998): 181–204.

6 For the politicization of the term, see Riccardo Bavaj, "'The West:' A Conceptual Exploration," *European History Online*, November 21, 2011, accessed May 26, 2022, http://www.ieg-ego.eu/bavajr-2011-en.

7 Ines Prodöhl, "'A Miracle Bean': How Soy Conquered the West, 1909–1950." *Bulletin of the German Historical Institute*, Washington, DC, 46 (Spring 2010): 111–29; Matthew Roth, *Magic Bean: The Rise of Soy in America* (Lawrence: University Press of Kansas, 2018).

8 Joshua Specht, "Commodity History and the Nature of Global Connection: Recent Developments," *Journal of Global History* 14, no. 1 (2019), 145–50; Steven C. Topik and Allen Wells, "Commodity Chains in a Global Economy," in *A World Connecting*, ed. Emily S. Rosenberg (Harvard: Harvard University Press, 2012), 592–812, here 598–99.

9 On the history of the soybean in the United States, see most recently Matthew Roth, *Magic Bean*; much shorter but clearer in following causes for the rise of soy in America is Christine M. Du Bois, "Social Context and Diet: Changing Soy Production and Consumption in the United States," in *The World of Soy*, eds. Christine M. Du Bois, Chee-Beng Tan, and Sidney Mintz, 208–33 (Chicago: University of Illinois, 2008). However, Thomas Sorosiak, "Soybean," in *The Cambridge World History of Food*, vol. I, 422–26, ed. Kenneth F. Kiple (Cambridge, UK: Cambridge University Press, 2000) is less convincing. In contrast to the title of the volume, Sorosiak focuses mainly on the history of the soybean in the United States and presents a rather uncritical narrative; for Germany, see Jürgen Drews, *Die 'Nazi-Bohne': Anbau, Verwendung und Auswirkung der Sojabohne im Deutschen Reich und Südosteuropa, 1933–1945* (Münster: Lit Verlag, 2004); Robert G. Fahs, "German Economic Diplomacy in Northeast Asia, 1917–1936" (PhD diss., University of Hawai'i, 1996); on the history of the soybean in Manchuria, a first attempt in a Western language has been made by David Wolff, "Bean There: Toward a Soy-Based History of Northeast China," *The South Atlantic Quarterly* 99, no. 1 (2000), 241–52; see also Hiromi Mizuno and Ines Prodöhl, "Mitsui Bussan and the Manchurian Soybean Trade: Geopolitics and Economic Strategies in China's Northeast, ca. 1870s–1920s," *Business History* (2019), 1–22, https://doi.org/10.1080/00076791.2019.1687688; Ines Prodöhl, "Dynamiken globaler Vernetzung: Mandschurische Sojabohnen auf dem Weltmarkt," *Zeitschrift für Agrargeschichte und Agrarsoziologie* 61, no. 2 (2013), 75–89; attempts at bringing various soybean stories together are made in Ernst Langthaler, "Gemüse oder Ölfrucht? Die Weltkarriere der Sojabohne im 20. Jahrhundert," in *Umkämpftes Essen: Produktion, Handel und Konsum von Lebensmitteln in globalen Kontexten*, eds. Cornelia Reiher and Sarah Ruth Sippel (Göttingen: Vandenhoeck & Ruprecht, 2015), 41–66; Ernst Langthaler, "The Soy Paradox: The Western Nutrition transition revisited, 1950–2010," *Global Environment* 11, no. 1 (2018), 79–104, https://doi.org/10.3197/ge.2018.110105; Christine M. Du Bois, *The Story of Soy* (London: Reaktion Books, 2018); in the early 1970s, William Shurtleff and Akiko Aoyagi started out researching soybean-based foods in Japan. In later years, they expanded their work thematically and are now best known for their databases and annotated bibliographies on all matters soy, see "Soyinfocenter," accessed June 22, 2022, https://www.soyinfocenter.com.

10 Giorgio Riello, *Cotton: The Fabric that Made the Modern World* (Cambridge, UK: Cambridge University Press, 2013).

11 John Soluri, *Banana Cultures: Agriculture, Consumption, and Environmental Change in Honduras and the United States* (Austin, TX: University of Texas Press, 2005); Anna Lowenhaupt Tsing, *The Mushroom at the End of the World: On the Possibility of Life in Capitalist Ruins* (Princeton, NJ: Princeton University Press, 2015).

12 Iván T. Berend, *An Economic History of Twentieth-century Europe: Economic Regimes from Laissez-faire to Globalization* (Cambridge, UK: Cambridge University Press, 2006), 63; Roger Middleton, "The Great Depression in Europe," *The Oxford Handbook of European History, 1914–1945*, ed. Nicholas Doumanis (New York, NY: Oxford University Press, online 2014), https://doi.org/10.1093/oxfordhb/9780199695669.013.11.

13 American Soybean Association, *Proceedings of the American Soybean Association* 1 (1928), 9–11, 39–42.

14 For a strong emphasis on state actors in commodity chain studies, see also Jennifer Bair, "Global Commodity Chains: Genealogy and Review," in *Frontier of Commodity Chain Research,* ed. Jennifer Bair (Stanford, CA: Stanford University Press, 2008), 1–34; Jennifer Bair, "Analysing Global Economic Organization: Embedded Networks and Global Chains Compared, *Economy and Society* 37, no. 3 (2008), 339–64; Ernst Langthaler and Elke Schüßler, "Commodity Studies with Polanyi: Disembedding and Re-Embedding Labour and Land in Contemporary Capitalism," *Österreichische Zeitschrift für Soziologie* 44 (2019), 209–23.

15 Timothy J. LeCain, *The Matter of History: How Things Create the Past* (New York, NY: Cambridge University Press, 2017), 16.

16 Raj Patel, Jason W. Moore, *A History of the World in Seven Cheap Things: A Guide to Capitalism, Nature, and the Future of the Planet* (Oakland, CA: University of California Press, 2017); for an inspiring read of this and LeCain's book see Gregory Samantha Rosenthal's review in *Journal of World History* 30, no. 3 (2019), 459–64.

17 Diana Roy, "China's Growing Influence in Latin America," *Council on Foreign Relations,* last updated April 12, 2022, accessed May 26, 2022, https://www.cfr.org/backgrounder/china-influence-latin-america-argentina-brazil-venezuela-security-energy-bri; Karen Braun, "Plunge in U.S. soy exports to China in 2021 exposes Phase 1 flaws," *Reuters,* last updated February 9, 2022, accessed May 26, 2022, https://www.reuters.com/business/plunge-us-soy-exports-china-2021-exposes-phase-1-flaws-braun-2022-02-09/; see also Prabhu Pingali, "Westernization of Asian Diets and the Transformation of Food Systems: Implications for Research and Policy," *Food Policy* 32, no. 3 (2007), 281–98; for soy production in Latin America see in particular Pablo Lapegna, *Soybeans and Power: Genetically Modified Crops, Environmental Politics, and Social Movements in Argentina* (New York, NY: Oxford University Press, 2016); Gustavo De L.T. Oliveira and Susanna B. Hecht, eds., *Soy, Globalization, and Environmental Politics in South America* (London; New York, NY: Routledge, 2018).

18 Hsing-Tung Huang, *Science and Civilisation in China,* vol. 6, pt. 5, *Fermentations and Food Science* (Cambridge, UK: Cambridge University Press, 2000), 293. For foods made of soy, see the chapters in Du Bois et al., *The World of Soy.*

19 Qing Yong Xu, "A 'Fertilizer Revolution'? A Critical Response to Pomeranz's Theory of 'Geographic Luck'," *Modern China* 33, no. 2 (2007), 195–229, https://www.jstor.org/stable/20062667.

20 George Bronson Rea, "Beans: The Solution of the Commercial Situation in Manchuria." *The Far Eastern Review* 6, no. 10 (March 1910): 453–61, 486–89, here 455; Wolff, "Bean There," 245; Alexander Hosie, *Manchuria: Its People, Resources and Recent History*, 2nd ed. (London: Methuen & Co., 1904), 245.

21 Mark R. Finlay, "The Industrial Utilization of Farm Products and By-Products: The USDA Regional Research Laboratories," *Agricultural History* 64, no. 2 (1990): 41–52; Mark R. Finlay, "Old Efforts and New Uses: A Brief History of Chemurgy and the American Search for Biobased Materials," *Journal of Industrial Ecology* 7 (2003): 33–46; Ines Prodöhl, "From Dinner to Dynamite: Fats and Oils in Wartime America," *Global Food History* 2, no. 1 (2016), 31–50, http://dx.doi.org/10.1080/20549547.2016.1138366.

22 H.T. Montague Bell and H.G.W. Woodhead, *The China Year Book 1914* (London: Routledge, 1919/1920), 54.

23 William G. Clarence Smith, "The Battle for Rubber in the Second World War: Cooperation and Resistance," in *Commodities of Empire Working Papers*, no. 14 (November 2009), accessed May 2022, https://commoditiesofempire.org.uk/publications/working-papers/working-paper-14/; Jonathan Marshall, *To Have and Have Not: Southeast Asian Raw Materials and the Origins of the Pacific War* (Berkeley: University of California Press, 1995).

1 Soy around 1900 in a Global Context

As the demand for vegetable oil was rising in Europe in the first decade of the twentieth century, the soybean, grown in Northeast China, soon emerged as an alternative oil crop. Its oil was suitable for human consumption but also useful as a lubricant and for lighting. From 1908–1909 onward, dried but otherwise unprocessed soybeans were traded in large quantities to customers first in Great Britain and later in Denmark, Germany, and beyond as well. While this book explores how and why soybeans conquered the Western world in subsequent years, this chapter sheds light on the period before. It asks first which role soy played in Asia, and second why the beans—although they were known—did not find much use in other parts of the world until, suddenly, they became a commodity of economic value.

In each of the first two trading seasons of the emerging trade in soybeans from Asia to Europe—that is, 1908–1909 and 1909–1910, respectively—about 500,000 tons of dried soybeans were shipped to Great Britain. Thereafter, demand declined but remained at about 300,000 tons shipped annually to various European ports until the beginning of the First World War.[1] These large figures indicate that by the time Europeans discovered the bean's value, people in the region of their origin must already have been well experienced if not specialized in growing them. Infrastructure for transportation and a generally flourishing trade in soybeans seem likely preconditions for trade with Europe. All of this was indeed true, as will be shown in this chapter. It argues that in course of the nineteenth century, the soybean became a cash crop in Northeast China due to the rising demand for fertilizer in southern China and Japan. Soybean's economic value lay in its potential to enrich the soil with nitrogen, a much-needed macronutrient for any plant. Since soybeans also contained oil, they were first pressed, with the resulting oils then being used for human consumption, and the residue from the milling process serving as a fertilizer. This residue was often called bean cake, because of its round shape stemming from the milling process, or simply meal. China and Japan had thus established ways for utilizing the crop that in later years were merely adapted in Europe. One significant difference was that European customers were initially more interested in the

DOI: 10.4324/9781003255222-2

oil than in the cake; another was that the waste product served mainly as fodder and not fertilizer.

The bean's rising significance in nineteenth-century Manchuria was accompanied and enabled by geopolitical disputes between China, Russia, and Japan about precisely that region. In order to mark the land as Chinese, the Qing dynasty opened up the empire's hitherto unsettled Northeast for migration. The incoming migrants grew millet for daily consumption and soybeans for cash. The Russian empire, however, built two railways across the region and also encouraged settlement in order to increase its influence and establish semi-colonial structures in the region. In that way, facilities suitable for the transportation of soybeans, among other commodities, were at hand. As the third actor, the Japanese were also attempting to expand political and economic influence and gain a foothold on the Asian mainland. While in Manchuria they did not succeed until after the Russo-Japanese war, Japanese rice farmers were the main customers for soybean cake long before that. In other words, imperial struggles between China, Russia, and Japan led to the colonization and exploitation of Manchuria and eventually to the ever-expanding cultivation of soybeans in this region. European customers could rely on these already established structures when eventually they came to import vast quantities of soybeans.

To be sure, not all soybeans in the Far East were milled. They also served dietary needs and contributed to the daily intake of proteins, particularly among the lower classes. Those who could afford it, relied rather on meat as a source of protein. It was, however, precisely the bean's value as a food that European scientists were interested in in the years prior to its emergence there. Soybeans are rich in protein and fat, two macronutrients that people in central and northern Europe at the time usually obtained from meat, lard, eggs, fish, and milk. Some experts working at the intersection of nutrition, agriculture, and public health saw the soybean as a cheap and easily cultivated alternative to animal protein, but they attached little importance to soybeans being difficult to digest unless treated and processed in certain ways. They often recommended to barely soak them in water and then boil them for several hours, just as other dried beans; but as soybeans treated in this way remained unpalatable if not indigestible to many, their efforts did not meet with much success.

A few farmers in the United States, particularly in the Midwest and the South, were willing to try out soybeans as an emerging crop, simply because they would grow on their depleted soils. Many were suffering from the after-effects of years of near-monoculture in wheat, corn, and cotton, which besides overproduction had led to soils containing too little of the nutrients their established crops needed. Some discovered the soybean as an alternative, since the plant already in the growing period was technically able to fertilize their soils with nitrogen, but it remains open to question whether they succeeded in making use of the plant's fertilizing capacity. When it came to using the crop, they focused on forage, not food. Only Asian immigrants, mainly on the U.S. west coast, as well as groups promoting a vegetarian lifestyle, often for religious reasons, promoted the soybean as a food. Either way, all efforts were short-lived, and soybeans did not become a crop of any significance in U.S. agriculture at this time.

Manchuria and Its Beans

Up until the late nineteenth century, Northeast China constituted a distinct entity geographically and ethnically distinguished from the rest of the empire. It served as a reserve for the ethnic minority rule of the empire, which in Western writing has been transcribed as Manchu. The Manchu had prevented the migration of Han Chinese to the region for centuries and kept the hinterland as a reserve and imperial hunting ground for their own needs. While the people stemming from this ethnic group were Manchu, or bannermen, they never called their region of origin Manchuria. That term was invented in the early eighteenth century by Jesuits at the Qing court, who used it to mark China's northeast on maps. Through travelers and botanists, the term then found its way to Europe. In contrast, in China, the region's name was and is more commonly set in relation to the heartland and called Dongbei, or the Eastern Three Provinces, Northeast China, or simply Northeast. The term "Manchuria" has often been a source of disapproval because it was coined by foreigners in a semi-colonial setting and evoked imperial connotations. More than anything else, Japan's conquest of the region in 1932 and the founding of the puppet-state Manchukuo gave reason for Chinese writers not to make reference to the term at all. In scholarly writing, it has nevertheless become a common practice to use the terms synonymously.[2]

The region in question bordered Siberia and Far Eastern Russia to the north and east, but for a long time, the border between China and the Tsarist empire remained undefined. It was largely undeveloped and unsettled land, providing no initial need to formally claim it. Beginning in the late seventeenth century, both sides made attempts to define their border, but could not reach an agreement until the mid-nineteenth century. By that time, European powers, including Russia, were seeking to expand their territories by building formal and informal empires. Russia, which was defeated in the Crimean War against Britain, France, and Turkey (1853–1856), found that the Far East was an arena in which it could still expand and restore its international standing. China—or more precisely the ruling Qing dynasty—however, was weak due to the Taiping rebellion, a civil war lasting from 1850 to 1864 and because of the Second Opium War of 1856–1858. Russia exploited the situation to force China into giving up large territories the Qing had hitherto considered part of their empire. The Treaty of Aigun (1858) and the Convention of Peking (1860) forced China to give up territory north of the rivers Amur and Ussuri. Although this made things formally clearer, the everyday lives of the people on both sides of the border remained interwoven and their economic and social situation stayed dynamic.[3]

Besides difficulties with the Sino-Russian border, parts of Mongolia were also sometimes considered part of Manchuria, depending on the source. Only the borders to the Chinese mainland in the southwest and the Korean peninsula in the southeast were clearly defined. In between them was the Yellow Sea, a marginal sea to the Pacific Ocean. Since the focus of this book lies in the period after the treaties between Russia and China, I am applying a rather narrow understanding of Manchuria. It includes the three northeastern provinces of China—Heilongjiang, Jilin, and Liaoning—as well as the northern parts of Inner Mongolia (see Map 1.1). This area enclosed about 390,000 square miles of mainly unsettled and undeveloped land. With an extent as large as this, it covered about the same area as California, Nevada, and Arizona combined, or almost double the size of France. In the mid-nineteenth century, when the territory was still larger than my narrow definition, about two million people lived there.[4]

Most of the people living in the region's vastness had settled in the southern part along the fertile valley of the Liao River, where they cultivated sorghum as a food staple. They also grew wheat and soybeans, but because they were profitable trade items, they kept only a little of both. The Liao River was muddy but offered good transport possibilities in winter times. Horses and mules then pulled huge loads of soybeans and other commodities on sleds across the frozen riverbed. A cart drawn by six mules or ponies could carry up to three tons of produce over the frozen river. On average, they made 25 miles per day.[5] Given the rugged geography of the region and the rapid course of the river, this was advantageous over transport by cart or boat in the summer months.

At the city of Yingkou, the Liao entered the Yellow Sea, which served as a regular trading route between the Chinese mainland and the three northeastern provinces. In Yingkou, soybeans were either first processed or shipped as whole beans. Processing meant milling the beans, and while the oil often served local and regional markets, bean cake as the residue of this process was shipped long distances over the Yellow Sea and the Western Pacific Ocean to southern China. As early as 1750, soybean cake was shipped from here to regions on the lower Yangtze, and since the middle of the nineteenth century at the latest, whole beans and soybean cake were shipped to regions even further south. Here, the nitrogen-rich bean cake was needed to fertilize soil depleted from the cultivation of cotton, sugar cane, rice, and not least mulberries, which were needed to feed silkworms.[6] All items for trade from Yingkou had to wait for the spring as the water temperature in the northern part of the Yellow Sea is close to freezing in winter, and patches of drift ice and continuous ice fields form and hinder navigation between November and March.

In the nineteenth century, China experienced what has become known as unequal treaties, allowing foreign powers to exploit the country and establish informal empires. One of the unequal treaties was that of Tientsin of 1859, which ended the first phase of the Second Opium War. It led to the

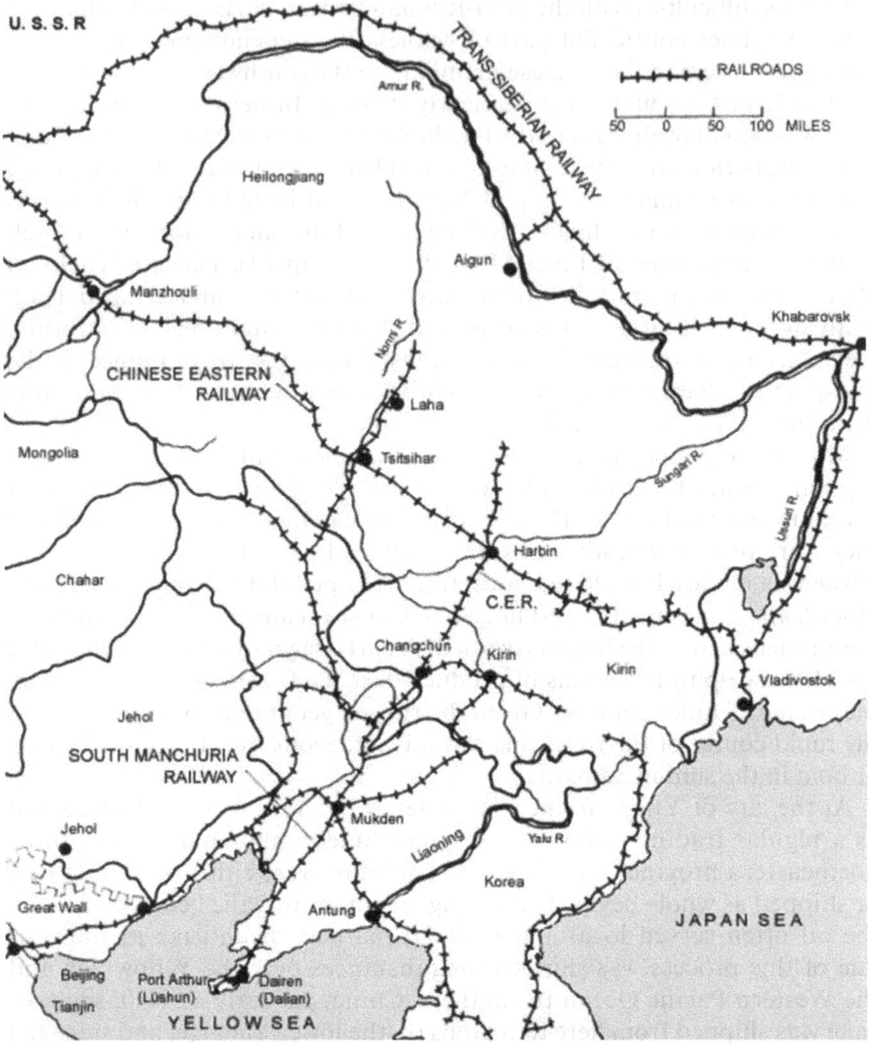

Map 1.1 Manchuria and its railways around 1920.

Source: © Routledge, Taylor and Francis, Elleman, Kotkin, eds., *Manchurian Railways and the Opening of China*, 2015.

opening of several Chinese ports to foreign trade, including Yingkou, and in addition allowed Christian missionary activities and legalized the import of opium.[7] Until the Russo-Japanese war of 1904–1905, when Dalian opened as another port for foreign trade, Yingkou remained the region's only port for trading commodities to and with destinations outside Asia. The emerging trade included silk, precious metals, and ginseng, but not yet soybeans.

They were known in Europe but hitherto not in demand, and thus mainly traded to regions further south in China.

It was an expression of the Manchus' power to keep the area unsettled and undeveloped, although the overpopulated northern regions of China urgently needed additional land. Thus, many settlers simply arrived in Manchuria and started making a living rather informally. In the 1860s, the local authorities' and the Beijing central government's growing need for money eventually led to the release of large tracts of land, but it was not before the end of the 1870s that immigration restrictions on the Han Chinese were lifted completely.[8] Now, the opening of the Northeast was part of the Qing Dynasty's efforts to modernize China politically and to unite the multiethnic empire under what was in some respects a national idea. The relaxed settlement policy was followed by the withdrawal of further privileges for the bannermen and attempts to bind the region more closely to China socially and administratively, such as through the expansion of military bases.[9] Settlement was naturally followed by agricultural development, an expansion in infrastructure and trade activities.

It is difficult to trace national and international trade activities for this region as contemporary sources capture only scattered numbers and instances. In Yingkou, the British-dominated Imperial Maritime Customs kept records of the trade activities affecting them since the opening of the port, but only recorded the tonnage of foreign-flagged vessels and not trade within Asia. In 1891, for example, the Imperial Maritime Customs recorded 372 steamships plus 61 sailing vessels. Not recorded were the large junks that handled the bulk of Asian cargo, i.e., the soybean trade. The number of junks amounted to 1662 in the same year, almost four times that of foreign ships. This comparison illustrates how extensive the tonnage was although it is rare to find concrete figures or other English-language sources for it.[10]

Nevertheless, in 1894, A.R. Agassiz from the Imperial Maritime Customs in Shanghai made some estimations to calculate current and forecast future trade developments. He conducted a thorough study of how Manchuria transformed from an undeveloped hinterland into a region of rapid agricultural and industrial growth thereby becoming an area of interest to foreign powers. According to his calculations, the value of all soy products, including whole beans, cake, and oil exported from Manchuria in 1894 accounted for about 1.5 million pounds sterling and was more than ten times that of silk.[11] A significant difference between the two products was that soybeans and their lightly processed products were shipped mainly to China and Japan, while silk found its way to Europe.

Destinations and Uses

Among the few figures available concerning the soybean trade at the time is one regarding the arrival of produce in Yingkou. For the winter of 1890–1891, Agassiz reported that approximately 100,000 tons of produce were brought to this port. They had reached there on 547 carts, drawn by a total of 2,340 mules and ponies, and awaited processing and further shipment, which was only possible in the spring, after the ice had thawed and the sea once again became navigable. While the precise proportion of soybeans remains obscure, it is known that they were by far the region's most important cash crop and thus the main commodity on these carts. Whatever else people were able to trade, its volume was somewhat negligible compared to beans.[12] Agassiz's numbers thus illustrate the vast amount of beans being shipped annually from Yingkou already in the 1890s.

Another source describing the economic development in Manchuria is Alexander Hosie's book *Manchuria* from 1901. Hosie was the British consul in Yingkou and carefully composed the social, political, and economic situation in the region. Hosie estimated that soybeans and soy products such as bean oil and cake accounted for 78 percent of all goods exported from Northeast China. Other sources confirm Agassiz's and Hosie's observations regarding the increasing Manchurian soybean trade at the time. Tsao Lien-en, also from the Imperial Maritime Customs, reported more than 65,000 tons being shipped from Yingkou in 1867, with almost twice as much—120,000 tons—only seven years later. There was an additional 77,500 tons and 67,000 tons of bean cake in the same years, respectively. With 1,500 tons and 776 tons bean oil in the respective years, trade in this item was rather negligible and even declining. Notably, this tremendous increase in soybean exports occurred when trade was still limited to Japan and southern China. "The European market was then not yet dreamed of," Tsao Lien-en wrote.[13]

Soybeans brought to Yingkou had various uses, with food being only one of many. Soy's economic value lay in its oil's suitability for cooking, and soybean cake, which served as fertilizer and fodder. Putting soybeans in relation to other foods available in traditional China and paying closer attention to how the human body reacts to the soybean helps us to understand why its value as a food was below that of its value as oil and cake. Recent scholarly work dates the earliest mention of soybeans to fragments of an ancient Chinese text from around 1000 B.C., indicating that the plant had already acquired some significance back then. In ancient China, soybeans were traditionally considered one of the five staple grains, with rice, wheat, and two different varieties of millet being the other four. Of these five, wheat and soybeans were considered coarse food, or inferior grains, because they were less appealing and difficult to digest when boiled.[14] While rice and millet became soft and slightly sweet, this did not apply to boiled soybeans and wheat. The introduction of the stone rotary mill (around 500–200 B.C.) changed the status of wheat as it yielded flour suitable for making bread. Soybeans, however, remained rather unappealing, even when ground.

As long ago as the second century A.D. texts are known that refer to bloating caused by eating too many soybeans over a long period of time. In fact, soybeans contain what is now known as antinutrients, that is, plant compounds that reduce the body's ability to absorb essential nutrients. Legumes such as peas and beans generally contain a high amount of such antinutrients, but even within this group soybeans stand out, and it is apparent that people have long been aware of this. Scholars suggest that the crop nevertheless remained an integral part of the traditional Chinese agriculture and diet because it grew well even on poor land, did not deplete the soil, and provided good yields even in years when weather conditions damaged other crops.[15] The soybean was, in a way, an emergency crop suited as food in years of famine and hardship and used as fertilizer and fodder when there were more appealing foods on offer. Thus, they were held in low esteem by the ancient Chinese but kept as part of their diet.

Making soybeans more appealing and their essential nutrients accessible required preparation techniques such as soaking, grinding, sprouting, and fermenting, which then resulted in tofu, soy milk, soy sauce, miso paste, and many others. None of these techniques were recent inventions when soybeans were traded in large quantities at the port of Yingkou around 1900—quite the contrary. In the late nineteenth century, Dutch sinologist Gustaaf Schlegel read through a variety of historical texts of Chinese origin and found evidence for a food item related to tofu mentioned as early as the second century B.C. Being a linguist, Schlegel traced issues related to language, not changing eating habits. Nevertheless, he described a method for making tofu, which was prevalent around his own time. According to him, the beans were first soaked in water for several hours. Thereafter, they were ground, and the resulting thin white mass was then heated up to boiling. The froth was skimmed, and the fluid strained through a cotton cloth. The filtrated fluid was then put in brine, which turned the fluid into a gelatinous mass. The consistency of this form of fresh tofu was similar to cream cheese, and though it did not last long, it was possible to press out a good deal of water, a method which gave it a cheesy texture and increased its shelf life.[16]

Schlegel also traced the mentioning of soy sauce back in time and apparently found evidence of it as long ago as the first century A.D. Again, he combined his linguistic research with a hands-on approach and described a method for making soy sauce he had observed himself. The beans were first boiled and then mixed with an equal amount of wheat or barley, salt, and water and then left to ferment for two to three months, after which the liquid was pressed and strained. The fermenting of soybeans was a pungent business and Schlegel reported on the "disagreeable stench" emanating from the jars used for making soy sauce.[17]

As interesting as Schlegel's research and observations are, they also provide evidence for the making of food from soybeans being a time-consuming process. After all, it seems unlikely that the rising trade in soybeans in the late nineteenth century and the large tonnage arriving year by year at Yingkou was caused by an increased interest in soybeans as food alone. On the contrary, additional sources even seem to suggest that soybeans were neither particularly highly valued nor necessary to serve in order to secure a sufficient intake of protein. Agassiz reported that people in Manchuria fattened their pigs with soybean cake, making pork cheap and plentifully available. Besides pork, goat meat, beef, and mutton were also part of the regular diet, suggesting that there was no urgent need for additional protein resources from soybeans. Tofu "was an article of diet more for the laboring than the upper classes of Chinese," wrote another contemporary observer.[18] And since soybeans hardly contained any carbohydrates, they at no time competed with millet, rice, or wheat. In other words, people had a variety of protein-rich foods at hand and rarely depended on the inferior soybean.

Beans arriving in Yingkou around the 1900s were either shipped as whole beans or crushed in one of the many oil mills located in the city. The extracted oil was used for cooking and baking but also served purposes unrelated to food, such as for lighting and lubrication. The residue of the milling process was a valued fertilizer and shipped to regions where the soils had been depleted by modern agriculture, such as sugar-cane cultivation in southern China or rice fields in Japan. In addition, soybean cake was used as fodder for livestock. Even beans leaving Yingkou as a raw product were eventually mainly processed into oil and a nitrogen-rich residue at their destinations.[19]

Japanese farmers found soybean cake from Manchuria to be a highly effective fertilizer, especially for rice paddy fields. For them, the cake was a cheaper and more effective alternative to fish meal. Since the seventeenth century, fish meal and dried fish had been imported from Ezo (Hokkaido) to the Kinai region, where the demand for commercial fertilizer was intense due to its advanced and concentrated commercial farming of cotton, tobacco, indigo, and *natane* (Japanese rapeseed). Due to overfishing, however, Hokkaido herring became scarce and thus expensive, and Japanese fertilizer merchants began promoting Manchurian soybean cake. In the late 1890s, the trade volume increased drastically. Simultaneously, the demand for soybean products in southern China was diminishing as cotton and sugar plantations there went into decline. By 1899, Japan's purchases of soybean cake exceeded the total amount of all soybean products shipped to southern China. From then on, most of the soybeans grown in China's Northeast, as well as most of the soybean cake, was shipped to Japan.[20] This pattern did not change until 1927, when Germany became the largest customer of whole soybeans.

Railway Imperialism

"Everything depends, at present, upon the export trade, and the growth of the export trade depends upon [...] the improving of the means of communications and facilities for transporting goods," wrote A.R. Agassiz in 1891 about Manchuria and its further economic development.[21] Agassiz was to be proved right; just a few years later a railroad was built, and further ways of economic exploitation were facilitated, which boosted trade. Besides, the railroad became also an expression of the imperial rivalries between China, Russia, and Japan.

Russia had been planning to build its Trans-Siberian Railway across Siberia and the Asian parts of Russia in the direction of Vladivostok since 1891. From early on, these plans, however vaguely, included the idea of an alternative route through the two Chinese provinces of Heilongjiang and Jilin, which would not only have resulted in achieving a shortening of about 340 miles but also gaining increased economic and political power in Northeast China. Tsarist Russia wanted to strengthen its geopolitical position against other European powers by formally and informally building up the empire. The idea for shortening the railway route by having it run through Northeast China, however, did not go unchallenged among Russian officials as initially the railroad was intended to connect the empire's European center with its regions in the Siberian taiga and peripheries in the Far East. The railroad would fail to achieve this goal were it to be built through China.

Nevertheless, plans became more concrete during the Sino-Japanese War of 1894–1895, which was fought largely on Chinese territory, namely Manchuria. The war made clear Japan's growing aspirations to expand into mainland Asia while it also revealed the weakness of the Qing dynasty.[22] Japan's victory and its consequently strengthened position provoked tensions with Russia, which now began planning a railway line through Manchuria as a supplementary route to the Trans-Siberian Railway in order to bolster its strategic and commercial position in Asia. At the instigation of Russian Finance Minister Sergei Witte, Russia offered China its support against Japan in return for permission to build a railroad through the Northeast. In 1896, the treaty was sealed, and the Chinese Eastern Railway (CER) was built between 1897 and 1903. While the Trans-Siberian Railway still skirted around China's Northeast, the CER ran through it between Chita and Vladivostok.

Being now connected by land and sea, Vladivostok was envisioned as an important hub in the Far East, but in terms of trade, it came with the disadvantage of freezing over for several months in winter, making the water unnavigable. Thus, only two years after Russia had concluded the contract over the CER, Russian negotiators strong-armed China into another agreement also meant to further strengthen the Russian empire's position in Manchuria. Through this additional treaty, Russia leased an ice-free region several hundred miles further south of Vladivostok—the Liaodong Peninsula in the Yellow Sea. In addition, China granted a concession for the construction of a second railway line, the so-called South Manchurian Railway (SMR). It was to run perpendicular to the CER in the direction of Dalian and Lüshun Port, back then known as Port Arthur or Royojun. Just as the CER, the SMR also opened in 1903 (see Map 1.1).[23]

Historical research has shown that the work on the railroads proved to be extremely arduous and frustrating for both the colonizers and the colonized. It certainly came at the expense of many people.[24] For the soybean and its trade, however, the railway was nevertheless crucial. It proved quite fundamental in promoting the economic development of the region. In fact, the two railway lines were exemplary of a global phenomenon later framed as railroad imperialism, a term that describes how great powers harnessed spaces for economic development while marking them as part of their respective empires.[25] Thanks to the railway, Manchuria became literally connected to the world as hitherto unknown business opportunities emerged. American Baldwin locomotives, for example, were shipped in component parts from Philadelphia and then assembled in Shanghai, Canton, or Hong Kong under U.S. supervision.[26] In addition, the railway attracted labor and thus further migration. The influx of manpower contributed to developing the region not only through construction work but also by its sheer presence. It paved the way for new markets for global goods such as cotton and tobacco from the United States. The newly established railroad company also managed the surrounding countryside, as not only the route but also an unspecified surrounding area were declared extraterritorial territories of the Tsarist Empire. Thus, the company was involved in the extraction of raw materials necessary to build the lines and erect accommodations as well as other facilities for workers and settlers. Finally, Russian migrants who either came as workers or to settle in the area also permanently fell under the administrative responsibility of the railroad company. Its headquarters were in Harbin, a rapidly growing metropolis where the two railways met—the CER, running between east and west, and the SMR, between north and south. In later years, Harbin was to become the fourth central transshipment point for soybeans and other commodities, along with Yingkou, Vladivostok, and Dalian.[27] In the years to come and as shown in Chapter 2 of this book, these two railroads formed important transportation routes in the long-distance trade of soybeans.

Although China was unable to counter such industrial projects, it was not as powerless as it might first appear. In order to incorporate the Northeast more fully into the Chinese heartland, in the 1890s, the central government in Beijing instigated important administrative reforms. Having earlier merely opened the region for settlement, an outright settlement policy was now initiated in order to mark the land as Chinese through the sheer presence of Han Chinese migrants. Although the policies, based on generous land grants, were poorly organized and led to numerous cases of abuse—the favorable purchase prices for arable land attracted speculators—these efforts nonetheless helped Manchuria to develop. Attracted by the positive economic prospects were migrants from China's overpopulated north, but also Han Chinese who due to the Boxer Rebellion in 1900 had to flee or resettle from the more densely populated and controlled parts of the country. In the years between the opening of the region in the 1860s and the Japanese occupation in 1931, between 28 and 33 million people migrated from China to Manchuria, and at least 13 million Russians moved into Central Asia and

Siberia over this period. While Chinese migrants embarked on a short sea voyage across the Yellow Sea, those coming from Russia used the railway.[28]

In addition, seasonal migrant workers arrived on an annual basis to help in agriculture. Around 1900, from Yantai in northern China alone about 20,000 young men arrived in Yingkou on steamships every spring.[29] The number of those arriving from other ports or taking junks, which was still the predominant means of transportation, remains beyond our knowledge and possibly also our imagination. In any case, the successive incorporation of the Northeast into the Chinese mainland was the Qings' response to Russia's and Japan's imperial claims. The total population, which was at merely two million by the mid-nineteenth century, had rapidly risen to 17 million around 1900, with the majority now living along the railway tracks. The Sino-Japanese War had thus triggered a massive economic and social change.

Crop Talks in Europe and the United States

At the time Russia, China, and Japan were in dispute over vast land masses in the Far East, relatively little was known about Manchuria's most important cash crop in other parts of the world. In nineteenth-century Europe, the soybean had found a way into expert circles concerned with botany, agriculture, and public health, but people at large had never heard about the plant, and most had not come across it. In the United States, the situation was similar, even though it seems that a few farmers, especially in the Midwest and the South, showed an interest in trying out the cultivation of soybeans. That, however, came not out of curiosity but due to poor harvests in other crops.

An early mention of the soybean in a European source is Engelbert Kaempfer's *Amoenitatum exoticarum,* published in 1712. Kaempfer was a German naturalist, physician, and explorer who traveled to many places in Russia, India, Persia, and Japan, among others, and made detailed medical observations and extensive descriptions of plants, including the soybean. Another early indicator of the plant's presence among botanists is the Swedish botanist Carl von Linné, who gave it the botanical name, *Glycine soja.* Nowadays, this term refers to the wild variety, while in plant taxonomy soybeans are known as *Glycine max.* Nevertheless, the plant's baptizing according to Linné's standards shows that he must have been familiar with it. In the course of the nineteenth century, the plant gained entry into some botanical gardens. It is known that the Alte Botanische Garten in Munich, the city's first botanical garden founded in 1809, was working on the soybean as early as 1815. The Royal Gardens in Kew, London, published on them in 1865, while the Bergius Botanic Garden in Stockholm did not include soybeans in its research until after 1900.[30] Generally speaking, the crop had entered circles of botanical expertise to a limited extent but was rather treated as an exotic plant.

There was one agronomist from the Austrian-Hungarian empire, however, who set out in earnest to change that. Friedrich Haberlandt was under the false impression that in Asia the soybean was chiefly used for human nutrition, and, after analyzing the bean's chemical components, tried to establish it as a foodstuff in Austria and beyond as well. Haberlandt, who had never been to Asia to gain knowledge about soybean cultivation and use, acquired seed samples of 20 different soybean varieties at the Vienna World's Fair in 1873 and then started cultivation trials at the botanical fields of the University of Natural Resources and Applied Life Sciences in Vienna. Later on, he sent seed samples to other scientists and farmers all over Europe and encouraged cultivation trials. In 1877, about 160 people in various places in Austria-Hungary, Germany, Poland, the Netherlands, and Switzerland participated in a series of trials. In this way, Haberlandt was able to share his enthusiasm for soy with other experts. However, he was unable to establish soy beyond this circle. One of the reasons for Haberlandt's failure was that when it came to the uses of the soybean, he had focused on food and disregarded the crop's possible applications as fertilizer or fodder. Another reason for his lack of success was that when attempting to establish soybean-based foods, he failed to introduce Asian cooking styles but suggested grinding the beans and adding the resulting flour to dishes according to European culinary conventions. He did not consider any changes in eating habits, treating the beans just like other pulses with which he was familiar.[31] That soybeans in turn were rejected, however, was not only a matter of distaste but also one of indigestion. The high amount of antinutrients in soybeans needed to be broken down through certain techniques, for instance those long proven in Asian-style foods such as tofu, or they would otherwise cause bloating.

Haberlandt died only a few years later in 1878. Other agriculturalists continued working on soybeans and tried to establish them among farmers, but neither did their efforts bear much fruit. In 1881, Bavarian agriculturalist Ernst Wein wrote a short compendium with practical information intended to teach farmers how to grow, treat, and harvest the beans. Although he was most concerned with their cultivation, he also included a few pages on how to make use of them once harvested. Being well aware that soybeans can cause indigestion, he—contrary to Haberlandt—issued advice on Asian-style foods and described a method for making miso paste. In addition, Wein pointed out the beans' value as fodder and wrote in detail on the advantages of adding soybeans to cattle feeds and the quality of the resulting milk.[32] Yet, soybeans failed to catch on in Austrian, German, or any other European agriculture. The simple reason for this was that varieties prevailing back then did not thrive in most parts of Europe because it was too cold during the growing period.[33]

On the other side of the Atlantic, the situation was similar insofar as people at large would not know much about the soybean either. Compared with Europe, however, there were two significant differences in the United States.

Firstly, in the Midwest and in the South climactic conditions for growing the beans were much better than in Germany and Austria. Secondly, farmers who tried them out did so to improve their soils and to provide their livestock with fodder, not to feed people in the first place. The seeds reached Northern America by means of travelers such as former sailors, or migrants distributing them further to early horticultural societies, which then passed them on to farmers. Later, American historians and agriculturalists centered the early years of the soybean in the United States on certain events that fit well with key parameters in U.S. history and memory. According to one of these accounts, U.S. naval officer Matthew Perry played a major role in introducing the soybeans in the United States. Through what became known as gunboat diplomacy, Perry, in 1852, forcibly opened Japanese ports to American trade, and, among other things, returned to the United States with several varieties of the "Japan peas," as they were called back then. Another typical narrative features the soybean playing a certain role during the Civil War as a coffee bean substitute. Each of these and other episodes have their historical evidence, but the actual scale to which soybeans were cultivated in the nineteenth century remained nevertheless almost insignificant.[34]

Some people would promote soybeans as food, most prominently maybe Charles Langworthy, who in 1899 published an appendix on "Soy Beans as Food for Men" to the *Farmers' Bulletin,* a publication of the USDA. The text originated in an environment of experts working on metabolism and nutrition. Best remembered from this circle is Wilbur Atwater, Longworthy's boss within the USDA, who is considered the father of modern nutrition research. In his article, Langworthy argued for soybean-based foods to increase the daily intake of proteins because it was most cost-effective. For preparing the beans, he stood more in the tradition of adjusting the soybean to Western eating habits, just as Haberlandt had done in Austria. Such a perspective on soybean-based foods, mainly as soybean flour, was shared widely among experts in the United States and abroad in years to come, as we will see. For the time being, Langworthy certainly contributed to securing more attention on soybeans, but it remains doubtful whether people actually ate them.[35]

Instead, there is more evidence that American farmers included soybeans in their crop rotation to improve their soil and to provide their livestock with protein-rich feed. Toward the end of the century, the *Farmer's Voice,* a weekly, farm-related newspaper from Illinois, published an article on cultivating and using soybeans. The article was based on agricultural textbooks and letters the paper had received from farmers and agriculturalists working at various colleges or affiliated experiment stations. Most of those sharing their knowledge were located in the Midwest, but the article reflects some nationwide interest in the soybean as it included reports from Virginia, North Carolina, and Massachusetts as well. None of the contributors considered growing soybeans in order to eat them, and neither was anyone interested in extracting the oil within, as became the practice in later years. At this time, American farmers considered soybeans as a pasture crop, and only a few would actually harvest either the beans or the entire plant to keep it as fodder for the winter months. In addition, they grew soybeans to fertilize their soils.[36]

The soybean can in fact have a beneficial effect as a fertilizer, and this characteristic makes it reasonable to include it in crop rotations, at least at first sight. The bean's roots are comprised of nodules that can form a symbiosis with certain bacteria, which can "fix" and thus enrich the soil with nitrogen from the air. Nitrogen is one of the three main macronutrients plants generally need in order to grow, with phosphorus and potassium (or kalium) being the other two. Nitrogen has thus been a sought-after fertilizer for centuries and was naturally to be found in livestock manure. It was not before the early twentieth century that chemists worked out how to produce nitrogen artificially. Prevailing alternatives were legumes such as clover, alfalfa, and most peas and beans, all of which had root nodules able to form a symbiosis with bacteria, allowing farmers to naturally enrich their soils with nitrogen from the air. "Poverty forbids the thought of buying manures; we farmers keep so little stock we cannot make much, and fertilizers are out of our reach," wrote the *Farmer's Voice* on the matter, and suggested the growing of soybeans.

The only downside with using soybeans and other peas and beans as green manure was that each legume needed its own specific bacteria to develop the capacity to fix nitrogen. When the particular bacteria were not yet part of the soil, the respective legume would take nitrogen rather than release it to the soil, just as any other plant. As neither this knowledge nor the bacteria for soybeans were yet widespread in the United States, the results of using the crop as green manure were limited.[37] On the other hand, as most farmers trying out soybeans did not make use of them other than having their cattle or hogs graze the fields, the soil was in any case fertilized with their droppings.

Even though reports on soybeans generally remained scarce, farmers did not seem to have any opposition to the idea of growing them. Quite the contrary: many were looking for an alternative crop to clover in their crop rotation. Clover was a legume just as the soybean and also had the ability to enrich the soil with nitrogen. However, in many places, clover no longer prospered due to the soil being depleted of nutrients from the overproduction of wheat and corn. Farmers were thus on the lookout for an alternative crop. It also helped that in 1898, the USDA began to research unfamiliar crops and their potential usage in U.S. agriculture and various industries. Around that time, only about eight soybean varieties were known in the country.[38] That the USDA now also began investigating the soybean demonstrates a generally rising interest in the crop. One farmer and agriculturalist from the Minnesota School of Agriculture would even predict a very bright future for the crop: "We may expect the soy bean to be one of the most valuable plants in cultivation."[39]

For the time being, however, the soybean constituted a negligible crop in U.S. agriculture, even in the Midwest, where farmers were more inclined to trying them out. Agriculture there was heavily characterized by the production of meat and fodder, in addition to wheat. Even though farmers there were generally better off than small-scale farmers in the South, who remained unproductive and unprofitable, they also experienced hardship at times. Besides, not all those working in agriculture were farmers; sharecroppers often lived without land and hope, also in the Midwest. What made matters worse was that when the prospect of selling more corn or wheat arose, crop rotation was not always followed. Farmers then hoped to earn more money, only to end up with less. Planting the same crops on the same land led to depleted soils and overproduction, which in turn led to reduced income, making it difficult for farmers to earn a living.[40] Since clover would no longer thrive and farmers were on the verge of losing an important fodder and fertilizer all at once, some tried out soybeans as an emergency crop. However, the acreage grown with soybeans was still so small that it was not yet registered in agricultural statistics.

Back in Europe, it was not before the First World War that the legume as a crop for European agriculture was given any more attention, a situation most likely caused by the prevailing food shortages. In order to stimulate new interest, another book was published for which Haberlandt's son, Gottlieb, was given the honor of writing a foreword. Instead of spurring on the general enthusiasm, Haberlandt junior simply pointed out that the book would not "assert essentially new points of view, new facts." Instead, it would just repeat what had been known for the past 40 years. Gottlieb Haberlandt even outright complained that his father's "Schützling" ("fosterling") was still not being cultivated in Central Europe.[41] And yet again, when it came to making use of the beans, Haberlandt and the author of the book, Maurice Fürstenberg, were most concerned with establishing them as a food. According to Fürstenberg, the soybean had the potential to radically change if not revolutionize human nutrition, and he suggested that cheap soy proteins should replace more expensive animal proteins.

Certain agricultural and dietary expert circles, it seems, did not depart from their once-established idea of achieving permanent acceptance of the soybean as a food item, despite the fact that people continued to dislike dishes containing soybeans. Interestingly enough, Fürstenberg was most likely not even aware of the cultivation experiences and uses of soybeans in the American Midwest as he did not mention them at all.

Bridging Cultures

Since soy contains no starch but is nutritious due to its high protein and oil content, it was well proven as a food for diabetics in Asia, a fact European and American medical practitioners and scientists often pointed out as well. In 1890, the *Druggist's Bulletin* of Detroit, Michigan, reported on the "freedom of sugar-making constituents" in soybeans and proposed a loaf of bread made of soybean flour for diabetics. Twenty years later, the British medical journal *The Lancet* published the results of experiments according to which the addition of soybeans to ordinary diabetic food was able to significantly reduce the amount of sugar in the human body. Nevertheless, it remains an open question to which degree any soybean-based food was available to diabetics at the time and if it was actually eaten. Other contemporaries rather complained that soybeans, particularly breads made of their flour, were not fully established among diabetics even though their benefits were known. "It may be (and we will even charitably suppose so) that this lamentable fact is only due to ignorance," complained sinologist Gustaaf Schlegel. He provided no reasons for his assertion, but it is possible these breads still contained the bean's antinutrients and therefore caused digestive problems.[42]

When it came to soybean-based foods, in the late nineteenth century, it was only soy sauce that Europeans and Americans seem to have valued. Hardly any contemporary source failed to mention the certain delicacy the condiment would lend to hearty dishes. All over Europe, soy sauce received entries in general encyclopedias that express a certain familiarity with it.[43] Soy sauce came ready-made from a shelf in a food store; it was an urban luxury, and Europeans likely imported it from Japan. Country-dwellers, on the other hand, who encountered first-hand experiments with the crop on their farms, hardly processed their beans into soy sauce or any other Asian-style foods, as the preparation methods occasionally described by various authors remained foreign to them. In the United States, however, soy sauce was in fact manufactured by Asian immigrants and then sold to their community and beyond. Sources indicate that the production of soy sauce went hand in hand with a growing demand of soybeans, and it is likely that immigrants grew the beans themselves. However, since cultivation numbers for soybeans were not yet recorded, the acreage devoted to the crop in earlier years remains unknown but was in any case small. Also, import numbers remained so small that they were not tracked, again indicating the mere niche soy sauce had found.[44] Besides, when it comes to staples, dietary habits generally change very little over time and only with great difficulty. It was one thing to add a little soy sauce to a Sunday roast, but quite another to switch the roast for tofu altogether.

Interestingly enough, in Europe, it was not only European agriculturalists and nutritional experts who tried to promote the soybean as a food. Another protagonist was Chinese anarchist and global intellectual Li Shizeng. Li was born in 1881 to a father who held influential positions at the Qing court, especially when it came to China's foreign relations. When, in 1902, the Qing court began to establish diplomatic ties with France, Li's father arranged for his son to accompany the newly appointed ambassador. Here, Li first studied agriculture at the École Pratique d'Agriculture in

Montargis and, after graduation in 1905, furthered his education in biology and chemistry at the recently established Institut Pasteur in Paris. During these years, Li was drawn to anarchist ideas and also came into contact with other like-minded Chinese, including Zhang Jingjiang and Wu Zhihui. They formed the core of the so-called Paris Group, a circle of young Chinese intellectuals who worked hard to topple the Qing government.

Besides their intellectual ambitions, Li and the Paris Group were also active on the business front. They started to import Chinese products and ran their own Chinese teashop, as well as a small printing press.[45] With capital stemming from officials within the Chinese government and headquarters in Tianjin, in 1909, Li eventually founded a company making soybean-based foods just outside of Paris. He had the necessary equipment shipped over to France and employed 24 Chinese workers at the plant. They made tofu, soybean milk, soybean flour, coffee substitutes, and the like. In far-away Singapore, the *Weekly Sun* reported on the French Chinese soybean plant as the "most up-to-date factory in France and perhaps in Europe."[46]

The quantities of soybeans imported for this and possibly other adventures in the late nineteenth and early twentieth centuries were too marginal to be entered into national statistics. Disparate sources indicate that there were some imports, in Britain for example around 12,000 tons annually in the early 1900s.[47] These numbers testify that there was some limited interest in and knowledge about the soybean, but no more than that. Just as the amounts shipped to France at the time, likewise the output of Li's plant remains unknown. To further foster interest in Europe and the United States, Li applied worldwide for patents to make soybean-based foodstuffs. He eventually teamed up with a French agriculturalist to publish a series of articles titled "Le Soja" in which he discussed the nutritional benefits of soybeans. He wanted the crop to become more widely known, thereby promoting his own soybean-based foodstuffs.[48] However, as interesting as Li's activities for establishing the soybean as a food in Europe were, they did not achieve much success. Despite spreading the word and actively engaging in promoting soybean-based food, people would hardly begin to include it in their daily diet, neither boiled, fermented, or otherwise processed.

In the United States, the situation was only slightly different. Admittedly, many a business offering tofu started in various states, particularly along the west coast, where the Asian immigrant population was at its highest, but their customers were largely other immigrants from similar social, cultural, and culinary backgrounds. Other than that, only a few Americans were interested in eating soy, and often for religious reasons, such as the Seventh-day Adventists. Through their understanding of a healthy lifestyle, they promoted a vegetarian diet.[49] With that, soy had found a small entry as food in a few circles on both sides of the Atlantic, but to societies at large, the crop was still barely visible.

Conclusion

In the late nineteenth century, imperial disputes over Manchuria turned this formerly vast and unsettled hinterland into a region of growing economic significance. Over the course of only some 20 years, the region became settled and was connected to various parts of the world by means of railroads and ocean shipments. Japan's demand for soybean cake spurred the economic development of the region further but also led Manchurian agriculture to specialize in the soybean. Alexander Hosie, the British consul in Yingkou, concluded that "they are, in a word, the wealth of Manchuria."[50] They were, however, also the region's crux. While the need for fertilizer in southern China and Japan triggered the demand for soybean cake, Chinese migrant settlers offered the product's supply and Russian railways its transport. At the same time, this was no peaceful economic exchange but one interwoven with imperial rivalries between the three empires. The Sino-Japanese War was a first brutal climax in the dispute, and the Russo-Japanese War of 1904–1905, which was again mainly fought in China's Northeast, became so as well.

In around 1900, soybeans were not completely unknown in Europe but interest from industry, agriculture, or society at large was rather limited. Few visionaries highlighted the bean's value as a foodstuff by pointing to its high fat and protein content. However, European cooking methods for dried beans and peas were not applicable to soybeans. They contained different antinutrients than those beans and peas so far available in Europe, which made it harder for the human body to digest them. Thus, enthusiasm for the soybean as a foodstuff remained limited. The following chapters will show that this situation remained for the years to come, but it also shows that soybeans nevertheless gained entry into the Western world—just not as food.

In the first decade of the twentieth century, soybeans found their way to first British and then other European markets. In 1910, the renowned London-based Linnean Society gathered to study soybean seed samples and listen to a lecture by botanist John Henry Holland about the cultivation and use of the crop.[51] In retrospect, Holland seemed one of few contemporaries who was not concerned with promoting soybeans as a food, even though he mentioned that they could be and had been eaten for centuries. Instead, Holland highlighted other uses of the crop—as fertilizer, fat, and feed. He stressed that soybeans had been grown in small quantities in the United States, where they were valued as green manure. In Europe, he explained, the bean's principal use was currently for its oil, and the residue of the milling process was suitable for feeding livestock.

In fact, something had happened that led to a rise in import figures, but it had little to do with nutritional experts promoting the idea of eating soy to improve general health and avoid hunger crises. Those voices could still be heard, but a need for fat led soy to a different customer segment than that for vegetable foods rich in proteins.

Notes

1 "Annual export of beans and their products through Dairen, Newchwang and Vladivostok," compiled by Mitsui & Co., in Tokuji Hoshino, *Economic History of Manchuria* (Seoul: Bank of Chosen, 1920), after 218. A trading season lasted from November 1 of one year to October 31 of the next.

2 Mark Gamsa, *Manchuria: A Concise History* (London: I.B. Tauris, 2020), 6; Mariko Tamanoi, *Memory Maps: The State and Manchuria in Postwar Japan* (Honolulu: University of Hawaii Press, 2009); Shun-Hsin Chou, "Railway Development and Economic Growth in Manchuria," *The China Quarterly* 45 (1971): 57–84, here 57.

3 Gamsa, *Manchuria*, 42; Sören Urbansky, *Beyond the Steppe Frontier: A History of the Sino-Russian Border* (Princeton, Oxford: Princeton University Press, 2020), 30–34.

4 Alexander Hosie, *Manchuria: Its People, Resources and Recent History*, 2nd ed. (London: Methuen & Co. 1904), 135–42.

5 A.R. Agassiz, "Our Commercial Relations with Chinese Manchuria," *The Geographical Journal* 4 (1894): 534–56, here 539.

6 Kenneth Pomeranz, *The Great Divergence: China, Europe, and the Making of the Modern World Economy* (Princeton, NJ: Princeton University Press, 2000), 226; Norman Shaw. *The Soya Bean of Manchuria* (Shanghai: Inspector General of Customs, 1911), 16. There has been some scholarly debate about the significance of the trade in bean cake as fertilizer to southern China, see Yong Xu, "A 'Fertilizer Revolution'? A Critical Response to Pomeranz's Theory of 'Geographic Luck'," *Modern China* 33, no. 2 (2007): 195–229, https://www.jstor.org/stable/20062667.

7 Shortly after Yingkou's opening, the British administration relocated the port nearer to the river's mouth to make it more accessible to steamships. In addition, it renamed the place Newchwang, but the name originally referred to yet another small port city nearby. Robert Nield, *China's Foreign Places: The Foreign Presence in China in the Treaty Port Era* (Hong Kong: Hong Kong University Press, 2015), 166; Agassiz, "Commercial Relations," 535. In this monograph, I use the term Yingkou.

8 Wolfgang Seuberlich, *Zur Verwaltungsgeschichte der Mandschurei (1644–1930)* [Berlin 1943], ed. Hartmut Walravens (Wiesbaden: Harrassowitz Verlag, 2001), 46–47; James Reardon-Anderson, *Reluctant Pioneers: China's Expansion Northward, 1644–1937* (Stanford: Stanford University Press, 2005), 71–84.

9 Seuberlich, *Verwaltungsgeschichte*, 70.

10 Agassiz, "Commercial Relations," 540–51; similarly, but for 1898 and 1899, Hosie, *Manchuria*, 259–60.

11 Agassiz, "Commercial Relations," 541.

12 Agassiz, "Commercial Relations," 539.

13 Tsao Lien-en, "The Marketing of Soya Beans and Bean Oils," *Chinese Economic Journal* 7, no. 3 (September 1930): 941–71, here 948–49.

14 Hsing-Tsung Huang, "Early Uses of Soybean in Chinese History," in *The World of Soy*, eds. Christine M. Du Bois, Chee-Beng Tan, and Sidney Mintz (Chicago: University of Illinois, 2008), 45–55, here 45–46.

15 Huang, "Early Uses," 45–46; Thomas Sorosiak, "Soybean," in *The Cambridge World History of Food*, vol. 1, eds. Kriemhild Coneè Ornelas and Kenneth F. Kiple (Cambridge, UK: Cambridge University Press, 2000), 422–26, here 422.

16 Gustaaf Schlegel, "The Chinese Bean-Curd and Soy and the Soya-Bread of Mr. Lecerf," *T'oug Pao* 5, no. 2 (1894): 135–47, here 138–39. Hosie, *Manchuria*, 183 described a similar process for making tofu.

17 Schlegel, "The Chinese Bean-Curd," 136, 140–42. The off-putting smell is confirmed by Hsing-Tung Huang, *Science and Civilisation in China,* vol. 6, pt. 5, *Fermentations and Food Science* (Cambridge, UK: Cambridge University Press, 2000), 293.
18 Agassiz, "Commercial Relations," 540. The region's staple was sorghum (millet), which was usually consumed locally. Wheat and rice, in contrast, also grew in Manchuria, but both were cultivated for trade. Rice was twice as expensive as sorghum and considered a luxury food. See also, Adachi, *Manchuria*, 178–79; U.S. Department of Commerce and Labor, *Soya Bean and Products*, Special Consular Reports, vol. 41 (Washington, DC: Government Printing Office, 1909), 6.
19 Agassiz, "Commercial Relations," 541–42.
20 *Report on Progress in Manchuria, 1907–1928* (Dairen: South Manchurian Railway Co., 1929), 116; David L. Howell, *Capitalism from Within: Economy, Society, and the State in a Japanese Fishery* (Berkeley: University of California Press, 1995); Hiromi Mizuno and Ines Prodöhl, "Mitsui Bussan and the Manchurian Soybean Trade: Geopolitics and Economic Strategies in China's Northeast, ca. 1870s–1920s," *Business History,* published April 22, 2019, https://doi.org/10.1080/00076791.2019.1687688.
21 Agassiz, "Commercial Relations," 555.
22 On Japan's expansionism, see, among others, Ramon H. Myers. "Japanese Imperialism in Manchuria: The South Manchuria Railway Company, 1906–1933," in *The Japanese Informal Empire in China, 1895–1937,* eds. Peter Duus, Ramon H. Myers, and Mark R. Peattie, 101–32 (Princeton: Princeton University Press, 1989); Yoshihisa Tak Matsusaka, *The Making of Japanese Manchuria, 1904–1932* (Cambridge, MA: Harvard University Asia Center, 2001); Sherman Cochran, *Encountering Chinese Networks: Western, Japanese, and Chinese Corporations in China, 1880–1937* (Berkeley, CA: University of California Press, 2000).
23 On the construction of the CER see, among others, Ralph E. Glatfelter, "Russia, the Soviet Union, and the Chinese Eastern Railway," in *Railway Imperialism*, eds. Clarence B. Davis, Kenneth E. Wilburn, and Ronald E. Robinson (New York, NY: Greenwood Press, 1991), 137–54, here 140–41; Sarah C.M. Paine, "The Chinese Eastern Railway from the First Sino-Japanese War until the Russo-Japanese War," in *Manchurian Railways and the Opening of China*, eds. Bruce A. Elleman and Stephan Kotkin (Armonk, NY: M.E. Sharpe, 2010), 13–36; Rosemary K.I. Quested, *"Matey" Imperialists?: The Tsarist Russians in Manchuria, 1895–1917* (Centre of Asian Studies, University of Hong Kong, 1982); Sören Urbansky, *Kolonialer Wettstreit: Russland, China, Japan und die Ostchinesische Eisenbahn* (Frankfurt/Main; New York, NY: Campus Verlag, 2008), 23–53; Jürgen Osterhammel, *China und die Weltgesellschaft. Vom 18. Jahrhundert bis in unsere Zeit* (München: Beck 1989), 218–21.
24 Glatfelter, "Russia," 140–41.
25 See Ronald Robinson, "Introduction," in *Railway Imperialism*, eds. Davis, Wilburn and Robinson, 1–6; Frtihjof Benjamin Schenk, *Russlands Fahrt in die Moderne: Mobilität und sozialer Raum im Eisenbahnzeitalter* (Stuttgart: Franz Steiner Verlag, 2014), 114–18; Bruce A. Elleman, Elisabeth Köll, and Y. Tak Matsusaka, "Introduction," in *Manchurian Railways and the Opening of China,* eds. Elleman and Kotkin, 3–9; for China, the phenomenon is best described in Elisabeth Köll, *Railroads and the Transformation of China* (Cambridge, MA: Harvard University Press, 2019).
26 Hosie, *Manchuria*, 48.
27 On Harbin and its rise under Russian and Chinese rule see James Carter, *Creating a Chinese Harbin: Nationalism in an International City, 1916–1932* (Ithaca, NY: Cornell University Press, 2002); David Wolff, *To a Harbin Station: The*

Liberal Alternative in Russian Manchuria, 1898–1914 (Stanford, CA: Stanford University Press, 1999); Mark Gamsa, *Harbin: A Cross-Cultural Biography* (Toronto: University of Toronto Press, 2020); Blaine R. Chiasson, *Administering the Colonizer: Manchuria's Russians under Chinese Rule, 1918–1929* (Vancouver: UBC Press, 2010); as well as the contributions to *Itinerario* 35, no. 3 (2022), special issue on "Ethnic Ghettos and Transcultural Processes in a Globalized City: New Research on Harbin" (eds. Frank Grüner and Ines Prodöhl). To varying degrees, all of these works analyze the semi-colonial settings in Harbin and touch upon the importance of the railway for trade and exchange, but none pays special attention to the city as a trading hub for soybeans.

28 Seuberlich, *Verwaltungsgeschichte*, 71; Adam McKeown, "Global Migration, 1846–1940," *Journal of World History* 15, no. 2 (2004): 155–189, here 158–59, https://www.jstor.org/stable/20068611.

29 Hosie, *Manchuria*, 178–79.

30 *Samen-Catalog des königlich botanischen Gartens zu München 1815,* Bayerische Staatsbibliothek, 4 Bavar. 1588; "List of Publications," *Bulletin of Miscellaneous Information (Royal Botanical Gardens, Kew)*, no. 121 (January 1897), 7; Veit Brecher Wittrock and Hans Oscar Juel, *Catalogus Plantarum Perennium Bienniumque in Horto Botanico Berigiano* (Stockholm: Isaac Marcus' Boktr-Aktiebolag, 1891).

31 Friedrich Haberlandt, *Die Sojabohne: Ergebnisse der Studien und Versuche über die Anbauwürdigkeit dieser eingeführtenden Culturpflanze* (Vienna: Georld, 1878), 103–10; Ernst Langthaler, "Friedrich Haberlandt's Failed Vision: Soy in European Food Cultures, 1873–1945," *Arcadia* (Spring 2018), no. 3, https://doi.org/10.5282/rcc/8177.

32 Ernst Wein, *Die Sojabohne als Feldfrucht: Zusammenstellung der vorliegenden Cultur- und Düngungsversuche für den praktischen Landwirth* (Berlin: Verlag von Paul Parey, 1881), 42–49.

33 Contemporaries, or at least those in Germany, would not, however, accept that poor climactic conditions were the main reason for the beans' low esteem in German agriculture, and rather point to the lack of interest and knowledge among farmers, see Maurice Fürstenberg, *Die Einführung der Soja. Eine Umwälzung der Volksernährung* (Berlin, 1916), 21.

34 Thomas Sorosiak, "Soybean," in *The Cambridge World History of Food,* vol. I, ed. Kenneth F. Kiple (Cambridge, UK: Cambridge University Press, 2000), 422–26, here 423; Theodore Hymowitz, "Introduction of the Soybean to Illinois," *Economic Botany* 41, no. 1 (1987): 30–31; Matthew Roth, *Magic Bean: The Rise of Soy in America* (Lawrence, KS: University Press of Kansas, 2018), 3–4.

35 USDA, *The Soy Bean as a Forage Crop,* by Thomas A. Williams, with appendix "Soy Beans as Food for Man," by Charles F. Langworthy, Farmers' Bulletin, no. 58 (Washington, DC: U.S. Government Printing Office, 1899); Roth, *Magic Bean,* 5–6.

36 "What Two Legumes Can Do," *Farmer's Voice* (April 15, 1899), 8; similar accounts are "Japan Pea," *The Country Gentlemen* 5, no. 15 (April 12, 1855): 232; "Drought-resisting Crops," in *Prairie Farmer* (May 26, 1900), 5.

37 It was known in agricultural circles that soybeans needed the bacteria to form nodules and enrich the soil with nitrogen, see "Drought-resisting Crops," in *Prairie Farmer* (May 26, 1900), 5; "Brown's Crop Talk," *Farmer's Review* (December 26, 1914), 2. In the 1920s, agriculturalists from the USDA still doubted how widespread this knowledge was and whether farmers would observe the practice of inoculating their beans; Jay C. Hackleman, "The Future of the Soybean as a Forage Crop," *Agronomy Journal* 16, no. 3 (1924): 228–36, https://doi.org/10.2134/agronj1924.00021962001600030016x; see also Chapter 4 of this book.

38 Edwin G. Strand, *Soybean Production in War and Peace* (Washington, DC: U.S. Department of Agriculture, 1945), 1–2.
39 "Drought-resisting Crops," in *Prairie Farmer* (May 26, 1900), 5.
40 R. Douglas Hurt, *American Agriculture: A Brief History* (West Lafayette, IN: Purdue University Press, 2002), 217.
41 Fürstenberg, *Die Einführung,* preface by Gottlieb Haberlandt (author's translation).
42 H.H. Rusby, "Soja," *Druggist Bulletin* 4, no. 4 (April 1890): 113; "The Use of the 'Soy Bean' as a Food in Diabetics," *The Lancet* 176, no. 4556 (1910): 1844–45; Gustaaf Schlegel, "The Chinese Bean-Curd," 146.
43 Haberlandt, *Sojabohne,* 12; "Soja," in *Brockhaus' Conversations-Lexikon,* 13th ed. (Leipzig: F.A. Brockhaus, 1882–1878), here vol. 14 (1886), 903; "Soja," *Illustreret norsk konversationsleksikon* (Oslo: Aschehoug, 1907–1913), here vol. 6 (1903), 972–73; "Souï," *Nouveau Larousse illustré* (Paris: Larousse, 1878–1907), here vol. 7 (1898), 762; "Soja," *Meyers Konversations-Lexikon,* 3rd ed. (Leipzig: Bibliographisches Institut, 1874–1884), here vol. 14 (1878), 734.
44 Roth, *Magic Bean*, 21; for the difficulties of changing food habits see Alexander Nützenadel and Frank Trentmann: "Mapping Food and Globalization," in Alexander Nützenadel and Frank Trentmann, eds., *Food and Globalization: Consumption, Markets and Politics in the Modern World* (Oxford; New York, NY: Berg, 2008), 1–18.
45 Arif Dirlik, *Anarchism in the Chinese Revolution* (Berkeley: University of California Press, 1993), 81; Gotelind Müller-Saini, *China, Kropotkin und der Anarchismus: Eine Kulturbewegung im China des frühen 20. Jahrhunderts unter Einfluss des Westens und der japanischen Vorbilder* (Wiesbaden: Harrassowitz, 2001), 208. I am grateful to Christiane Sibille and Rudolph Ng for assisting me with research on Li Shizeng.
46 "A Chinese Factory in France," in *Weekly Sun*, March 4, 1911, 10, accessed June 21, 2022, http://eresources.nlb.gov.sg/newspapers/Digitised/Article/weeklysun19110304-1.2.40.
47 "Soy Beans," *Journal of the Royal Society of Arts* 58, no. 2994 (April 8, 1910): 519, http://www.jstor.org/stable/41339108.
48 *Li Yu-Ying (Li Shizeng), History of His Work with Soyfoods and Soybeans in France, and His Political Career in China and Taiwan (1881–1973), Extensively Annotated Bibliography and Sourcebook*, compiled by William Shurtleff and Akiko Aoyagi, June 8, 2011, accessed June 21, 2022, https://www.soyinfocenter.com/pdf/144/LiYy.pdf.
49 Matthew Roth, *Magic Bean,* 15–26.
50 Hosie, *Manchuria*, 245.
51 "Soy Beans," 519.

2 Commodifying Soy in Europe

Technological Change, Imperialism, and Globalization

From 1908–1909 onward, soybeans were being sold to a specific but growing market in Europe, namely that for fatty raw materials in the production of margarine, soap, and paints, among others. In this chapter, I will show that soybeans entered European markets before the First World War as a resource for further processing, not as a commodity with its own value. The resource it delivered was fat. I argue that the interplay between three simultaneous processes enabled the beans' transfer to regions outside Asia. Key to soybeans becoming a crop of global significance were technological developments in Europe, mainly in the field of chemistry. Scientific knowledge and technological developments in Europe during the Second Industrial Revolution were a prerequisite to soybean's entry into markets outside Asia. They triggered a demand for a variety of raw materials, with fat being one of them. The demand for fat in Europe was closely watched by the Japanese trading house Mitsui[1], which successfully offered soybeans from Northeast China to European customers from 1908 onward. What followed were numerous shipments of soybeans to Europe, first mainly to the British port of Hull, but later elsewhere too, and Mitsui became the primary player facilitating this trade. The trading house had established itself as one of the few powerful companies in Manchuria in the course of the Russo-Japanese war.

Equally important for soy's commodification outside Asia was Japanese imperialism, that is its policy and practice of extending power and domination in Manchuria, among other regions. From the late nineteenth century, Japan aimed at acquiring territory on the Asian mainland, and the outcome of the war provided it with such a foothold. Japan now controlled parts of southern Manchuria, including the strategically important city of Dalian and parts of the SMR, the railway which ran from this port up to Harbin. With that, the door was open for Mitsui and other powerful companies, which in turn were expected to economically control the region. Political protection provided by the Japanese empire in the form of subsidies or privileges, as well as Mitsui's particular business practices with Chinese farmers, enabled it to ship soy around the world at a rate and a scale that was previously unknown. Japanese imperial encounters turned Manchuria into

DOI: 10.4324/9781003255222-3

the main growing region for the bean on a worldwide basis. This process, however, was less caused by European demand for soybeans as it was by meeting Japan's own needs in soybean cake as fertilizer.

However, without rapid lines of communication and transportation, Mitsui would not have been able to watch the European market and ship the beans to it. A generally globalizing world was thus the third driving force behind soy's global encounters. Most important in this respect were quick lines of communication and transportation, as in this case provided by the CER and SMR, in addition to Chinese railways built in competition with the major two. Besides railways, ships and telegraphs facilitated the transfer of information and goods and were needed for gathering information, organizing trade, and securing markets.

The chapter draws on a wide array of sources. Contemporary scientific publications regarding fats in food and industry are complemented by trade statistics and reports from the governments in Great Britain and the United States. Americans feared for their business interests in Manchuria and thus kept a close eye on its market; their reports are thus a rich source of material. Japanese actors often published statistics and promotional material about Manchuria in English, not least to present their activities in China as projects of modernization. These publications must be read critically and analyzed in light of their origins, but they nevertheless help to understand all interests in soy at the time.

Fat: Lubricant of Modernity

Fat is important for every living being—it is essential for life. Even though no other food contains energy in such a high concentration as fat, the consumption of fat is of greater importance than the mere intake of sufficient calories. To eat fat is to stay healthy, as fat is essential for the absorption of certain vitamins. In addition, a lack of some fatty acids can lead to deficiency diseases. In other words, fat, vitamins, and human development, or productivity, are mutually dependent. This link and the resulting importance of fat for human well-being has been known since the mid-nineteenth century.[2] Considering this substance's significance as a food and—as will be shown—nonfood resource, it seems appropriate to define fat in the first place. I will then reflect upon fatty raw materials, their uses, and markets around 1900, a time when soybeans had not yet entered Europe as a raw material for fat.

Chemically, fats are triacylglycerols (or triglycerides), and these in turn are esters of three fatty acids and glycerol (or glycerin). Triacylglycerols are found in all living organisms, but they can have different chemical and physical properties, which is because there are a variety of fatty acids. Among other individual characteristics, the various fatty acids permit different chemical aggregate states at room temperature. Solid triacylglycerols are often referred to as fats, while liquid ones are called (fatty) oils. Chemists prefer to use triacylglycerols as an umbrella term; however, in this context, *fat* seems a simple and reasonable alternative when addressing both forms.[3]

Nowadays, the overabundance of fat seems a burden, particularly when in terms of body mass and the link between being overweight and heart disease, diabetes, and many other human maladies. The unlimited availability of fat, however, is a rather more recent historical development: until the mid-twentieth century, Western societies had only limited resources of it available. Fat is the main component in certain animal products such as butter, margarine, lard, and whale oil, and it is found to varying degrees in all seeds. Traditionally, the choice of fat for human nutrition was closely linked to its general availability, no matter whether its origin was animal or vegetable. Sesame is considered the oldest oilseed crop consumed by humans. Even though scientists are divided over the question of whether its domestication first occurred in Africa or in India, for both regions the event dates back to the ancient world.[4] In the early modern period, African slaves brought sesame to Northern America, where it has been an integral part of the black population's cuisine ever since, particularly in the southern United States. Even for other regions, archeologists and botanists have been able to date the use of certain seeds as oil crops back to prehistoric periods. In southern Europe, olives have been used for oil production since the Bronze Age.[5] Central Europe focused on animal fats, alongside a few oil plants such as flax, poppy, and hemp, while northern European countries specialized in whaling.

For the better part of the nineteenth century, this conventional pattern remained more or less the same. People would eat what was available and tasted good, and kept less palatable fats for nonfood needs, such as tallow for soap and candles. Most vegetable oils were also considered less palatable; rapeseed oil had mainly been used for lighting purposes and as a lubricant, palm oil in soap making, and linseed in paints. Toward the end of the century, however, the processing of fat benefitted significantly from technological and scientific achievements stemming from the advancing or further specializing of industry. Findings in modern chemistry and physics led to sophisticated material syntheses, of which fat was only one raw material among many others. However, for this commodity, the new knowledge led to fundamental changes in terms of production, processing, use, and consumption.

A first milestone in the processing of fat was the invention of margarine in France in the late 1860s. In this case, scientific knowledge met with political efforts to supply the population with sufficient amounts of fat. Due to increasing political tensions with Prussia as well as rising prices for butter, the French government was looking for a cheap, durable, and healthy substitute product. Napoleon III initiated a competition for an alternative to butter that would initially be used primarily in the military and in poorhouses. The result, which was principally based on beef fat, was the forerunner of today's margarine. Although dairy farmers almost everywhere put up massive resistance to its introduction, margarine soon became popular in Europe and North America simply because it was less expensive than butter and lard.[6] This margarine, however, relied on solid fats from animals and did not have much in common with the product as we know it today, which is produced from vegetable resources.

While Europeans worked on butter substitutes, U.S. entrepreneurs and chemists made efforts to stretch lard, which was in common use in baking and cooking. They worked with stearin or tallow and also attempted to make use of cottonseed, a fatty raw material that the United States had in abundance. Being a waste product particular to the southern states, the seed's oil had so far found little use in the food sector since its odor and brownish color were off-putting. In 1899, the American food chemist David Wesson developed a process that removed these unsightly characteristics from the oil, suddenly turning it into a product suitable for human consumption. Refined cottonseed oil, marketed under the brand name Snowdrift and later Wesson Oil, could now be used for frying or to make salads. In the years to come, refining techniques became central for the processing and use of vegetable resources on both sides of the Atlantic. Tangy tastes, odors, and colors, which had often hindered their use as food, could now be successively eliminated.

Another issue with oils was that they could only be used as an additive to margarine or lard in smaller quantities because their low melting point led to the diluted product becoming too soft. Converting fluid into solid fat was thus another milestone in the processing of fat. In 1901, German chemist Wilhelm Normann succeeded in doing so with a technique that became known as fat hardening. This process enabled companies such as Procter & Gamble in the United States or the forerunners of today's Unilever in Europe to replace animal fat with cheaper vegetable fat. Margarine slowly but steadily became a product based on formerly fluid resources, such as vegetable or whale oil, as both were much cheaper than animal fats.[7] Vegetable shortening suitable for baking and cooking did not have the same taste as lard but could be used in the same way. In 1911, Procter & Gamble launched a cheap frying and baking fat based on cottonseed oil called Crisco, which was marketed very successfully in the United States by means of a vast advertising campaign. It is still available today.[8]

As a result of these chemical insights and the possibilities to change the characteristics of certain fats, the market for fat changed. Margarine and shortening containing formerly fluid resources, such as cottonseed oil or whale oil, became increasingly prominent, not least because they were cheaper than pure fats such as butter or even lard. Around 1900, margarine consumption in Prussia was at 100,000 tons per year, but by 1913 that amount had more than doubled. Even so, less margarine was being consumed than butter, which was at 350,000 tons in 1913, but the share of the former was rising constantly.[9]

Even though by far the largest and most sought-after market for fat was that for food, there have always been other markets for fat and these additional industries also benefitted from newer processing insights. The flexibility in the use of fatty raw materials around the time soybeans appeared on the European market is essential to the plant's history, even if most soybean oil went into the production of margarine. A look at various end products and thus possible uses for soybean oil thus helps in understanding the complexity of the global fat market.

The most common examples from the long history of uses for fat in nonfood applications are oil lamps and soap. In addition, fat served a lubricant, and its usage as such rose tremendously with the ongoing industrialization. Further fat-based products were paints and varnishes, as they protected all sorts of machines against erosion, and their markets grew with the industrialization too. The production of these products also became simultaneously specialized as a benefit of newer chemical insights. Then there was dynamite, invented in the 1860s, which was manufactured from glycerin, a component in fat. There were other uses for fat to come in the course of further technological developments, eventually turning fat into a lubricant of the modern age. Beginning in the late nineteenth century, the beauty industry made advances with numerous products based on fat, such as lipsticks, lotions, and creams; waterproof fabrics such as oilcloth were just as suitable for the dining table as they were as clothing for the military; in times of limited electrical supply, candles were still to be found everywhere; printing ink relied on fat, as did early plastics.

Petroleum, which is mostly used today for the purposes mentioned here, was far from ubiquitous in the late nineteenth and early twentieth centuries, thus organic fats were in high demand either during the production process or as an ingredient of the final products themselves. But not all fats were used to an equal extent in this nonfood sector. Fats from animal origin were preferred for direct consumption as food, while vegetable oils were kept for technical or industrial purposes. They often had strong aftertastes and, before the advent of refining and deodorization, were considered unpalatable.

The possibilities for using fats in nonfood items seemed endless around 1900. Nevertheless, we can elucidate the market by sorting the various end products into three major groups. A first significant market for fat in nonfood use lay in the manufacture of soaps, detergents, and cleaning agents. This sector expanded rapidly throughout the nineteenth century, as the example of Britain illustrates. While the British consumed 24,100 tons of soap annually in 1801, by 1851 the figure had risen to 85,053 tons. By 1912 the figure had quadrupled again to 366,000 tons. This rising demand for soap was not solely caused by new hygiene standards but by geopolitical expansions as well. A prerequisite to more soaps for private households was access to adequate raw materials, and tropic palm oil from British Nigeria became soap's most important ingredient. Mindful of these developments, contemporaries saw the soap industry as the market with the strongest growth rates for fat worldwide.[10]

The soap industry had even more to offer than hygiene products. When producing soap, the fatty acids were separated from the glycerol and then converted. Besides various soaps suitable for cleaning, other compounds and transformations yielded end products that were still soaps in their chemical composition but had little in common with them in a conventional sense. These included plaster and zinc ointments as well as aluminum soaps used for waterproof fabrics and oilcloth blankets.[11] Even though this market was still emergent, the invention of these products indicate the growing demand for fat.

A second significant market for fat in nonfood uses lay in the production of paints, varnishes, and lacquers. Traditionally they were based almost exclusively on linseed and tung oils because these dried in the air, leaving a protective film on the coated surfaces. Chemical insights made it possible to stretch linseed and tung oils to some extent with semi-drying oils such as cottonseed, linseed, or eventually also soybean oil. The result was cheaper than the original, but also of inferior quality. Paints diluted in this way often formed drops and usually remained sticky, but as the demand for paints stayed high so too did the use of fat in their production.[12]

Finally, a growing third market for fat was in the field of chemical synthesis, which, among other things, made it possible to replace wood with synthetic materials, such as linoleum and early plastics for furniture and the lining of railroad cars or kitchens. In chemical synthesis, the use of fat was particularly promising as it included the manufacture of such diverse products as artificial leather, sheet metal, wool fabrics, glue, and early substitutes for rubber.

All these chemical insights resulted in a bigger market for fluid fats and their imported raw materials. Home-grown vegetable resources were usually not at hand and animal fats were in any case far too expansive and in short supply anyway, as the rising demand for affordable margarine and shortening proved. Scientific knowledge had thus transformed the entire fat market. It was shifting toward greater flexibility and broader possibilities in terms of raw materials and end products.

In reviewing these developments, Carl L. Alsberg and Alonzo E. Taylor, two American nutritionists, pointed out in 1928:

> Hydrogenation, refining, deodorizing, stearin pressing, winterizing, and a large number of other technological processes which have been evolved in the course of the last 150 years have all had one object: to make one fat substitutable for another.[13]

Even though the transformation of fat had its limits, replacing one fat with another without much loss in quality decoupled the end product from the availability of a particular raw material. In turn, fat-processing industries became less dependent on crop failures, fluctuating quantities of animal resources, or economic and social unrest. However, the increasing diversity made the entire market rather complex, even for experts like Alsberg and Taylor. They noted that the information available on fatty raw materials and their uses was inadequate and unsatisfactory because their origins were so diverse and their markets so numerous.[14]

Import Dependencies

The changing and generally expanding use of fat leads to the assumption of a rising demand for fatty raw materials in the late nineteenth and early twentieth centuries worldwide. Europeans required more resources both to feed a growing population and to keep the wheels of industry turning. The latter's demand was met with supplies from overseas, while home-grown resources, essentially animal fat such as butter or lard, tended to be used for direct consumption as food. Imported vegetable resources were often processed into margarine and lard substitutes, for example, or found applications in consumer goods such as soaps, the manufacture of tin cans, woolen fabrics, or linoleum.

This development is reflected in contemporary sources, but with the fat market being so confusing, it remains difficult to locate comparable data regarding resources, trading patterns, markets, and outlets. The first survey on the global fat market—or, more precisely, the market for fat from vegetable sources—was published by the International Institute of Agriculture (IIA) in Rome in 1923. The IIA was an international organization founded in 1905 with the aim of recording global agricultural statistics as comprehensively as possible. The institute specialized in processing national data collections in an internationally comparative manner. The survey on fat goes back in time to 1909.[15] Incidentally, 1909 is also the year from which soybean imports in Europe rose significantly. While the data collected in the survey naturally does not allow us to trace the rising demand for fat prior to that year, it is nevertheless a good reflection of the supply and demand of the most sought-after sources of vegetable oil at the time of the arrival of the soybean as an additional fatty raw material in Europe.

According to the survey, all major European powers imported additional fat to meet their demand, but the preferred resource varied widely from country to country, as the following example from 1909 illustrates. Germany, still one of the great European powers at that time, mainly imported linseed (437,000 tons) as well as palm nuts and kernels (231,000 tons). Copra, the dried flesh of the coconut, was the third main imported resource, with imports by weight registered at 112,000 tons. Great Britain, however, recorded 610,000 tons of cottonseed and 305,000 tons of linseed as its foremost imports of fat-containing resources.[16] When looking at the figures by weight, it seems that the total imports in both countries were equal; however, the amount of fat varies significantly in the respective resources, and the quantity of imported raw materials does not equate to the amount of fat obtained.

Copra and palm nuts, both preferred in Germany, were among those vegetable raw materials containing the highest amount of fat, copra containing

60–75 percent and palm nuts yielding 35–40 percent. At room temperature both had a soft but not liquid texture which made them attractive for modifying margarine and lard. In addition, they could be used in a wide range of products and did not require much processing. Cottonseed and linseed, with similar chemical characteristics, applications, and prices, represent the other end of the spectrum.[17] Their oils remained fluid at room temperature, had a strong odor and off-taste, and required further alteration when used in foodstuffs. Cottonseed contained about 17 percent fat and linseed around 35 percent, and their oils were among the least expensive on the world market.

Despite the challenges of analyzing the data given for Germany and Great Britain in the example above—not to mention the global trade in fatty raw materials at the time—the IIA's survey is testimony to the contemporary world order. Preference for a certain resource was hardly based on its chemical characteristics or the amount of fat it contained, but rather on where it came from. The European powers often gave preference to their colonies and the raw materials that could be obtained from them. India, for example, was the main producer of cottonseed, and Great Britain the main recipient. Peanuts stood out with a comparatively high amount of fat (approximately 50 percent), but, in contrast to all other fat resources, were scarcely imported by European countries, except for France—because Senegal, by that time a French colony, was a major producer. Linseed, mainly imported by Germany, Great Britain, and Belgium, was grown in India and to an even greater extent in Argentina. While Indian linseed served British needs, independent Argentina supplied Germany and Belgium. As neither European country had access to colonies specialized in the cultivation of oil palms or coconuts, each relied on supplies from independent or seemingly independent regions. The German demand for copra was served by the Philippines, which prior to the First World War was by far the largest area for the cultivation of coconuts and had by that time just lost its struggle for independence from the United States.[18] As will be shown in Chapter 3, Germany's focus on importing soybeans after the First World War was based on the consideration that the trade was not controlled by any other European power.

The data published by the IIA generally confirm the old European world order, but there are some striking exceptions. Throughout the early 1910s, Germany had a preference for palm nuts and kernels and was by far the main importing country of this resource. Palm trees were primarily grown in Nigeria, then a British colony, and in French West Africa, but neither France nor Great Britain imported significant amounts of these commodities prior to the First World War.[19] Explaining this seemingly paradoxical observation would require further research, but it could be that French and British oil mills considered the processing of palm nuts and kernels as too costly compared to existing production methods.

The survey further shows that the demand for fats rose steadily in the years prior to the First World War. They were mainly used in the manufacture of foodstuffs, soaps, paints, and various synthetic products, but there were also areas of use that proved to be stagnant or in slight decline despite a generally rising demand for fat. Such declining markets were those for lubricants and illuminants. The Industrial Revolution had initially created an increased demand for greases and oils since steam engines for cotton spinning, mining, railroads, and shipping required regular lubrication. From about 1850 mineral oils were also used for this purpose but did not yet completely replace organic raw materials. Instead, mixtures of petroleum and tallow or lard were often used, while rapeseed oil turned out to be particularly useful in shipbuilding. In fact, up to the First World War, rapeseed oil was by no means considered palatable and was solely sought after for technical uses, such as for lighting or as a lubricant. What led to the decline of the market for fat-based lubrication was major the advancement of internal combustion and electric engines as they replaced steam engines. Another declining market was for oil lamps and candles. With the increasing electrification of public spaces and private households, especially in the urban centers of Europe and America, candles, and oil lamps fell into less frequent use, in particular after 1900.[20]

To sum up, it should be noted that fats have become increasingly modifiable and versatile since the late nineteenth century. They have turned into a valuable raw material not only for foodstuffs but also for a large variety of end products. Chemical and technical knowledge had made highly sophisticated manufacturing processes possible, and manufacturers in Europe were on the lookout for raw materials to supply the growing population with food and an increasing range of consumer goods.

The Advent of the Soybean in Europe

The Dalian-based Mitsui trading house had a branch in London which had been established to facilitate the company's rice business but also to report back on the European markets. The office in London had apparently noticed the increasing demand for fat in Europe and in the late fall of 1906 made an initial attempt to offer soybeans as a fatty raw material in Britain. This attempt failed because the beans had drawn moisture on their journey and arrived rotten. A second attempt in the following year reached the port of Liverpool undamaged and the beans were successfully launched as an oil crop. Fats were generally sought after at the time, but failures of Indian linseed crops had triggered a rising demand for inexpensive alternatives. Contemporary sources vary when it comes to the quantity of soybeans Mitsui shipped to Europe in the years prior to 1908, yet everything indicates that they were trial shipments and the volumes rather small. Other sources report that Mitsui was not the only player seeking to launch the soybean on European markets. Moiseevich Kabalkin, a Harbin-based Russian grain merchant, tried to do so at around the same time as well but was apparently less successful.[21]

The beans Mitsui sent came from Northeast China, which at that time was divided by different spheres of influence. Due to the semi-colonial conditions, no standardized trade statistics reflecting the soybean business are available. Manchuria had two ports open to international trade, with Dalian being under Japanese control and Yingkou under the British. A third port, Vladivostok, was close to the region but on Russian territory (see Chapter 1). The various port authorities employed different ways of measuring soybeans, either by weight or by volume, and in addition, each actor involved in the international soybean trade, whether Chinese, Russian, Japanese, or British, worked in various units and currencies. At times the numbers contradict each other or show a small cross-section only.[22] Of great value, therefore, are trade statistics prepared by Mitsui itself. Their statistics provide information not so much on their own trade than on the total trade in soybeans, soybean cake, and soybean oil between 1907 and 1917 from all ports relevant for the soybean trade.[23]

Mitsui's trade statistics show that almost 500,000 tons of whole soybeans went to Britain in each of the two first trading seasons of greater significance, 1908 and 1909 (see Figure 2.1). These beans were shipped in roughly equal amounts from either Dalian or Vladivostok. A soybean trading season began on November 1 of a given year and lasted until October 31 the following year, which meant that everything that was registered for the year 1908 did not in fact reach Europe before 1909, and so on. This minor note is important since from an Asian perspective the soybean trade with Europe began in 1908 while European accounts on the arrival of the soybean as a commodity of trade usually point to 1909 as the beginning; naturally, both are correct.

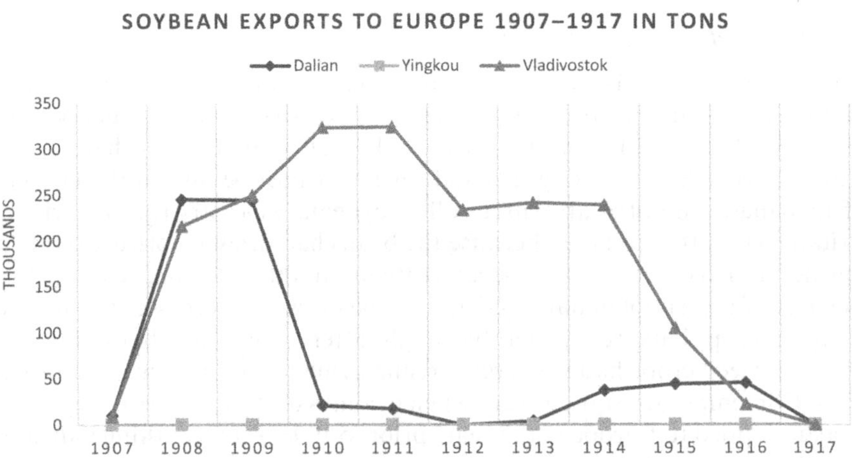

Figure 2.1 Export of whole soybeans by port of export to Europe, 1907–1917.

 Based on information from "Annual export of beans and their products through Dairen, Newchwang and Vladivostok, compiled by Mitsui & Co.," in Tokuji Hoshino, *Economic History of Manchuria* (Seoul: Bank of Chosen, 1920).

Soon after the first ships carrying dried soybeans from Manchuria arrived in Great Britain, the U.S. Department of Commerce requested that consuls in Europe and Asia report on the soybean, its cultivation, and its use. In their replies, most European consuls emphasized the utility of cheap soybean oil in the manufacture of margarine and soap and predicted great economic potential for the soybean in general. John L. Griffith of Liverpool reported:

> A valuable oil, used largely in the making of soap, is extracted from the bean, and it is anticipated that the meal and cake manufactured therefrom may compete very seriously with American cotton-seed cake.... There is no doubt, however, that the soya-bean cake and meal will be used more and more in this country, provided a sufficiently low price is maintained.[24]

While the use of the byproduct from the milling process as fodder became reality at a later point, in 1909 concerns were still high among farmers that soybean cake would negatively affect the livestock fed with it and their meat. Robert P. Skinner, a U.S. consul in Hamburg, reported on "evil effects known to result from the direct feeding" of soybean cake and referred to the maldigestion caused by it. Consul general Soren Listoe of Rotterdam reported on experiments with feeding soybean cake to cattle, which all ended in diarrhea. They all attested to the great potential of the soybean's use both as a vegetable oil resource and also as fodder once farmers understood how to feed their livestock with it. However, at that early stage, most consuls provided only limited information as the products were still too unfamiliar.[25]

In fact, the soybean trade affected U.S. sales of cottonseed to Britain to at least some degree. Soybeans contained between 14 and 21 percent fat, which was similar to cottonseed, and when they became available in Europe, it was against cottonseed that they primarily competed. Contemporary soybeans were inexpensive and provided an oil that was suitable for similar end products. In December 1909, British newspapers reported on a decline in demand for cottonseed and linked it to the rising demand for soybeans. *The Economist*, one of the first newspapers to report on the new commodity, reported that many British oil mills had temporarily switched over their facilities entirely to the processing of soybeans.[26] To which degree this statement can be trusted remains doubtful, especially in light of the fact that Britain imported significant amounts of cottonseed and linseed (610,000 tons and 305,000 tons, respectively) that year.[27] The additional 500,000 tons of soybeans it received in the same year according to Mitsui's statistics nevertheless show the great demand for fat in Britain. The overall picture is that soybeans filled a specific niche in the market and were making advances in Europe.

For the years from 1910 onward, Mitsui's numbers show the strong position of Vladivostok as the main port for shipping soybeans to Europe. On average almost 300,000 tons were shipped annually between 1910 and 1914 from the port (see Figure 2.1).[28] This finding implies that soybeans shipped to Europe came mainly from the northern, Russian-controlled part of Manchuria and were transported by rail on the Russian-controlled Chinese Eastern Railway to Vladivostok. In terms of colonial preferences, this transport pattern seems paradoxical at first sight—Mitsui was a Japanese company, so why would it prefer the use of a Russian railway over the use of the Japanese-controlled SMR? However, the CER kept its rate for the transport of goods eastwards (to Vladivostok) particularly low and in the opposite direction, toward Harbin, where the CER joined the SMR, high. Historian Blaine R. Chiasson showed that with this pricing policy the CER was a loss-making business, but that the Tsarist empire sought to offset these losses with subsidies from 1908 onward in order to attract business.[29] In fact, the CER attracted Mitsui and its soybeans with this policy, which in turn explains why most of the beans destined for Europe were shipped past the Egersheld lighthouse in Vladivostok.

Mitsui's trade statistics show further that European oil mills received even more whole soybeans than Japanese customers. Even though exports of whole soybeans to Japan increased steadily from around 130,000 tons in 1907 to 350,000 tons ten years later, the annual average in this period was at 186,000 tons and thus much lower than exports to Europe. Instead, Japan took large amounts of soybean cake, peaking at 850,000 tons in 1917. Figure 2.2 shows that soybean cake exports from Dairen to Japan were steadily rising, while those from Yingkou declined. In contrast, European buyers took only negligible quantities of soybean cake, and then only in the early stages of the

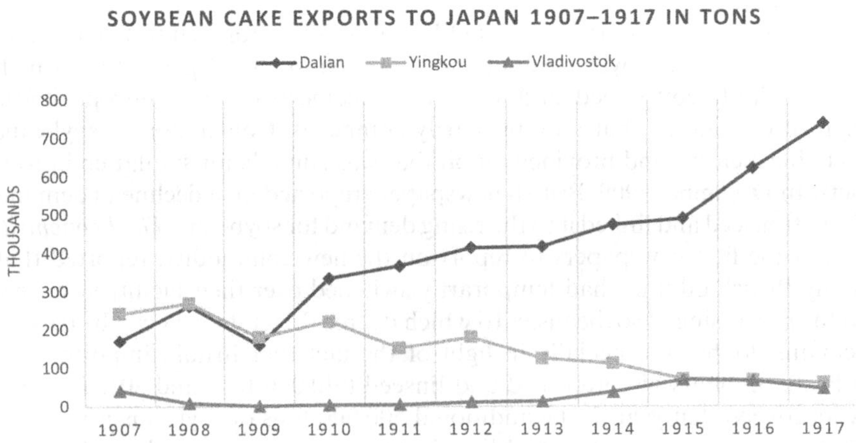

Figure 2.2 Export of soybean cake by port of export to Japan, 1907–1917.

© Author. Based on information from "Annual export of beans and their products through Dairen, Newchwang and Vladivostok, compiled by Mitsui & Co.," in Tokuji Hoshino, *Economic History of Manchuria* (Seoul: Bank of Chosen, 1920).

global soybean business. It seems reasonable to assume that these shipments were of a rather experimental character. Being specialized in providing oil and fodder, European oil mills were keen to avoid the import of ready-made soybean cake, but it remains an open question to which degree they were involved in keeping trade in this product as low as possible.

Japan's interest in soybean cake exceeded the European interest in whole soybeans by far, confirming that Japan remained the main customer for soybeans in general in this period. As Japan was mainly interested in soybean cake, Mitsui could theoretically have offered soybean oil to its European customers instead of whole beans. That way, oil mills in Manchuria would have processed even more beans, and while the oil was headed toward Europe, the cake could have been brought to Japan. In reality, however, Europe received only minimal amounts of soybean oil—less than 30,000 tons annually before the First World War—as transporting oil turned out to be too cumbersome and costly compared to shipping dried beans for further processing in Europe.

At the beginning of the twentieth century, soybean oil was usually shipped in wicker baskets lined with waxed paper. Such containers were hardly suitable for repeated loading and further transportation on steamships. They often leaked on the high seas and spoiled other goods. Metal barrels formerly used for petroleum had to be thoroughly cleaned so as not to contaminate the vegetable oil, which in Europe was destined to be a food item, among other uses. Great hopes were pinned on the tanker with regard to the transport of liquids worldwide. In 1911, the British envisioned transporting petroleum in one direction and soybean oil in the other.[30] Tankers indeed became a common sight on the world's oceans after the war, and by the end of the 1920s, they handled 20 percent of global freight traffic, generally carrying mineral oils. Soybean oil was also transported in tankers after the war, but whether they carried petroleum in one direction and soybean oil in the other remains doubtful because cleaning the tanks gave rise to additional costs and longer waiting times.[31]

Soybean oil processed in Dalian and other parts in southern Manchuria was mainly consumed locally or regionally, and Mitsui circumvented the logistical problems of cleaning tankers by offering whole dried beans to Europe. British buyers did not mind this—quite the contrary. British oil mills were able to process a wide range of oilseeds and fruits, and soybeans posed no challenge while they also provided an additional source of income. Only in the context of the First World War, when fats and oils became increasingly important for military use, did soybean oil enter Europe to a greater extent than before, but numbers remained at around 41,000 tons even in the peak years 1915 and 1916, before rapidly declining.[32]

At the very beginning of the trade with Europe, in 1909 and 1910, the beans that arrived in Great Britain also remained there. Other European countries also were in search of affordable oil sources and adept at handling oil crops of all kinds, but for them the whole, uncrushed soybean disappeared in the shoals of their customs regulations. Since in plant taxonomy soybeans are legumes, or pulses, they had to be declared as such when imported. In the early nineteenth century, many European countries levied duties on the import of vegetables in order to protect their national agriculture, which for soybeans meant the imposition of import taxes and thus higher total costs. In the German Reich, for example, an import duty of 20 or 40 Reichsmark per ton was levied on pulses, depending on whether the import originated from a contracting country or not. It was not until 1910 and at the insistence of the Association of German Oil Mills that soybeans could be declared as oilseeds and thus imported duty-free.[33]

On the European continent, British oil mills thus initially held a monopoly in the handling of soybeans and exported the resulting products to Denmark, Belgium, Germany, Norway, and Sweden, and occasionally also to Italy and Turkey.[34] The extent of this early trade remains unknown as the amounts handled were often too small be registered. There is, however, evidence that Great Britain traded about 70,000 tons of soybean cake to other European countries.[35]

For most of the European countries, customs regulations changed around 1910, resulting in an increase in soybean imports. In the years up to the First World War, Great Britain remained the main importing country, but Denmark, the Netherlands, and Germany also showed great interest. Due to their chemical properties and low price, soybeans were generally required in the production of margarine and soap and the byproduct from oil extraction was turned into feed.[36] Only occasionally did foodstuffs made from soybeans reach the market. In 1913, for example, Soyama-Werke in Frankfurt am Main began operations and offered soy milk and flour. Other companies followed, offering soy coffee, or products inspired by Asian soy dishes.[37] However, these foods are likely to have retained their exotic status and are unlikely to have reached the market on a large scale.

Japan and the Global Soybean Trade

While Mitsui's collection of data is of great value regarding Manchuria's total trade, it falls short in revealing what part the company itself played in this trade. For an article published in 2019, Hiromi Mizuno and I found evidence that Mitsui's success immediately triggered fierce competition from European trading firms, such as Jardine, Matheson & Co., the largest trading company in the Far East, which was founded by two Scotsmen in 1835; Samuel & Co., the forerunner of Royal Dutch Shell; and Butterfield & Swire, a London-based trading company. These European firms had become large and powerful by establishing offices in Hong Kong and Shanghai and later in Yokohama (Japan) in the nineteenth century to trade in cotton, opium, tea, and so on. However, they missed out on the soybean trade. According to sources we worked with, all European firms combined exported only 162,000 tons of Manchuria soybeans to Europe in 1909, or less than one-third of the total amount of 500,000 tons of beans shipped that year.[38]

There is further evidence of Mitsui's strong position and European firms' relative weakness. In January 1910, the U.S. Department of Commerce and Labor reported on the British soybean market and that Mitsui managed to contract 400,000 tons of soybeans from the previous year's harvest to British buyers.[39] This confirms that Mitsui secured about two-thirds of the total trade in that year (1909 in Figure 2.1). Other contemporary sources reported that Mitsui even had to charter ships from various European trading houses, including those of Samuel & Co. and Jardine, Matheson & Co. to get the beans to Europe. These firms, in turn, entered the soybean trade rather indirectly.[40]

With Mitsui holding the biggest share in the soybean trade, the question remains who and what Mitsui was. How did it become, and secure its position as, an important trading actor in Manchuria and which role did soybeans play in its businesses? The trading house was part of a much larger group known as the Mitsui *zaibatsu*. From the end of the nineteenth century onward the term *zaibatsu* was applied to large, family-owned conglomerates with various branches, subsidiaries, and outsourced companies that played a major role in shaping the Japanese economy and on which the Meiji government depended to implement its modernization and industrialization plans. Up to this day, Mitsui is one of the largest trading companies in Asia and its parent enterprise, Mitsui Group, is one of the largest corporate groups worldwide.

Because of its special structure and its politico-economic influence on the Japanese empire, Mitsui *zaibatsu* enjoys not only a long but also a well-researched history encompassing most of its branches and sub-companies.[41] The roots of the *zaibatsu* go back to the Japanese Tokugawa period. In 1673, Takatoshi Mitsui opened a kimono-tailoring shop in Edo (Tokyo), laying the foundation of what would become a multi-industry company. In 1680, the tailor shop was soon joined by a currency exchange office, and shortly thereafter, Mitsui became the financier of the Tokugawa government as well as local lords. By the time of the Meiji Restoration in 1868, the company had risen to be one of the wealthiest in Japan.

At that time, ending the unequal treaties imposed on Japan by Western powers in the 1850s was among the Meiji government's highest priorities. The Opium Wars in China were closely watched in Japan, and to avoid a similar situation at home, the Japanese government set the goal of catching up economically and militarily. Capital was central to meeting this aim as it enabled the purchase of new technologies that would preserve the country's self-reliance and independence. However, because of the unequal treaties, Western capital was tied to Western merchants with fixed trading routes and goods. By 1874, for example, European or American trading companies such as Samuel & Co. or Butterfield & Swire controlled 97 percent of all Japanese exports and 94 percent of all the country's imports. In an attempt to break out of these semicolonial structures and thus obtain foreign currency, the Meiji promoted, among other things, the establishment of their own trading houses. This was the context in which the Mitsui family founded one of the first trading houses in Japan in 1876: Mitsui Bussan, or Mitsui & Co., the name the company preferred to use in English-language transactions.[42] This trading company became responsible for the soybean business, among others, and is referred to as only Mitsui here. In the same year, Mitsui Bank, Japan's first private bank, was founded.

The largest *zaibatsu*, such as Mitsui or Mitsubishi, were instrumental in developing mines, establishing shipyards, processing textiles, and developing infrastructure with the help of the Japanese government. In the 1880s, they bought these industries from the government and transferred them into independent companies which nevertheless remained affiliated with the parent enterprise. The *zaibatsu* Mitsui purchased Japan's largest coal mine and established the Mitsui Mining Company. In this way, the divisions and influence of the resulting business conglomerate grew. The three businesses—mining, banking, and trading—built the three pillars of the Mitsui *zaibatsu,* which besides had industrial companies owned by various combinations of these businesses and their subsidiaries.[43]

The trading company was central to the acquisition of foreign capital and therefore constantly expanded its business areas. It observed foreign markets, conducted research, and invested in developing new business areas. Mitsui sent young employees to European and American universities, and its managers benefitted from the social networks that the family's top management maintained with the business families of the Rothschilds, Krupps, Vanderbilts, and Morgans.[44] In 1877, a year after the Mitsui trading house was founded, branches were established in London and Shanghai, while Paris, Hong Kong, New York, and Tianjin soon followed along with other cities worldwide. These branches sometimes also took on consular duties as Japan had not yet established diplomatic offices in some of the countries. The fact that large companies took on consular duties was not novel to international relations at the time and was a common practice, in particular, for smaller countries such as Norway and Switzerland. In the case of Japan, it proves how powerful not only the *zaibatsu* but also the trading company in particular had become and how far economic and political interests were interwoven with the firm.

The company's involvement in the Manchurian soybean trade had its roots in the late nineteenth century when, in 1896, it entered a partnership with Chinese trading agents in Yingkou. This partnership seemed necessary because there was a great demand for soybean cake in Japan, but the soybean trade was largely dominated by Chinese wholesalers. In Japan, the nitrogen-rich cake was used to fertilize paddy fields. Dealing with Chinese traders in order to obtain reasonably priced soybean cake seemed a promising enterprise and Mitsui eventually managed to gain a firm foothold in the trade. The company's share of the trade in soybean cake to Japan was only 13 percent in 1897, but by 1906 was almost entirely in its hands alone.[45]

While this development proves Mitsui's strong position in Northeast China, it was not only caused by entrepreneurial good fortune, as international relations in the Far East in general and the Russo-Japanese War more specifically played a key role in strengthening Japan's position in Asia and consequently Mitsui's role too. There had been latent conflicts between China and Japan since the late nineteenth century, and Japan's ambitions on the Asian mainland had become more pronounced since disputes about Korea and the First Sino-Japanese War (1894–1895). Japan grew politically and economically stronger, and its claim on parts of Manchuria only ten years later was a consequence of these developments.

Japan was also able to extend its position in the Far East because it did not need to fear the intervention of the European powers. From 1902–1923, the Anglo-Japanese Alliance bound Britain and Japan together in safeguarding their respective interests in China, Korea, and India. British anxieties over Russian expansion in Asia, particularly in Afghanistan and India, were the strategic reasons behind the alliance. Historian Ian Nish has shown that for the British government, Manchuria and Korea were lesser concerns.[46] For Japan, on the other hand, the alliance acknowledged the existence of Japanese rights on mainland northeast Asia and helped to extend its economic and political interests there. It prevented, for instance, France from entering the Russo-Japanese War on the side of the Russians. Russia and France had their own alliance, but France feared its entry into the war would trigger Britain's entry into it too. Even though it was very difficult for the Japanese government to obtain loans in London to fight the war, it nevertheless succeeded in doing so, and historian Janet Hunter suggested that this was only possible due to the formal link between the two governments.[47]

The Russo-Japanese War was fought on Manchurian territory, where Han Chinese farmers initially increased soybean cultivation to provide both sides with food and fodder. When Russia imposed a strategic embargo on soy and fish to trigger a long-term food crisis in Japan, it hit Japan hard because it was dependent on both products.[48] Thus, the Japanese military let Mitsui's trade representative immediately follow the combating forces to buy soy from farmers and thus meet the domestic demand for fertilizer. In return for the soybeans, Mitsui offered cotton, thereby bartering with the Chinese and utilizing both directions of transportation.[49] Now being in more direct contact with the farmers laid the ground for the rise of the company in Manchuria.

In addition, Japan's victory over much greater Russian forces led to profound changes in the balance of power in China's Northeast. Before the war, the region was under the increasing influence of Russia, but now Japan entered the scene and began competing for influence and resources as well. The outcome of the war gave rise to far-reaching geopolitical changes in the Far East which guaranteed Japan the position of a politically and economically strong actor in Northeast China. As defined in the Portsmouth Treaty, Japan leased the strategically well-situated Liaodong peninsula and renamed it Kwantung. In contrast to the other port regions, this peninsula was ice-free all year round and therefore valuable for military and economic operations. Besides this, Japan took over large parts of one of the two major railways Russia had begun to build. The SMR ran from Harbin southward to the city of Dalian and the section between Changchun and Dalian was now under Japanese control. The railway company of the same name became a central economic actor in the region (see Map 1.1).

With these geopolitical changes, northeastern China was divided into three spheres of power, each of which sought to strengthen and expand its influence. The northern part, which bordered Siberia and encompassed the provinces Heilongjiang and northern Jilin, was under Russian control. The economic and cultural center of the region was Harbin, which by means of the CER connected with Vladivostok, Russia's major port in the Far East. Japan claimed southern Manchuria, which included the southern part of Jilin, Fengtian, and the leasehold area of Kwantung. The former Port Arthur, renamed to Ryojun by the Japanese, served as headquarters for the Japanese military administration while Dalian became an important economic and cultural center in the south. Especially after the official opening of international trade in 1907, Dalian rapidly developed into a transportation hub and transfer point for goods from rail to sea and vice versa. The rest of Manchuria was under the control of various Chinese warlords who fought for power and influence in the region.[50]

The Japanese claim to the Asian mainland was rooted in trade interests, and these were an expression of Japan's economic modernization course mentioned earlier. At the beginning of the twentieth century, the country's economy was comparatively weak. Although Japan recorded annual export growth rates of 8.5 percent, which was far above the world average of 3.4 percent, its share of world trade was small compared with that of the major European powers and the United States.[51] The country's economic policy was geared toward increasing this share by becoming a serious international trading partner. Manchuria, along with Korea, was considered one of the most important areas in achieving this goal.

While Japan clearly had economic interests in Manchuria, its presence in China was also an expression of imperial power, and companies such as the SMR or Mitsui played a key role in this respect. The SMR was not only a means of transporting people and goods but also an enterprise of gigantic proportions, as the number of businesses related to it show. In 1911, for instance, the obligatory railway business included the operation of six further lines besides the main line and thus altogether more than six hundred miles of rails. In addition, the company operated hotels and agricultural or geological experiment stations along the railway tracks and provided gas and electricity to the city of Dalian. The Japanese built the port with cutting-edge technologies and added breakwaters, piers, and a dockyard capable of accommodating vessels of 5,000 tons, with a storage capacity of more than 100,000 tons of cargo.[52]

In a marketing brochure, the SMR boasted of offering "the shortest and quickest route between Europe and the Far East."[53] Given the north-south course of the actual railway versus the east-west direction of the advertised connection, this advertising slogan seems paradoxical at first. However, a few years earlier, the SMR had incorporated a regular ship passage from Dalian to Shanghai, from where people and goods traveled further to Europe. With this route, the crossing to Great Britain in fact took two days less than taking the voyage entirely by ship from the Russian port of Vladivostok.[54]

With control over rail and shipping in the southern part of Manchuria, Japan secured a firm foothold as an economic and political player in the Far East. The SMR was a quasi-governmental company for safeguarding Japanese commercial interests. Other companies that played into Japan's imperial economic policy in Manchuria were the Yokohama Specie Bank and Mitsui. At that time, Mitsui was already well established within the *zaibatsu* Mitsui, and compared to other Japanese trading companies, held a privileged position within the empire. In 1909, its peak year, the company handled 24 percent of Japan's total import and export business. It was the only Japanese company allowed to trade rice with Europe and it enjoyed privileges for trading coal from Manchuria.[55] While the SMR built and maintained the infrastructure in Manchuria's south, Mitsui handled the global trade business, and the Yokohama Specie Bank provided both with the necessary financial resources. A contemporary American observer judged the interplay of these three companies as together forming the artery of Manchuria's economic development, and historical research has shown that this was indeed the case.[56]

Mitsui was powerful because it was supported by the Japanese government and it worked hand in hand with other major Japanese companies in Manchuria. Further contributing to its success in the soy trade were some business strategies against which European companies could not compete. Contemporary sources report that some European firms invested in advance purchases by buying the beans from the farmers well before they were harvested. When the farmers could not (or would not) deliver their harvest as agreed, the buyers lost both beans and money. Mitsui avoided future trading and worked with Chinese trading partners, albeit without relying solely on them.[57] Another advantage Mitsui had over its European competitors was that it had trained its sales representatives in Mandarin as well as Chinese culture and trading practices, which in turn meant that local agents were less important to the business. Mitsui's people were able to determine future cultivation capacities at an early stage, anticipate crop yields, and sound out business possibilities in a more informed manner than their competitors.[58]

The Anglo-Japanese alliance afforded British firms no predominant position among foreign business in Japan or the Japanese-controlled territory in Manchuria. In fact, the alliance enabled Japan to strengthen its position to the disadvantage of Britain, but the pattern of trade was not a consideration when the alliance was negotiated in 1902, nor when it was revised in 1905. Japan's share of world trade remained relatively minor in comparison with that of Britain. Nevertheless, the alliance confirmed the growing unwillingness and inability of the British government to sustain its preeminent position in the global economy, as economic historian Janet Hunter has shown.[59] This meant in essence that British firms lost their position in Manchuria and were not even able to sustain their interests from the British-administered port of Yingkou.

Prior to the opening of Dalian to international trade in 1907, Yingkou was a flourishing hub for international trade, with the flow of goods in and out of Northeast China, including the intra-Asian soybean trade, coming under the control of British merchants. With the advent of Japanese actors in Northeast China, Yingkou lost a once-important customer, Japan, and its preferred commodity, soybean cake (see Figure 2.2).

In fact, the Liao River-Yingkou route through Manchuria described in Chapter 2 had decisive disadvantages in the face of rail and the competing harbors of Dalian and Vladivostok. The Liao had been the most important river for transportation in southern Manchuria in the nineteenth century, but even back then constant flooding and silting at the mouth of the river had posed major challenges. Despite British, Chinese, and Russian efforts to solve this problem in order to enable steamers to access the port, the transportation of goods continued to rely on small, low-draft junks that could navigate the shallows. In addition, limited wharfage space became a severe problem as the volume of trade increased.[60] Last but not least, the British administration in Yingkou put Japanese merchants at a disadvantage by imposing fees on them that they could avoid in Dalian and Vladivostok.[61] The impact of this practice was to be seen in the declining trade in soybean cake from Yingkou to Japan (see Figure 2.2). Although some soybeans were still transported along the Liao toward Yingkou, these were mostly traded regionally or within mainland China.[62] With the rising strength of Mitsui and Japan in Manchuria, the role of Yingkou—and thus Great Britain—in the international soybean trade steadily declined.

Japanese and American Competition in China's Northeast

For Japanese companies in Manchuria, competition came not only from Britain. The region was a contested space, full of actors of different origins and with varying interests, as historians have recently shown.[63] Manchuria was a region of immigration, which also attracted businesses, and besides British, Chinese, Russian, and Japanese companies, American ventures also tried to secure a stake in its economic prospects. U.S. American trading interests were wider-ranging than soybeans and comprised of crops with greater significance to their economy such as cotton and tobacco. The United States tried to uphold the trade in American cotton and tobacco to Manchuria and, in return, participate in the newly arising trading opportunities.

China's Northeast was a particularly vital sales region for American cotton. With its opening for settlement and the arrival of Han Chinese migrants in the late nineteenth century, actors in the United States sought to expand the cotton trade to this region as well. Soon after the Russo-Japanese War, however, they essentially lost this business due to aggressive Japanese business practices. According to the *New York Times*, in 1905 U.S. companies exported goods worth 52 million U.S. dollars to China, of which cotton products to the Northeast, at 24 million U.S. dollars, accounted for nearly half alone. In subsequent years sales declined steadily and by 1909 the value of cotton exported to Manchuria had fallen to 7.5 million U.S. dollars, a decline of 70 percent in a mere four years. Even though these numbers do not reflect shifting sales values or any other fluctuations, the drop remains significant.

These figures were presented in an article by the U.S. consul in Mukden, Frederick D. Cloud, who laid open the dilemma for American cotton traders. He illustrated how serious the loss of the Manchurian market for American cotton producers generally was, not only regarding what was lost already but what would be lost in the future too. Manchuria was "one of the largest and most valuable undeveloped regions in the world," thus its market was anticipated to grow steadily. At stake were thus continuously expanding sales opportunities.[64]

American cotton was pushed out of Northeast China by means of an interplay between the trading house Mitsui, the Yokohama Specie Bank, and the railway company SMR. Supported by the Japanese government, these three set up a cartel to push cotton produced in India and processed in Japan into the region, and as a result Mitsui succeeded in almost completely taking over the region's cotton trade within just a few years after the end of the Russo-Japanese War. The same happened to the American tobacco trade as well, and in a similar manner.

Japan's aggressive business strategies have been described in recent historical studies. Sherman Cochran analyzed the competition between Western, Japanese, and Chinese corporations in China and covered the cotton trade as well. Others, such as Kozo Yamamura or Seiichiro Yonekura studied Japanese businesses in Manchuria as a forerunner of modern capitalism while focusing on the takeover of the cotton and tobacco trades.[65] Yet other scholars focused on the U.S. perspective on China and emphasized what became known as the Open Door Policy. This policy originated in the late nineteenth century with the secretary of state John Hay, who in 1899–1900 issued a series of memoranda calling for international access to the Chinese market. While Open Door was intended to provide all entrepreneurs regardless of their origin with equal trading conditions in China, it was first and foremost set up to support U.S. business interests. The Japanese takeover of the cotton trade clearly ran counter to that intention; in fact, the cotton trade proved the difficulty of implementing it, as both Bruce Elleman and Gregory Moore have shown in their respective studies.[66]

While scholars have covered many aspects of the rivalry between Japan and the United States in China's Northeast, the link to soybeans is still missing. Soybeans are not merely another commodity and thus an example of this competition. Americans had no interest in them at that time. It was rather thanks to soybeans that the Japanese cartel was able to push American cotton out of the market in the first place. As a result of the Russo-Japanese War, the economy in Manchuria was in turmoil and farmers simply didn't have the means to pay for imported goods such as American cotton fabrics.[67] Indian cotton was not only cheaper than American cotton but was also offered to the Chinese in exchange for soybeans, not money. Japanese rice farmers, on the other hand, largely depended on soybean cake to fertilize their rice fields. The recent war, with its embargo, had shown how crucial fertilizers were for averting food shortages. From the Japanese perspective, transporting Manchuria-grown soybeans in exchange for cotton all the way down to Dalian, having them processed there, and then importing the cake to Japan seemed very rational.[68] American companies, on the other hand, were unwilling to enter into bartering business practices, especially since they had little use for soybeans at that time. The Japanese cartel in Manchuria was thus more than an expression of imperial encounters—it also served to ensure basic requirements such as future food supplies in Japan.

Considering these circumstances, an early U.S. consular report concerning the global trade and interest in soybeans seems particularly interesting. As the first ships carrying dried soybeans from Manchuria to Europe were still being unloaded in early 1909, the U.S. Department of Commerce called on their consuls in Europe and Asia to report on the soybean, its cultivation, and its use. American cottonseed producers had requested such investigations as they feared the competition from soybeans in their markets for oil and fodder. All consuls attested to the great potential of the soybean's use both as a vegetable oil resource and as fodder once farmers understood how to feed their livestock with it. However, at that early stage, most consuls provided only limited information as the products were still too unfamiliar.[69]

It is the speed with which the Americans drew up the international comparisons in the soybean trade that makes the quoted report particularly interesting. At a time when information traveled by mail and telegraph and had to be printed to reach its audience, the processing time of barely a few months between the arrival of the first soybean cargo in early 1909 and these reports in the early summer of the same year is astonishing. Soybeans and cottonseed oil served the same end products—margarine, soap, and dyes—and in addition, the respective byproducts of the milling process served as fodder. The actual competition between soybeans and cottonseed at that time could not be determined as the imported quantities of soybeans were still so marginal that the commodity had not even been given its own entry in British trade statistics, and yet Americans still feared the competition.

What if Mitsui and the soybeans threatened to push cottonseed out of European markets in a similar manner to how they had pushed American cotton fabric out of Manchuria? In actuality, this would not happen as the demand for cheap oil resources in Europe was high and the market was large enough to absorb both cottonseed and soybeans. Nevertheless, American experiences in Manchuria explain their vigilance in Europe and the reports the consuls sent back home.

Frederick D. Cloud's account of the situation in the *New York Times* has shown the devasting effect Mitsui's success had on American cotton traders in Asia. In November 1909, the U.S. government made a pivotal effort to assert American trade interests in Manchuria, and it is this final attempt that shows how deeply intertwined economic and political interests were at that time. Secretary of State Philander C. Knox argued for neutralizing the two major Manchurian railways to strengthen China's political rights in Manchuria. He argued that neither the Russians nor the Japanese had fulfilled their commitments, signed in the 1905 Portsmouth Peace Treaty, not to interfere with any state in its commercial activities. Masked as part of Open Door, Knox proposed that Russia and Japan sell their railway rights to China and that China borrow the money to do so from the United States, Britain, France, and Germany.[70] The plan would have likely harmed the Anglo-Japanese alliance and was generally met with little interest. The SMR, after all, was an important link in the cotton and soybean trade to and from Manchuria, and if Japan lost control over it, it lost control of that trade as well. The reference to strengthening China's political rights was nothing more than a weak attempt to divert attention from the United States' own economic interests in Manchuria. The example of the soybean and its commodification outside Asia thus illustrates the extent to which processes of globalization were not only shaped by economic actors but were also accompanied by political support.

From then on, U.S. actors could only watch the exploitation of Manchuria and its trade. In his article, consul Cloud in Mukden concluded that the call for Open Door was no more than empty words and that the United States would no longer be able to make any capital out of Manchuria. He wrote that "open door in Manchuria is nothing more than a beautiful myth, a millennial dream."[71]

Other accounts of the situation pointed in the same direction. The U.S. ambassador in Beijing, William J. Calhoun, reported bitterly to the State Department in 1911:

> The recent increase in the production of the soya bean in Manchuria is not devoid of a serious political aspect in view of the cupidity of the Japanese, which, it is fair to presume, is further aroused by the not unnatural desire on their part to partake of, if not control, this great source of wealth, and there is thus injected a further factor into an already complex and difficult problem. The question naturally arises, Who is to control the great trade of the future in this Manchurian product?[72]

These connections between imperialism and globalization were beautifully expressed by yet another American contemporary. George Bronson Rea, who edited an English-language journal in Shanghai at that time and later rose to become an official U.S. advisor to the Manchukuo government, also judged the economic and diplomatic interconnections of the soybean:

> It is a far cry from high diplomacy to the humble Soya Bean, yet, we hold to the belief that the past and present commercial situation and ultimate solution of the vexatious Manchurian problem is bound up in the control of this one product.[73]

Who would have thought that soy, so inconspicuous outside Asia, would be attributed such enormous significance in international politics?

The United States was not strong enough to compete successfully with Japan, which in American eyes was not playing fair. In 1916, Stanley K. Hornbeck, who in later years became one of the most influential China specialists in the State Department, concluded regarding the actions of Japanese companies:

> None of these methods of doing business can be declared to be a direct violation of the principles of the open door. They do, however, constitute an indirect interference—on the part of the Japanese government—with the natural course of equality of opportunity.[74]

Despite these insights, the United States officially adhered to Open Door even after the First World War. Hornbeck traveled to the Paris peace negotiations in 1919 as a delegate of the Wilson administration. He was a staunch and influential advocate of Open Door, even though neither he nor any other American succeeded in explaining how through it, China would experience territorial and administrative integrity, as was proclaimed. At the Paris peace negotiations, he firmly believed that the United States was in the right position to pave the way for collegial international cooperation regarding trade, concessions, and investments in the Far East. However, progress was slow and Hornbeck's efforts in Paris were essentially in vain. The agreements loosely reached among the United States, Great Britain, France, Germany, Japan, and Russia were by no means binding because the other countries had little interest in giving up their economic prerogatives in China.[75] As a result, the United States could neither sustain its cotton business nor enter the soybean trade.

Soybeans in the First World War

To be sure, the U.S. government could not actively influence trade patterns in Manchuria, and it remains open to question whether it even had an influence on the emerging soybean trade at home. In any case, the interest in soybean oil in the United States came about from a generally rising demand for fat, just as in Europe, and this increased during the First World War. But while Europeans almost exclusively obtained whole beans, Americans preferred to import the processed oil only.[76] The reason for this lies in the then nearly non-existent infrastructure for processing oil crops on the U.S. west coast. In Seattle, the main trading port for soybeans coming over the Pacific, only a relatively small oil milling industry had developed. So, despite the risk of oil spoilage or leakage—contemporary sources put the loss from leakage at five to ten percent—soy first entered the U.S. market as oil only.[77]

The Japanese trading company Mitsui lists the United States for the first time in 1910 when they shipped 50 tons of soybean oil across the Pacific. This quantity was still too small for U.S. trade statistics; here, soybeans, or more specifically soybean oil, did not appear until two years later, when it recorded 11,000 tons. In the following years, imports remained lower than that until they surged from 1916 onward, peaking at 152,000 tons in 1918. In the four years from 1916 to 1919, Americans imported a total of 427,000 tons of soybean oil worth 92 million U.S. dollars. Thereafter, the figures quickly fell back to levels below 10,000 tons. One way of understanding the rise in soybean oil imports during the war is to compare them to U.S. cottonseed oil production, a generally strong domestic sector for the production of fat. The amount of imported soybean oil was equivalent to just under one-fifth of the cottonseed oil produced in the United States in the same years, 1916–1919.[78]

American industries relying on fatty resources thus obtained a noteworthy amount of soybean oil to meet their demand during the war years, but what were these industries, and what was the oil used for? In 1920, the Tariff Commission, an agency of the Department of Commerce, published a *Survey of the American Soya-bean Oil Industry*. The *Survey* provided information on a large variety of different customer products made entirely or partly of soybean oil. For the sake of simplicity, I have grouped them and identified two categories—that is, soaps and foodstuffs. The first category encompasses not only soaps for personal use but also detergents for clothes and dishes, while foodstuff refers to margarine and lard substitutes.

The imported soybean oil was primarily used for products in the first category, soap. It did not displace any other oil used in the production of soap but was used in addition to existing fat resources to meet rising demand. The *Survey* shows that in 1912 a total of 123,000 tons of various fats were processed by the U.S. soap industry; by 1917, the amount had nearly doubled to 231,000 tons. Soap was primarily composed of tallow, but it was possible to add fluid oils to some degree, depending on the final product and its desired consistency. Usually, cottonseed oil was added, but domestic resources of both tallow and cottonseed were limited while demand for soap was growing. The tremendous increase in soap production in only five years was thus only possible thanks to additional, imported commodities, namely soybean and coconut oils. The use of soybean oil in soap production increased more than a hundredfold from 536 tons in 1912 to 56,000 tons in 1917.[79] Even though the increasing use of soybean oil in soap production is astonishing, it did not become the most important oil in this sector. Coconut oil was even more preferred in soap production, as was cottonseed oil. Nevertheless, soybean oil ranked third among all vegetable resources used in soap production in the years under consideration here.

It seems that the United States depended on soybean oil imports, especially during wartime, to serve the rising demand for fat. In an article for the American Asiatic Society from 1919, an official in the State Department wrote about the importance of soybean oil supplies in the United States and concluded:

> [I]f Manchuria did not come to the rescue during these days of war, some of our greatest soap factories would have been hard pressed, even to the point of closing, for lack of raw material.[80]

Similar to soap making, soybean oil did not displace any other oil in the food sector either, i.e. in the production of margarine and lard substitutes. It was added to already available and established raw materials, as figures for the production of lard substitutes show. In 1916, lard substitutes were composed mainly of domestic raw materials, with cottonseed oil ranking first, followed by stearin and peanut oil. Only two years later, its main ingredients and their rank had shifted: now lard substitutes were made of mainly cottonseed oil, followed by soybean oil and stearin. In 1916, only 6,500 tons of soybean oil were used for lard substitutes. In 1918, this figure was about four times as high at slightly over 26,000 tons. During the same period, the consumption of peanut oil for making lard substitutes also increased, but by one-and-a-half times only, from 8,000 to 12,600 tons.[81] Even though soybean oil had gained a notable place in the manufacture of lard substitutes within just two years, it had not necessarily displaced peanut oil. Rather, soybean oil was added due to the rising demand for but limited domestic supplies of peanut oil. Chinese farmers and their Japanese trading partners could easily process surplus supplies and ship them to the United States, while American farmers had difficulties servicing the increased demand.

To a much smaller degree than in soap and foodstuffs, soybean oil was also used in the manufacture of paints, varnishes, and lacquers. Paints required oils that would harden when exposed to air. Linseed oil is the best example of so-called drying oil, and flaxseed was grown domestically for this purpose. Poppy seed and tung oil were also drying oils but had to be imported from overseas, which was difficult given the wartime conditions. Simultaneously, acute wartime needs such as corrosion protection for matériel led to the rise in demand for drying oils in all warring countries. Soybean oil was considered a semi-drying oil and remained sticky when turned into paints, but it was possible to use soybean oil to dilute drying oils. No figures are available for the use of soybean oil in the making of paints, and it is unlikely that it was used to a large extent. However, I have included paints here because the USDA conducted chemical research regarding the use of semi-drying oils in paints and also worked on soybean oil for this purpose. In addition, the Paint Manufacturers Association became involved in various USDA campaigns to encourage American farmers to cultivate soybeans.[82] Paints remained an imagined, potential use for soybean oil in subsequent years, and firms would continue researching it, but it did not yet form an industry.

This outline of the U.S. use of soybean oil in the manufacture of soaps and foodstuff has focused on imported supplies. In addition to imports, Americans had some domestic supplies at their disposal during the war. Those quantities remained small and provided no competition for Manchurian beans. However, the period marked the first noticeable rise of soybean cultivation in the United States and will be treated as part of the rise of soybeans in U.S. agriculture in Chapter 4.

After the war, Americans quickly lost interest and the need for soybean oil from Manchuria. The reasons for this sudden decline remain open to question at this point, but it is likely that the emerging overproduction of crops such as linseed, cottonseed, and peanuts led to a drop in their respective prices and, in turn, made the use of soybean oil in soaps and foodstuffs less attractive. In addition, soybean oil reportedly had an aftertaste, and the margarine and lard substitute made of it was apparently less palatable than those made of other resources. Regardless of the specific reasons, the decline in imports illustrates that soybean oil was no longer attractive. It was a substitute when wartime shortages required additional resources, but it was not considered to be of much value thereafter. Interestingly, in Europe soybeans as a foodstuff would share the same fate.

Shortages in Europe

In 1915, a soy flour with the product name *Vaterland* began to circulate in some German cities.[83] It was probably intended to provide strength and energy in times of hardship, but the fact that soy flour was apparently commercially available in the midst of the war raises the question of whether Germany had access to soy despite the British blockade. Another hint to the prominent place of soy during the war is provided by a Japanese publication in which soy is attested a "very important part in the world's food supply."[84] The quote comes from an SMR publication which regularly reported in English on Manchuria's economic transformation. It stressed Japan's presence in the region in terms of progress and modern development. Nevertheless, the question remains of whether soy was available in Europe and the United States during the First World War.

To be frank, soybeans did not play a particularly prominent role in the war, either for the Central Powers or for the Entente, despite the German soybean flour and Japanese propaganda regarding the role of soy in the First World War. Britain was still one of the major importing soybean countries at the time, but the amount was constantly declining during the war. In 1915, approximately 170,000 tons of soybeans were imported, but in 1917, it were only 25,000 tons, and by 1918, none at all.[85] The fact that the quantities of soybeans available in all warring nations were steadily declining is confirmed by Mitsui's export figures (see Figure 2.1).

While the supply of soybeans stopped, the demand for fat in Europe remained high and grew even stronger. During the war, they were also mainly needed for food, whether at the front or at home, and they were consumed either directly as margarine, butter, baking, and frying fats or indirectly in the form of cheese, milk powder, fish, and eggs. In addition, raw materials containing fat were now needed to maintain or manufacture war materials. The First World War was characterized by immense material battles, which were only made possible because armaments could be produced on an industrial scale for the first time. To keep not only machine guns and howitzers but also bicycles or submarines and many other war materials running, vast quantities of lubricants and rust inhibitors were needed. Fat was further in demand for the manufacture of products that were not exclusively, but nevertheless, in the context of the war, primarily needed for the front, such as rubber boots, candles, dynamite, cans, lamp oil, and waterproof fabrics. All this together resulted in an even greater demand for numerous resources, but especially for fat. In Europe, however, this demand was not met with soybean oil.[86]

In *The Chemists' War*, historian Michael Freemantle used Britain as an example to highlight the central importance of glycerol in the production of explosives, particularly cordite. When in the 1860s Alfred Nobel succeeded in producing nitroglycerin, or dynamite, his invention triggered the demand for glycerol as the main starting material, and the same was the case for cordite, invented in 1889. The amount of glycerol among different fats varied, but the fruits of coconuts and oil palms contained comparatively large amounts. With glycerol being a component of fat, the availability of imported raw materials was central to the war effort. According to Freemantle's calculations, a single factory in Scotland processed 135 tons of glycerol alone in 1917.[87] The British government thus focused on obtaining those materials high in glycerol and stopped the import of soybeans because the transport route was too long and the yield in glycerol too low. Thus, the significant decline in soybean imports in Britain was essentially due to cargo bottlenecks.[88]

In Germany, the situation was barely any different. There, people on the home front suffered from all manner of food shortages. The German Reich had no concept of food security and there was also a lack of necessary information on how to obtain the various raw materials.[89] Government officials had not paid much attention to the dependence on imports, not even in such key areas as concentrated feeds and fertilizers, both of which were necessary to ensure food supplies. With the start of the war, duty exemptions on imports of butter, lard, and margarine were granted, and from December 1914 this also applied to oils as well as oilseeds and fruits. Until 1915, there were still imports of oilseeds from neutral countries such as Holland and Denmark or from cod liver oil, such as from Norway. However, the British blockade soon prevented these imports.[90]

In this context of a generally deteriorating supply situation in the first and second years of the war, soybeans also received increased attention as a source of fat and protein among the Germans. Overall, the distribution of soy was characterized by similar coordination difficulties as the general supply of food among the German population, so that the availability and use varied greatly. Often, only soy flour was available because the oil was needed elsewhere. The Soyama-Werke in Frankfurt and presumably other companies too offered a meat or sausage substitute based on soy flour, and in the city administration of Cologne, Konrad Adenauer, who after the Second World War became German chancellor, tinkered with a bratwurst consisting of blood and 40 percent soy flour.[91]

Elsewhere again, soy flour was offered directly, but without pointing out its special features. There is no doubt that soy flour was well suited to averting food shortages because of its high protein and fat content. However, the designation as soy *flour* was misleading because it contained hardly any carbohydrates and was suitable for baked goods only to a limited extent. In addition, soy flour went rancid comparatively quickly. What the population was left with, then, was often only a stale aftertaste. But it was not everywhere that soy flour alone was offered. The city of Dresden, for example, gave whole soybeans to the population, which led to considerable resentment, not least because the beans are difficult to digest. Due to the uncertainty in handling and processing soy, it was not infrequently regarded by the population as an inferior substitute product.[92]

As varied and uncoordinated as the use of soy was, it came to a standstill in the course of 1916 because supplies were interrupted by the British blockade. From then on, Germany faced severe food shortages. If soybeans were available at all, they merely supplemented scarce food supplies. Since supplying the fighting troops with armaments and food was a priority, supply shortages of any kind affected the civilian population. However, research has shown that the availability of food varied from region to region, and while rural areas were reasonably self-sufficient, the inhabitants of large cities often suffered greatly from the miserable distribution of food.[93]

To remedy the shortage in fat, the German Reich initiated experiments in extracting fats from animal bones and encouraged the collection of fats from wastewater for reuse, for example in the manufacture of candles. At the same time, civilian consumption had to be rationed and campaigns were launched to collect and dispense seeds containing fats and oils, such as beechnuts.[94] The success of these measures was doubtful, but their implementation illustrates the high demand. In parts of the Reich, people were encouraged to grow soy itself. There was no shortage of advisors, but implementation failed to materialize due not only to the lack of acceptance and negative experiences but also to the unfavorable climatic conditions in Central Europe.[95]

Surpluses in Asia

Given the interruption in trade caused by the First World War, it is useful to ask how the war changed trade patterns in Asia. What happened to the quantities of soybeans not shipped to Europe? What impact did the war, and ultimately the Russian Revolution of 1917, have on both the Asian soy trade and geopolitics in the Far East?

Before the war, Vladivostok was a central hub for Manchurian soybeans, and, from 1910 onward, many more soybeans were shipped to Europe from there than from Japanese-controlled Dalian. Vladivostok was an important port in the soybean trade because the Tsarist empire supported transport on the CER, which ran toward the city. At the beginning of the war, subsidies were cut, bringing the CER into financial difficulties and making it unattractive for trading companies like Mitsui.

In *Administering the Colonizer*, historian Blaine R. Chiasson has pointed out that the Russian Revolution entailed a number of problems for the Russians in this region, which eventually resulted in Russia losing its imperial influence in northern Manchuria.[96] He showed that the Russian Revolution had a greater impact on changing geopolitics in the Far East than the First World War. After 1917, railroad cars that had brought goods to Russia did not return, which generally worsened transportation possibilities. In addition, the Chinese authorities were eager to exploit the weakness of their Russian neighbor and successfully pushed back Russian influence. In effect, Russia had to relinquish many of the privileges associated with the railway concession, even in regard to its management. Finally, a currency crisis that arose in the wake of the political turmoil affected transportation conditions on the CER.

An immediate consequence of this confusing situation was that soybeans piled up along the tracks. In 1917, about 70,000 tons of soybeans awaited shipment in Vladivostok with another 15,000 tons in Harbin.[97] In order to avoid the Russian railway, farmers in the north went back to loading their crops onto carts and taking them to the Japanese sphere of influence at Changchun, where the SMR transported them to Dalian. Soy that farmers nevertheless took to the CER was now eventually freighted back to Harbin and from there on to Changchun, where it was exported to the Japanese SMR. The SMR transported the beans southwards to Dalian, which in turn received more than double the amount of beans in the years 1917–1921 than it had previously.[98] Beans nevertheless piled up along the route. In the summer of 1919, U.S. consul Douglas Jenkins at Harbin estimated that 20 percent of the soybeans harvested in 1918 were still at stations along the CER.[99] However, Jenkins confirmed that the soybean trade remained in the hands of Japanese traders, first and foremost Mitsui. In turn, this meant that the Russian port of Vladivostok handled fewer and fewer goods and lost its position as a hub for international trade in course of the war and the Russian Revolution.

Conclusion

Chapter 2 showed how soybeans became a global commodity. From the Russo-Japanese War onward, soybeans entered a complex web of trade interests and international relations, particularly between Asia and Europe. Supported by government structures and thanks to rapid communications and transportation systems, the Japanese trading company Mitsui succeeded in trading the Manchurian beans to Europe, mainly Great Britain but also Denmark and Germany, from where they were distributed further.

In Europe, technical achievements since the late nineteenth century had led to a rise in demand for fat. While the beans and the region in which they grew were rather unknown to Western observers, the trade was not random, and neither was the role of the most important trading company. This chapter has shown that the first wave of globalization and Japanese imperialism were interdependent and intertwined. Mitsui was able to operate within the framework of institutionalized capitalism, meaning within governmentally created structures. The company faced strong competition but was able to consolidate and expand its position with the help of the Japanese government.

Officials in the U.S. Departments of Commerce and State were concerned about the emerging soybean trade with Europe and particularly the prominent role of the Japanese trading company Mitsui in it. They generally feared Japanese competition on the world market and gathered information on the soybean as a resource for fat and fodder in Europe. However, they could neither influence nor stop Japanese activities in the Far East. As a result, soybeans became a commodity in Europe used in the production of numerous industrial and consumer goods. This development was interrupted by the First World War when transportation was limited, and soybeans piled up in Manchuria while demand remained high in Europe.

Notes

1 The correct name is Mitsui Bussan, meaning Mitsui Trading Company. In their English-language communication, the company used Mitsui & Co. (see also *The 100-Year History of Mitsui & Co., 1876–1976*, Tokyo: Mitsui & Co., 1976, 62). For sake of simplicity, I refer to the trading company as Mitsui. When referring to the parent company with the same name, I explicitly say so or add the term *zaibatsu* to distinguish between them.

2 George O. Burr, "Dietary Need for Fat," *The Annals of the American Academy of Political and Social Science* 225 (1943): 40–42; Karl Brandt, "Production and Consumption of Fats and Oils," *Annals of the American Academy of Political and Social Science* 225 (1943): 210–15, here 210.

3 Paula Yurkanis Bruice, *Essential Organic Chemistry* (Upper Saddle River, NJ: Prentice Hall, 2010), 517–19. There is no other substance that has the same chemical structure as fat, but there are some that resemble it, such as mineral oils, waxes, and essential oils. Those are not triacylglycerols and are thus excluded from this definition of fat.
4 Dorothea Bedigian, "Introduction: History of the Cultivation and Use of Sesame," in *Sesame: The Genus Sesamum,* ed. Dorothea Bedigian (Baton Rouge, LA: CRC Press, 2010), 1–31.
5 David S. Shields, "Prospecting for Oil," *Gastronomica* 10, no. 4 (2010): 25–34.
6 Birgit Pelzer and Reinhold Reith, *Margarine: Die Karriere der Kunstbutter* (Berlin: Klaus Wagenbach, 2001), 24–28; William Shurtleff and Akiko Aoyagi, "History of Soy Oil Margarine," *Soyinfo Center. Soy from a Historical Perspective,* eds. William Shurtleff and Akiko Aoyagi, accessed July 6, 2022, https://www.soyinfocenter.com/HSS/margarine1.php; W.G. Hoffmann, "100 Years of the Margarine Industry," in *Margarine: An Economic, Social, and Scientific History, 1869–1969,* ed. J.H. Stuyvenberg (Liverpool, UK: Liverpool University Press, 1969), 9–36.
7 Gary List and Michael A. Jackson, "The Battle Over Hydrogenation, 1903–1920," *INFORM – International News on Fats, Oils and Related Materials* 18 (2007), 403–5; Pelzer and Reith, *Margarine*, 32–35.
8 Shields, "Prospecting for Oil"; Terri Lonier, "Alchemy in Eden: Entrepreneurialism, Branding, and Food Marketing in the United States, 1880–1920," *Enterprise & Society* 11, no. 4 (2010): 697–710; Susan Strasser, *Satisfaction Guaranteed: The Making of the American Mass Market* (New York, NY: Pantheon Books, 1989), 3–28, 293–95.
9 Pelzer and Reith, *Margarine*, 36.
10 The figures are from Yves Péhaut, "The Invasion of Foreign Foods," in *Food: A Culinary History from Antiquity to the Present,* eds. Jean Louis Flandrin, Massimo Montanari, and Albert Sonnenfeld (New York, NY: Columbia University Press, 1999), 457–70, here 458. Péhaut's work on historic fat consumption is pioneering, but he does not provide many sources. Carl Alsberg and Alonzo E. Taylor, *The Fats and Oils: A General View* (Stanford, CA: Stanford University, Food Research Institute, 1928), 88; Geoffrey Jones, *Beauty Imagined: A History of the Global Beauty Industry* (Oxford: Oxford University Press, 2010), 71–93, 97–150, pointed out that the demand for soaps and other cosmetic products rose continuously worldwide even in times of crisis, such as during the Great Depression or the two world wars.
11 Alsberg and Taylor, *Fats and Oils*, 9–10.
12 Alsberg and Taylor, *Fats and Oils*, 84.
13 Alsberg and Taylor, *Fats and Oils*, 36.
14 Alsberg and Taylor, *Fats and Oils*, 5. The complexity still exists today, and the exploitation of various fats remains a remarkably confusing industry, see Derek Byerlee, Walter P. Falcon, Rosamond L. Naylor, *The Tropical Oil Crop Revolution: Food, Feed, Fuel & Forests* (Oxford: Oxford University Press, 2017), 4–6, and, with respect to soybeans, 66–91.
15 International Institute of Agriculture, *Oleaginous Products and Vegetable Oils: Production and Trade* (Rome: International Institute of Agriculture, 1923).
16 *Oleaginous Products*, 39 (Germany), 42 (Great Britain).
17 USDA, *Statistics of Fats, Oils, and Oleaginous Raw Materials.* Statistical Bulletin, no. 24 (Washington, DC: Government Printing Office, 1928), 13.
18 *Oleaginous Products*, 32 (France), 10 (Belgium), 422–25 (cottonseed), 446 (peanuts), 426–29 (linseed), 448–57 (coconuts and copra). Similar in USDA, *Statistics of Fats*, 13; Walter Bartram, *Die Rohstoffversorgung der inländischen*

und ausländischen Ölmühlen-Industrie (Mannheim: Self-publishing, 1920), 34–50; Péhaut, "Invasion," 458–60.

19 *Oleaginous Products,* 458–59 (palm nuts and palm kernels).

20 Alsberg and Taylor, *Fats and Oils*, 20–43, 63–88.

21 Various sources report on the beginnings of the soybean trade between Asia and Europe: H.T. Montague Bell and H.W. Woodhead, *China Year Book 1913* (London: Routledge, 1913), 49; Additional information provided in H.T. Montague Bell and H.G.W. Woodhead, *China Year Book 1914* (London: Routledge, 1914), 51; Norman Shaw, *The Soya Bean of Manchuria* (Shanghai: Inspector General of Customs, 1911), 20–21; U.S. Department of Commerce and Labor, *Soya Bean and Products*, Special Consular Reports, vol. 41 (Washington, DC: Government Printing Office, 1909), 3, 29; "The Soya Bean," *The Times*, July 19, 1910, 63; Kinnosuké Adachi, *Manchuria: A Survey* (New York, NY: R.M. McBride & Co.), 1925, 159–60; George Bronson Rea, "Beans: The Solution of the Commercial Situation in Manchuria," *The Far Eastern Review* 6, no. 10 (March 1910): 453–61, 486–89, here 455–56; SMR, *Soya Beans in Manchuria* (Dairen: Agricultural Office, South Manchurian Railway Co., 1926), 1. On Kabalkin see David Wolff, "Bean There: Toward a Soy-Based History of Northeast China," *The South Atlantic Quarterly* 99, no. 1 (2000), 241–52, here 245.

22 E.g., K. Kabuta, "Vladivostok versus Dairen," *Manchuria Daily News. Monthly Supplement* (October 1, 1922): 3–133, here 3, provides export figures for Dalian and Vladivostok for the years 1912–1921. As far as the years are comparable, his figures contrast sharply with those I use (see Figures 2.1 and 2.2 in this chapter). Kabuta's text is obviously tendentious in emphasizing the advantages of Dalian, which is why I did not rely on him as a source.

23 "Annual export of beans and their products through Dairen, Newchwang and Vladivostok, compiled by Mitsui & Co.," in Tokuji Hoshino, *Economic History of Manchuria* (Seoul: Bank of Chosen, 1920), after 218; unless otherwise explicitly stated, the data in the text as well as in Figures 2.1 and 2.2 in this book refer to the same source. Years refer to trading seasons, e.g., data for the first year, 1907, refer to a year lasting from November 1, 1907, to October 31, 1908, which means that beans recorded in one year arrived in Europe only in the following year. The numbers are higher for the first two years in Hiromi Mizuno and Ines Prodöhl, "Mitsui Bussan and the Manchurian Soybean Trade: Geopolitics and Economic Strategies in China's Northeast, ca. 1870s–1920s," *Business History* (December 1, 2019), DOI: 10.1080/00076791.2019.1687688. I would like to correct the numbers herewith. The data I work with in this book are confirmed by other contemporary sources as well, and thus I find them more reliable (see Shaw, *Soya bean*, 20; "Edible Oils and the Soya Bean," in *The Economist*, March 12, 1910, 555–56). In Britain, soybeans were not yet listed separately in trade statistics and it is therefore difficult to double-check the actual amount imported.

24 *Soya Bean and Products*, 29.

25 *Soya Bean and Products*, 19–34.

26 "Oil and Cake Manufacture," *The Economist*, December 4, 1909, 1144–45; see also "Edible Oils" and "The Soya Bean."

27 *Oleaginous Products*, 42. Geographer Yves Péhaut ("Invasion," 460) estimated that major European ports specializing in oilseeds and fruits, such as Liverpool, Marseille, Hamburg, and Rotterdam, imported about 500,000 tons of fatty raw materials each year in the early twentieth century. At least for Great Britain, this number is too small.

28 The soya bean industry, consul Douglas Jenkins, Harbin consulate, to the U.S. Secretary of State in Washington, DC, August 18, 1919, NARA RG 59 Department of State Relating to Internal Affairs of China, 1910–1929, M 329,

Roll 183, File 893.61345/4. Jenkins confirms that Vladivostok was initially more important than Dalian for the soybean trade with Europe.

29 Blaine Chiasson, *Administering the Colonizer: Manchuria's Russians under Chinese Rule, 1918–1929* (Vancouver, BC: UBC Press, 2010), 101–2.

30 A.R. Agassiz, "Our Commercial Relations with Chinese Manchuria," *The Geographical Journal* 4 (1894): 534–56, here 542; see also Alexander Hosie, *Manchuria: Its People, Resources and Recent History* (London: Methuen, 1904): 245; Shaw, *Soya Bean*, 16, 21; U.S. Tariff Commission, *Survey of the American Soya-bean Oil Industry* (Washington, DC: Government Printing Office, 1920), 12.

31 Robert W. Morrell, *Oil Tankers* (New York, NY: Simmon-Boardmann, 1931), vii, 1–2; Erich Stietz, *Die Soja in der Weltwirtschaft: Ein Beitrag zur Ernährungs- und Rohstoffwirtschaft der Erde* (Bethel b. Bielefeld: Anst. Bethel, 1931) 27, 33; see also picture in South Manchurian Railway, "Port of Dairen," *Manchuria Daily News: Monthly Supplement,* 2 (November 1, 1922), 8–15, here 14.

32 Exports of soybean oil from Vladivostok were comparatively small. Dalian mainly supplied European and Japanese customers while Yingkou played a central role in intra-Chinese trade, see Hoshino, *History of Manchuria*, after p. 218 (numbers are recorded for 1914 and 1915).

33 Bartram, *Rohstoffversorgung*, 24. Soybeans were classified as dry vegetables in France too, with duties being so high that the import of soybeans was not profitable, *Soya Bean and Products*, 19–20.

34 *Soya Bean and Products*, 19–28.

35 U.S. Department of Commerce and Labor, "Oil-Seed crushing: The Present Status of the Industry in Great Britain," *Daily Consular and Trade Reports*, no. 3687 (January 17, 1910): 7.

36 *Report on Progress in Manchuria, 1907–1928* (Dairen: South Manchurian Railway Co., 1929), 166; Maurice Fürstenberg, *Die Soja: Eine Kulturpflanze der Zukunft und ihre Verwertungsmöglichkeiten* (Berlin: P. Parey, 1917): 20–26.

37 Joachim Drews, *Die 'Nazi-Bohne:' Anbau, Verwendung und Auswirkung der Sojabohne im Deutschen Reich und Südosteuropa, 1933–1945* (Münster: LIT, 2004), 34; Fürstenberg, *Soja*, 26–34.

38 Mizuno, Prodöhl, "Mitsui Bussan," 12.

39 "Oil-Seed Crushing," 7.

40 Bronson Rea, "Beans," 456.

41 On the role of the *zaibatsu* within the Japanese economy, see Kozo Yamamura, "The Japanese Economy, 1911–1930: Concentration, Conflicts, and Crises," in *Japan in Crisis: Essays in Taishō Democracy,* eds. Gail Bernstein, Harry D. Harootunian, and Bernard S. Silberman, 299–328 (Princeton, NJ: Princeton University Press, 1974); Kozo Yamamura, "General Trading Companies in Japan: Their Origins and Growth," in *Japanese Industrialization and Its Social Consequences*, ed. Patrick Hugh, 161–99 (Berkeley, CA: University of California Press, 1976); Michael Y. Yoshino and Thomas B. Lifson, *The Invisible Link: Japan's Sogo Shosha and the Organization of Trade* (Cambridge, MA: MIT Press, 1986); Seiichiro Yonekura and Sara McKinney, "Innovative Multinational Forms: Japan as a Case Study," in *Leviathans: Multinational Cooperations and the New Global History*, eds. Alfred D. Chandler and Bruce Mazlish, 105–31 (Cambridge, UK: Cambridge University Press, 2005). After the Second World War, all *zaibatsu* were restructured and transformed into modern corporate groups by order of the Allied Control Council. For the history of the *zaibatsu* Mitsui and the Mitsui Group, see, among others, Mizuno and Prodöhl, "Mitsui Bussan," 5–10; John G. Roberts, *Mitsui: Three Centuries of Japanese Business* (New York, NY: Weatherhill, 1973); Seiichiro

Yonekura, "The Emergence of the Prototype of Enterprise Group Capitalism. The Case of Mitsui," *Hitotsubashi Journal of Commerce and Management* 20 (1985): 63–104.

42 *The 100-Year History*, 62.

43 Yamamura, "General Trading Companies"; Yonekura and McKinney, "Innovative multinational forms"; Yonekura, "The emergence of the prototype"; Nakamura, "The Present State."

44 Yonekura, "Emergence of the prototype," 372; Yamamura, "General Trading Companies," 169–71.

45 Mizuno and Prodöhl, "Mitsui Bussan," 9.

46 Ian Nish, "The First Anglo-Japanese Alliance Treaty," in *Anglo-Japanese Alliance* by Ian Nish, David Steeds, and Ayako Hotta-Lister, LSE STICERD Discussion Paper No. IS/02/432 (April 2002), accessed July 16, 2021, http://eprints.lse.ac.uk/6884/1/Anglo-Japanese_Alliance.pdf

47 Janet Hunter, "The Anglo-Japanese Alliance and the Development of the International Economy," in *Studies in the Anglo-Japanese Alliance, 1902–1923* by Gordon Daniels, Janet Hunter, Ian Nish, and David Steeds. LSE STICERD Research Paper No. IS/2003/443 (January 2003), accessed July 7, 2021, https://papers.ssrn.com/abstract=1162039.

48 Shaw, *Soya Bean*, 20; *Soya Bean and Products*, 25; "Soy Beans," *Journal of the Royal Society of Arts* 58, no. 2994 (April 8, 1910): 519, accessed April 20, 2022, http://www.jstor.org/stable/41339108; also reports on the importance of soybeans as a foodstuff during this war, although in respect to the Russian army only.

49 Bronson Rea, *Beans*, 456.

50 Stanley K. Hornbeck, *Contemporary Politics in the Far East* (New York, NY; London: D. Appleton, 1916), 263–64; Hoshino, *Economic History*, 226–27; Shun-Hsin Chou, "Railway Development and Economic Growth in Manchuria," *The China Quarterly* 45 (1971): 57–84, here 59.

51 Angus Maddison, *The World Economy: A Millennial Perspective* (Paris: Development Center of the Organization for Economic Co-operation and Development, 2001), 362.

52 Hoshino, *Economic History*, 84–88.

53 *South Manchuria Railway: Its Origin, Development and Phenomenal Rise to Importance* (Dairen: Manshu Nichi-Nichi Shimbun, 1911), title page.

54 *Soya Bean and Products*, 17.

55 Yonekura, "Emergence of the prototype," 86.

56 Hornbeck, *Contemporary Politics*, 276. This is confirmed by other contemporary sources, e.g., Adachi, *Manchuria*, 261–65; Hidemichi Akagi, "Japan's Economic Relations with China," *Pacific Affairs* 4 (1931): 488–510; Toyokichi Iyenaga, "Japan in South Manchuria," *The Journal of Race Development* 2 (1912): 373–98. Recent research has made the point as well, see Yoshiki Enatsu, "The Role of Private Companies in the Expansion of Japan's Interests in Manchuria in the 1920s: The Case of the Toa Kangyo Company (Toa Kangyo Kabushiki Kaisha)," *Chinese Business History* 15, no. 2 (2005): 1–2, 9–10; Ramon H. Myers, "Japanese Imperialism in Manchuria: The South Manchuria Railway Company, 1906–1933," in *The Japanese Informal Empire in China, 1895–1937,* eds. Peter Duus, Ramon H. Myers, and Mark R. Peattie, 101–32 (Princeton, NJ: Princeton University Press, 1989).

57 See Mizuno and Prodöhl, "Mitsui Bussan," 9 for details.

58 Sherman Cochran, *Encountering Chinese Networks: Western, Japanese, and Chinese Corporations in China, 1880–1937* (Berkeley, CA: University of California Press, 2000), 71–75; Yonekura, "Emergence of the Prototype," 386.

59 Hunter, "Anglo-Japanese Alliance."

60 Robert Nield, *China's Foreign Places: The Foreign Presence in China in the Treaty Port Era* (Hong Kong: Hong Kong University Press, 2015), 166–73.
61 Kang Chao, *The Economic Development of Manchuria: The Rise of a Frontier Economy* (Ann Arbor, MI: The University of Michigan, 1983), 4.
62 In contemporary statistics, trade with mainland China appeared as imports or exports from Manchuria. After 1907, Yingkou's imports and exports were mainly limited to imports and exports with China. Yingkou's rapid decline after 1907 was also observed in international newspapers, see "The soya bean," 63.
63 E.g., Sören Urbansky, *Beyond the Steppe Frontier: A History of the Sino-Russian Border* (Princeton, NJ, Oxford: Princeton University Press, 2020); Susanne Hohler, *Fascism in Manchuria: The Soviet-China Encounter in the 1930s* (London; New York, NY: I.B. Tauris, 2017); Mark Gamsa, *Harbin: A Cross-Cultural Biographie* (Toronto, ON: University of Toronto Press, 2021).
64 Frederick D. Cloud, "Why America is so interested in Manchuria," *New York Times*, March 27, 1910, SM 5.
65 Cochran, *Encountering Chinese Networks*, 78–81; Yonekura, "The Emergence of the Prototype"; Yamamura, "General Trading Companies"; Herbert P. Bix, "Japanese Imperialism and the Manchurian Economy, 1900–1931," *The China Quarterly* 51 (1971), 425–43, here 436.
66 Bruce A. Elleman, *International Competition in China, 1899–1991. The Rise, Fall, and Eventual Success of the Open Door Policy* (New York, NY: Routledge, 2015); Gregory Moore, *Defining and Defending the Open Door Policy: Theodore Roosevelt and China, 1901–1909* (Lanham, MD: Lexington Books, 2015).
67 In general little is known about Chinese who became part of a war that was not theirs, see Mark Gamsa, *Manchuria: A Concise History* (London: I.B. Tauris, 2021), 52.
68 Bronson Rea, "Beans," 455; British and American observers reported on Japan's dependency on soybean cake as fertilizer, see Shaw, *Soya Bean*, 20; *Soya Bean and Products*, 25.
69 *Soya Bean and Products*, 19–34.
70 "Proposal for the Neutralization of Railways in Manchuria," in *Papers Relating to the Foreign Relations of the United States, With the Annual Message of the President Transmitted to Congress December 6, 1910*, documents 194–240 (Washington, DC: Government Printing Office 1915), accessed July 21, 2021, https://history.state.gov/historicaldocuments/frus1910/ch31; Hornbeck, *Contemporary Politics,* 260–62, also reports on this proposal.
71 Cloud, "Why America is so interested in Manchuria."
72 American Legation in Peking to Secretary of State, June 17, 1911, NARA RG 59, Relating to Internal Affairs of China, 1910–1929, M 329, Roll 183, File 893.61345.
73 Bronson Rea, *Beans*, 455.
74 Hornbeck, *Contemporary Politics*, 263, 265–67.
75 Shizhang Hu, *Stanley K. Hornbeck and the Open Door Policy* (Westport, CT: Greenwood Press, 1995), 45.
76 Neither soybean cake nor whole soybeans were recorded as imported goods at that time as the imported quantities were too small. As for whole beans, Mitsui lists 825 tons in 1916, but less than 1 ton in 1917; see Hoshino, *History of Manchuria*, after 218; *Survey*, 7, confirms that American customers showed only meager interest in whole soybeans.
77 Initially the beans shipped from Kobe, after 1917 from Dalian, *Survey,* 12. Douglas Jenkins, American consul in Harbin, reported on the loss from leakage to the State Department, August 18, 1919, NARA RG 59 Department of State relating to internal affairs of China, 1910–1929, M 329, Roll 183, File 893.61345/4.
78 U.S. Department of Commerce, *Statistical Abstract of the United States: 1921, Forty-Fourth number.* (Washington, DC: Government Printing Office, 1922), 510, *Survey*, 7.

79 *Survey*, 19.
80 L.S. Palen, "The Romance of the Soya Bean," *Asia: Journal of the American Asiatic Society* 19 (January 1919): 68–74, here 69.
81 *Survey*, 19.
82 W.F. Washburn, *Soya Bean Oil, Flax Studies*. Bulletin of the North Dakota Agricultural Experiment Station, no. 118 (Fargo, ND: North Dakota Agricultural College, Government Agricultural Experiment Station for North Dakota, 1916), here 35–36.
83 Drews, *"Nazi Bohne,"* 34–38.
84 *Report on Progress*, 116.
85 Bartram, *Rohstoffversorgung*, 78.
86 There are many indications that fats and oils were in particularly high demand because of their versatile uses, but the background and circumstances are rarely explained, see Sir Llewellyn Woodward, *Great Britain and the War of 1914–1918* (London: Methuen, 1967), 350; Avner Offer, *The First World War: An Agrarian Interpretation* (Oxford: Clarendon Press, 1991), 66. For Germany, see Pelzer and Reith, *Margarine*, 49–50.
87 Michael Freemantle, *The Chemists' War, 1914–1918* (Cambridge, UK: Royal Society of Chemistry, 2015), 132.
88 Woodward, *Great Britain*, 484–97.
89 Wolfgang U. Eckart, "'Schweinemord' und 'Kohlrübenwinter': Hungererfahrungen und Lebensmitteldiktatur, 1914–1918," *Medizin, Geschichte und Gesellschaft*, 31 (2013): 9–31; The question of the degree to which Germans suffered from lack of food received much attention after the war and a growing scholarship has picked up the topic in recent years as well, see Alice Weinreb, *Modern Hungers: Food and Power in Twentieth-Century Germany* (Oxford: Oxford University Press, 2017), 13–48; Gesine Gerhard, *Nazi Hunger Politics. A History of Food in the Third Reich* (Lanham, MA: Rowman & Littlefield, 2015), 19–45.
90 Pelzer and Reith, *Margarine*, 49; Eckart, "'Schweinemord' und 'Kohlrübenwinter'," 10.
91 Drews, *"Nazi-Bohne,"* 37.
92 Drews, *"Nazi-Bohne,"* 34–38.
93 Offer, *First World War*, 21–78; Thomas Schindler, "Ernährung in der Krise: Anmerkungen zur Ersatzmittelbewirtschaftung in Marburg während des Kriegsjahres 1916, "*Zeitschrift des Vereins für Hessische Geschichte* 111 (2006): 219–36; Eckart, "'Schweinemord' und 'Kohlrübenwinter'," 17–26.
94 On the campaigns, see Pelzer and Reith, *Margarine*, 54–58; with specific reference to the situation in Marburg, Schindler, "Ernährung in der Krise," 221–30.
95 For example, with the help of Maurice Fürstenberg, *Die Einführung der Soja: Eine Umwälzung der Volksernährung* (Berlin: P. Parey 1916). On the state-sponsored cultivation trials, see Drews, *"Nazi-Bohne,"* 39–40.
96 Chiasson, *Administering the Colonizer*, 38–55, 101–2.
97 Mizuno and Prodöhl, "Mitsui Bussan," 16.
98 Kabuta, "Vladivostok versus Dairen," 9–10. The author of this source is tendentious in his favoring of Japan, but another source confirms the dramatic shift after 1917. According to *North Manchuria and the Chinese Eastern Railway* (Harbin: Chinese Eastern Railway, Printing Office, 1924), 284, the CER exported a yearly average of 170,000 tons to the SMR between 1913 and 1917. In the years 1918–1923, the yearly amount increased to 750,000 tons (ibid.).
99 Douglas Jenkins, The soya bean industry, American consul in Harbin to State Department in Washington, DC (August 8, 1919). NARA RG 59, Department of State Relating Internal Affairs of China, 1910–1929, M329, Roll 183, File 893.61345/4.

3 Fat and Feed in Germany

After the First World War, many a European food and agricultural enthusiast hoped that the soybean would soon be cultivated in Europe too. As climate conditions were not favorable, however, this would prove to be a rather difficult endeavor. Nevertheless, agronomists especially in Germany and Austria would make attempts to do so, but their breeding efforts were, naturally, time-consuming and did not result in the soybean being widely cultivated in Central or Northern Europe.[1] Even so, soy would gain a foothold at the time, but more as a commodity imported from the Far East than as a domestic crop. Germany, Denmark, and Great Britain were the largest soy-importing countries in Europe in the 1920s and 1930s. Just as before the First World War, the beans came from Northeast China, which in 1932 became the Japanese puppet state Manchukuo.

In Europe, the bulk of all imports was processed by oil mills with the oil being used primarily in the production of margarine and soap, and the residue as fodder. Soybeans thus had a dual use: while the main interest was first on the oil they contained, bean cake as the residue from the milling process became more and more relevant in livestock production. Manchuria also exported the two intermediate products, but European customers were most interested in whole soybeans. In 1927, one-third of all whole beans exported from Manchuria were purchased by German buyers (see Figure 3.1), and, due to the huge demand, Germany had become the largest importer of whole soybeans worldwide. In turn, soybeans had become a commodity of quite some significance in this country. Considering that in terms of quantity the soybean imports for 1928 equaled nearly half of all wheat imports in the same year, soybeans seemed to have gained a more than firm position in the German economy, food industry, and agriculture.

This chapter seeks to explore why the beans became a sought-after commodity in Germany, and what they were used for. One argument is that German oil mills were interested in the soybean not so much due to the chemical characteristics of its oil but because they were easily accessible and inexpensive. Germany was generally dependent on the import of oilseeds, and in this respect, soy was just one of many other resources, though one of increasing significance. Its benefit lay in providing cheap oil useful in

DOI: 10.4324/9781003255222-4

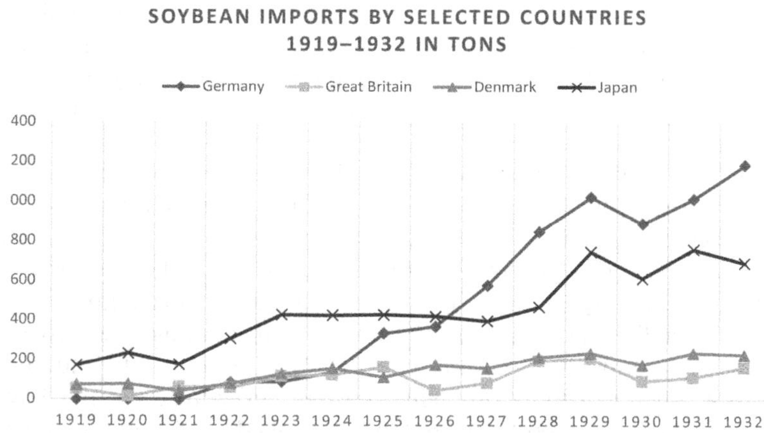

Figure 3.1 Soybean imports by selected countries in tons, 1919–1932.

© Author. Based on information from International Institute of Agriculture, ed., *Oleaginous Products and Vegetable Oils: Production and Trade* (Rome: International Institute of Agriculture, 1923), 442–43; International Institute of Agriculture, ed., *Oils and Fats: Production and International Trade*. Part 1 (Studies of principal agricultural products on the world market, no. 4) (Rome: International Institute of Agriculture, 1939), 71; and Erich Stietz, *Die Soja in der Weltwirtschaft: Ein Beitrag zur Ernährungs- und Rohstoffwirtschaft der Erde* (Bethel b. Bielefeld: Anst. Bethel, 1931), 31.

the food industry but also for the manufacture of other consumer goods. Another aspect in this cheap and available resource's favor was that the crop's cultivation and trade was not controlled by any other great power in Europe. In addition to emphasizing its low price, the eagerness of some German mills to use soybeans was due to resentment toward former war enemies. With the Treaty of Versailles, the German Reich had lost all its colonies and thus direct access to tropical oil crop resources. Some of my findings suggest that it was the result of the First World War and the global shifts in colonial possessions that led to German oil millers exploring materials from regions beyond European control; thus, the soybean was globalized by means of geopolitical changes in the wake of the First World War.

During the Weimar Republic, the soybean fully became a commodity on the German market, albeit one that was processed beyond recognition before the public consumed it. Paradoxically, even though Germans ate or otherwise consumed increasing amounts of soy, the beans never gained any value as a foodstuff in their own right. Instead, they became an industrial crop, used for further processing into oil and proteins. Moreover, the growth in soybean imports for the processing of oil brought lasting changes in agriculture: this period saw the rising value of soybeans as animal feed. With soybeans consisting of only about 16–20 percent oil, but approximately 40 percent protein, the residue from the milling process was not only enormous in its sheer volume but also made excellent concentrated feed.

Soybean fodder provided protein-rich muscle tissue, just as preferred in meat for human consumption. Thus, the average German consumed soy rather indirectly and unwittingly. As a result, soy was on everyone's lips—as margarine, Sunday roast, dessert, or lipstick—although hardly anyone was aware of it.

It was only in the Nazi period that soybeans came to be used as a direct foodstuff. Agricultural policy in Nazi Germany leaned heavily toward self-sufficiency and increasing the production of domestic crops and livestock. Such an approach met the demands of farmers, who dreaded the competition from globalized margarine, and in turn secured the support of farmers for the National Socialists. Political implications notwithstanding, the shift toward a policy expanding the domestic production of animal fats and proteins revealed a different supply problem. German agriculture did not have the means to yield enough fodder to feed the envisioned hogs, poultry, and cattle. The question thus became one of importing either feed or fat, but in reality, both of them, and the soybean offered the opportunity to kill two birds with one stone. On these grounds, the regime fostered soybean cultivation in southeastern Europe to increase the "domestic" cultivation of oil crops. In addition, Germany secured the beans' supply through a barter agreement with what had become the Japanese puppet state of Manchukuo. Despite these efforts, the provision of sufficient fodder became an increasingly unrealistic goal, especially with the country preparing for war. Thus, from 1936 onward, more attention was given to using the whole bean as food, such as in soybean flour to enrich breads, soups, sauces, and pastry with fat and proteins.

Providing the *Volk* with enough fat, preferably from homegrown livestock, was a challenge that not only concerned economists and agriculturalists. The new policy significantly reduced the amount of fat imports to save on foreign exchange, which, in the course of rearmament, was needed for obtaining metals. Because the people were highly affected by food shortages and were not able to consume enough fat, high-ranking Nazi officials addressed the interplay between butter and guns. They tried to convince ordinary Germans to accept shortages for what they believed was a better good: war. To historians, the line from butter to guns is not new. Gustavo Corni and Host Gies wrote the most comprehensive study on the link between food and the military build-up in Nazi Germany. They focused mainly on state control of the food industry and distribution and are excellent when analyzing the administrative challenges and internal contradictions regarding Nazi Germany's food policies. Likewise, Tim Schanetzky focused on economic policies and their consequences for food supplies and consumption. Reinhold Reith published on butter, margarine, and agricultural policies and pointed to the severe supply problems regarding fat.[2] As for soybeans, only Jürgen Drews and Ernst Langthaler have picked up the regime's efforts to foster their cultivation in southeastern Europe. Their studies are elaborate and grounded, but both fail to connect their results to the vast soybean imports from Manchukuo at the time. So far, only Robert

Fahs has analyzed German soybean imports from East Asia, although his ambition was rather to put Germany's economic diplomacy toward the Soviet Union, China, and Japan, not the German food situation, at the heart of his study. There is thus no study available that analyzes soybeans from southeast Europe and East Asia as elements of the same problem—namely serving Germany with fat, feed, and food.[3]

The following chapter is the first attempt to pull these various studies and approaches together by paying more attention to the crop's significance to the German economy and agriculture during the periods of the Weimar Republic and Nazi Germany. Reading contemporary sources with a focus on the beans, and asking what they were used for and why allows us to understand current approaches toward the crop. Agricultural and industrial developments in the Weimar Republic acted as an accelerator for the use of soybeans with which the Western world is nowadays familiar, as a fat resource and animal feed.

Import Dependencies and Technological Innovations in the Weimar Republic

In 1922, less than 85,000 tons of soybeans were imported into the German Reich. Only seven years later, in 1929, that amount had increased more than tenfold to over a million tons. No other country in the world matched this rapid growth in demand. A comparative look at the figures for other large soybean importers shows that German soybean imports were unique both in terms of their volume and the rate at which they grew annually. In only three years, from 1925 to 1927, the German Reich became by far the largest soybean importing country of any other (see Figure 3.1).

The data provided in Figure 3.1 show that German imports initially grew proportionally to those in Great Britain and Denmark and that it was not until 1925 that the German Reich began to import substantially more soybeans than the other countries.[4] While the data are interesting in themselves, they open up further questions such as why the demand for soybeans increased exponentially in the German Reich, and why Germans imported so much more soy than the other European countries. What were the beans used for, and what economic impact, for example in terms of processing and trade, did soy imports have for Germany?

Most of the data in Figure 3.1 were collected by the IIA in Rome. Besides its annual statistics, the institute oversaw individual studies on a range of key commodities for which it published information on cultivation, trade, processing, and consumption. One of the commodities given extra attention was fat from livestock, whales, seeds, and fruits. Fat was in short supply in all of Europe and heavily traded around the globe in the interwar period; thus, in 1923 and 1939, respectively, the IIA published two studies entirely dedicated to fat resources of global economic importance.[5] As for oilseeds and fruits, these studies provided background information on their climate requirements and further conditions for growing, methods for processing, international trade, national customs regulations, and consumption patterns. Soybeans were part of these studies because they were considered an oilseed and had been declared as such by all major European countries. Not all questions that arise in view of the extensive German soybean imports can be answered with the help of these studies, but they provide key clues, especially regarding the use of soy and its main products, soybean oil and cake.

The Margarine Boom

The data from the IIA show that, in Germany, oil extracted from soybeans went primarily into the production of margarine—that is, an all-purpose fat for frying, baking, and spreading on bread.[6] Most of the other imported fats or raw materials containing fat, such as oilseeds, were used for that purpose too. Minor amounts went into the production of soap, while the residue from the milling process was used as fodder.[7] As Germans were eating more and more margarine from the early twentieth century onward, production of it was a prosperous business. The demand for butter and margarine differed across social classes and the various German regions, but since margarine was more affordable, its popularity rose steadily. The fact that the two products were used in similar ways—mainly for spreading on bread, but also for baking and frying—also helped increase consumption rates. Around 1900, only about 170,000 tons of margarine were consumed, but by 1928 that figure had risen to 390,000 tons, a twofold increase. Thanks to this remarkable increase, by the late 1920s Germans were consuming about just as much margarine as butter, 7 kilograms of each per capita per year.[8]

Butter and margarine were not just any fat, but according to consumption numbers also the most important to the German diet. Together they accounted for more than half of the 1.4 million tons of fats the Germans consumed as food in the late 1920s. Other fatty foods consumed in significant amounts by the average German included lard and bacon, whereas edible tallow and vegetarian oils played only a minor role.

That margarine played such a prominent role in the 1920s was the result of the interplay of two classic parameters of globalization: political deregulation and technological achievement. While the German parliament offered the former, German chemists and oil millers worked on the latter. Combined, they aided margarine's entry into German markets and, with that, the globalization of soybeans. This process began around 1900 and was interrupted by the war, but thereafter accelerated, continuing well into the 1920s.

Since the early 1900s, margarine production had been boosted by a process in which liquid oils were turned into solid fat, known as fat hardening. It was Wilhelm Normann who patented the process in 1902. In the years to follow, various European and American companies developed the process further so that by the First World War they were able to produce a spread from liquid oils that would not drip off the bread. Additional chemical processes, such as full refining, eliminated unpleasant tastes and colors and helped improve the use of oils in margarine so that in the end it hardly mattered what fat the margarine was made of, at least in theory. In practice, taste and texture varied widely depending on the resources used and processes applied. The ability to exchange and substitute fats and oils allowed margarine manufacturers to operate independently of crop failures and price fluctuations, enabling them to replace raw materials in short supply with those available in abundance, or expensive ones with those more affordable. Added to this were new packaging techniques and machines that poured the margarine into forms and weighed it to the gram, helping to make margarine more attractive.[9]

The line between butter and margarine was not always easy to draw because butter could and at times even had to be mixed with other fats, primarily vegetable oils, and likewise margarine could, and at times had to, contain milk fat. Such practices were not driven by consumer demand but by political regulation requested by the dairy lobby. As butter was generally more expensive than margarine, dairy farmers feared a decline in the consumption of butter and thus their market for milk.

However, German agriculture was not able to provide enough fat resources, and the economy depended on imports. In reviewing these developments, the then Lübeck-based oil miller Walter Bartram wrote: "Without vegetable oils and fats, an adequate supply of fats was not even possible before the war."[10] Bertram made this statement shortly after the First World War, when he studied the global supply of fats and oils prior to building a career in the oil-milling industry, an endeavor that proved successful. He surveyed the market to assess his own business opportunities and, since hardly any oilseeds were grown in the German Reich, for him it was self-evident that Germany would need additional fat resources for domestic production and that oil mills would have to obtain their raw materials from suppliers abroad. He showed that the rising demand for margarine even before the war was not only caused by consumers' desires for inexpensive alternatives to butter, but also by the sheer need for fat resources in general.

In the years immediately following the war, butter was barely available on the German market, if at all, and then often diluted. Farmers held back their products in the hope of obtaining better prices on the black market or a few days later.[11] The German economy was suffering badly from hyperinflation. Unmanageable and difficult-to-calculate prices led to families reaching for low-priced alternatives for food and other household items. Margarine was one such low-priced alternative; however, at that time German margarine had an off-putting taste and texture and was by no means a quality product. It contained too much water and was made of less suitable oils such as fish oil or oil extracted from the feet of cattle. Farmers were not able to supply the population with adequate domestic fats, first and foremost from livestock, and they had nothing to spare for the margarine industry other than the cheapest and least-favored fats. With imported oilseeds being cheaper than domestic supplies, in theory, German oil millers could have reached for resources from overseas. However, as the German economy was in severe trouble in the course of the war and the subsequent Treaty of Versailles, they had no means to import oilseeds to supply the population with adequate fat alternatives either.

The situation only began to turn after 1923, when the German Reichsbank issued a new currency to put a stop to inflation. From then on, farmers marketed their products more regularly. Several other steps affected the fat market and, in combination, resulted in the skyrocketing import figures for soybeans from 1925 onward. Most important was the 1924 Dawes Plan which brought Germany to terms with the reparation payments being demanded by the other European powers. As part of the plan, Germany was able to take huge dollar loans from the United States, which boosted the entire economy, thereby also affecting the market for fat.[12] In due course, more fat became available on the German market, lard was imported from the United States, and butter and margarine of a high quality came from Denmark and the Netherlands.

As beneficial as these imports were for feeding the *Volk,* they did not have the same effect on the German economy because importing the finished products drained too much money from the country. In order to reduce the reliance on imports yet still meet the general demand for fat, on request of the German margarine industry in 1925 the Reichstag came to a new understanding of the fat market. It canceled import duties on oilseeds and oil fruits while increasing duties on oils to four Reichsmarks per ton, making importing them highly unattractive. This meant that the government was now focused on supporting the domestic processing of fat resources imported from abroad to meet domestic demand rather than having the market flooded with foreign products.[13]

This development is clearly reflected in the rise in import figures on fatty raw materials from that year onward. It explains why, beginning in 1925, soybean imports rose exponentially (see Figure 3.1). Likewise, rising soybean imports went hand in hand with declining oil imports. While in 1922, 42,000 tons of soybean oil were imported, by 1928 the figure was only 1,100 tons.[14]

Today's readers may wonder why the cultivation of German oilseed was not taken up as an alternative to imports. After all, the country's current agriculture is heavily characterized by oilseed cultivation, principally rapeseed, and each spring its cultivation turns entire landscapes into a sea of yellow. Yet, German rapeseed cultivation is the result of rather recent developments, as historian Sarah Waltenberger has shown.[15] In the interwar period, the country relied heavily on the import of fat-containing raw materials. In 1928, German oil millers extracted nearly 800 tons of oil from imported raw materials, while the yield from domestic oilseed, mainly rapeseed and flax, amounted to just 11 tons.[16] Imported raw materials such as copra, palm kernels, peanuts, or soybeans were far cheaper than domestic oil fruits. In addition, duty-free imports of inexpensive raw materials had a detrimental effect on the cultivation of domestic raw materials. As the latter were more expensive, cultivation rates declined even further.

With imported oilseeds playing such a significant role in margarine production, the question arises of which oils found their way into margarine, and what proportion of this was soybean oil. The answer is surprisingly simple, namely that German margarine was produced in different compositions depending on the raw materials available. The masterstroke of contemporary food chemists had been in creating a homogeneous product from heterogeneous raw materials. Rather than create a unique product based on highly specialized ingredients, the intention had been to become independent of the supply of specific raw materials. Contrary to the chemists' efforts (and success) in making a homogenous yet anonymous product, governmental statisticians as well as those at the IIA had the ambition to accurately list the individual ingredients. In light of these fundamentally contradictory intentions, the following numbers provide rather general information and do not account for every margarine available at the time.

In 1915, more than half of the fat content in an average German margarine was still of animal origin, mainly beef tallow. This share saw a steady decline in subsequent years; by 1928 the amount of animal fat in margarine was as low as six percent. The major ingredient in an average margarine, at 78 percent, was now vegetable oil, while whale oil accounted for 16 percent.[17] The seeds and fruits used had differing origins. A significant proportion, around 40 percent of the total fat content, was made up of coconut oil, which remained comparatively solid at room temperature and required less processing than more fluid oils. The proportion of soybean oil was around ten percent, as was that of peanut oil and palm oil.[18]

These figures illustrate that margarine was essentially a product of globalization. In addition, it had become an almost entirely vegetable product, not due to consumer demand but because of the availability of raw materials. A globalized market heralded the triumph of margarine as an inexpensive product derived from imported oilseeds. The war had dealt a decisive blow to the process of economic integration, yet it had not come to a standstill, and the world was once again connected. There were other areas that were less integrated, but the situation with fats suggests that global food production, trade, and consumption was increasing just as rapidly as before the war.

In view of the enormous growth in soybean imports, it may seem surprising that the share of soybean oil in margarine was a mere ten percent. The apparently low proportion can be explained by the general demand for fats and oils in Germany being many times greater than soybean oil alone could satisfy. Within Europe, the Germans not only led imports of soybeans, but also those of copra, the dried flesh of the coconut, and palm kernels. Figure 3.2 shows that Germany depended much more on imports of

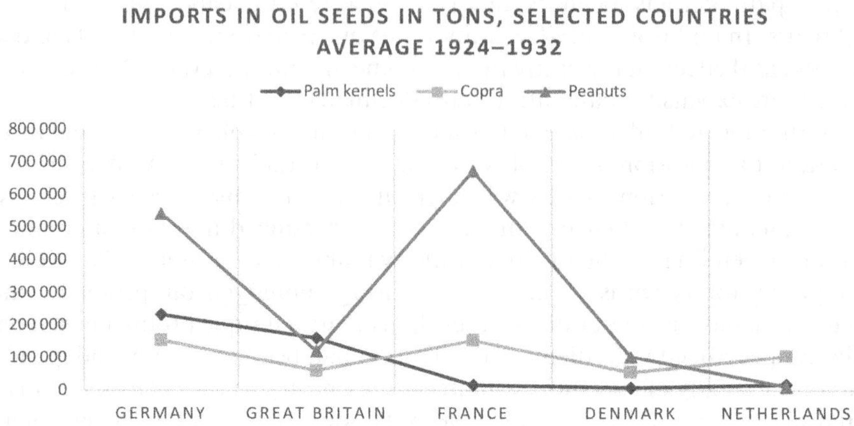

Figure 3.2 Top importing countries of palm kernels, copra, and peanuts annual average for the years 1924–1932 in tons.

© Author. Based on information International Institute of Agriculture, ed., *Oils and Fats: Production and International Trade.* Part 1 (Studies of principal agricultural products on the world market, no. 4) (Rome: International Institute of Agriculture, 1939), 31 (peanuts), 186–87 (copra), 229 (palm kernels).

vegetable oil resources than other European powers. It was only in peanut imports that France surpassed the German Reich.

It is difficult to estimate how large a share of the global trade soybeans had in all oilseeds and fruits, as they contained varying amounts of oils. The more oil any given raw material contained, the less of that raw material had to be imported, which explains the comparatively low imports of palm kernels and copra in all countries shown here. Despite the difficulties in comparing raw materials in order to assess the share of each one's oil on the world market, contemporary calculations suggest that the global share of oil from soybeans had reached nearly ten percent by 1924. With that, it had almost equaled the share of peanut oil and palm oil, which were at 13 percent each. Only the shares of coconut oil and linseed oil surpassed it, at one-fourth and one-fifth, respectively.[19] In other words, in terms of the global trade of their oil equivalent, soybeans ranked fifth and had thus established a firm foothold in the global market.

Notions of Independence in the Middle of Dependencies

As demand for fat was dependent on population densities and domestic supplies, the market for fatty raw materials differed from country to country. In the interwar years, Germany, Great Britain, and France were the world's leading importers of oilseeds, with Germany being particularly dependent on external supplies. This dependency had a history that reached back in time and was prevalent even prior to the war. Walter Bartram, the oil miller from northern Germany, wrote that before the First World War, Germany "ranked first among all countries in the import of oil raw materials." Providing a forecast, he stated that Germany's needs also in the years to come could only be met through extensive imports. To his mind, it was "not within the realm of possibility" for Germany to become independent of the world market for oil crops. Indeed, not even half of the 1.4 million tons of fat consumed annually as food in the 1920s was produced from domestic vegetable or animal resources. Given the sheer extent of German dependence on imports, the notion of self-sufficiency indeed seemed beyond reach.[20]

In fact, the German situation was complex. Peasants had no interest in cheap margarine displacing butter, and thus no incentive to increase the cultivation of domestic oil crops such as linseed, rapeseed, or sunflower. Meanwhile, they relied on the residue of the milling process to fertilize their soil and feed their livestock. In other words, they were just as dependent on imports to produce enough animal fat as German oil millers were to make margarine.

Besides soybeans, comparatively low-priced fat-containing raw materials included cottonseed and linseed. On the basis of price alone, German margarine producers could have also used either of the other two, but for a variety of reasons oils from them were barely used in its production. The United States was the world's largest producer of cottonseed, but in the interwar period its stocks mostly stayed within its domestic market. Supplies from Egypt, which was the second-largest cotton-growing region, were almost entirely imported by Great Britain and further processed there.[21] Linseed, on the other hand, was used in another economic sector. Flax was an oil plant and cultivated in Europe for centuries for its fiber and seeds, commonly known as linseeds. In the early twentieth century, flax was still grown in German fields, although only to a minor extent, and then mainly for its fiber, which was used for making cloth. As imports were much cheaper, growing flax for linseeds and then oil production was not profitable for German farmers. Linseed was in fact imported to a large degree. At about 370,000 tons imported annually either from Argentina or from Russia, it had been the most important oilseed before the war.[22] However, linseed oil was banned from margarine production from as early as 1920. That was only partly because the oil rapidly turned rancid and its taste was considered off-putting by many.[23] The main reason was that imported linseed was used in another sector, namely the production of paints and varnishes. Since linseed oil hardens when exposed to air—a huge, if not the most important benefit to this industry—all imports were absorbed by paint manufacturers. With that, neither cottonseed nor linseed were available to margarine producers. They resorted to the soybean because, of the three particularly inexpensive resources ostensibly available to them, it was the only alternative.

One contemporary Chinese observer even went as far as to claim that soybeans were in demand in Europe solely because they were cheap:

> At present, the European demand for soya bean depends entirely on their prices. The reason why Manchurian beans still retain their foothold in Europe is because that they are still among the cheapest oil products in the world, with the possible exception of cotton-seed.[24]

While soybeans were in fact among the cheapest oil resources on the market, it is too one-sided to focus solely on their low price as the only characteristic that made them attractive, especially in the German context. Manchurian soybeans apparently promised the Germans a certain independence from other empires and their resources. After all, Manchuria was "not directly subject to the control of the Entente powers," as one contemporary observer put it when praising the advantages of the soybean over other resources.[25] He was under the false impression that the Manchurian soybean trade was only subject to marginal control and that the German Reich would thus not find itself in any situation of dependency.

With the Treaty of Versailles, Germany had lost its colonies and thus its direct access to tropical raw materials. Walter Bartram was not the only oil miller to lament the "robbery of our colonies." In possession of colonies, he stated, Germany would be less dependent on the rest of the world market for oilseeds.[26] Tropical resources such as oilseeds, but also rubber, ebony, or other tropical fruits, were still available in the world market and prices were not necessarily more favorable for the empires of which these regions were a part. Nevertheless, empire and colony were interconnected and interdependent, which influenced trade patterns. The fact that France, for example, had only limited interest in the inexpensive soybean was because it relied mainly on peanuts from Senegal.[27] Great Britain and the Netherlands specialized in importing copra and the oil palm fruit because these commodities grew in their colonies. The British also almost completely absorbed all Egyptian cottonseed. The Germans did not have this access and felt highly disadvantaged. To some, the soybean offered a welcome alternative through which to avoid further humiliation.

I have shown in Chapter 2 that Japan was a strong actor in Manchuria and had nearly monopolized the soybean trade before the war, but this insight had not made its way to all German observers. Some emphasized an economic advantage stemming from the assumption that the soybean cultivation and trade were less regulated than other commodities. In 1931, economist Erich Stietz wrote a dissertation on soybeans in which he stated:

> The fact that Manchuria is still a disputed area, in which the preponderance of a political power cannot be spoken of, and therefore for the time being the danger of monopolization of soy is not to be feared for the German national economy, is to be judged favorably from the point of view of national economy.[28]

Stietz misjudged the situation, but his assessment reflects the German perception of geopolitics and global economy. Stietz and others focused on European empires; they were mentally bound to the time before the First World War, when the European concert had dominated the world. It seems as if they were not yet aware of the significance actors in the United States and Japan played in global trade and not least international politics. For them, soybeans still held a promise of independence that had otherwise been taken from them.

Regardless of such views, the soybean trade lay in the hands of just a few competing actors and Germany was in fact highly dependent on their prices, policies, and not least fluctuating fortunes. The Japanese trading company Mitsui, which had facilitated the soybean trade prior to the war, gained competition from European actors in the early 1920s. Two Danish trading firms, the East Asiatic Company and the Siberian Trading Company, had exploited the instable political and economic situation in northern Manchuria following the Russian Civil War and successfully established their businesses in Harbin. Political unrest and eventually civil war in China further helped to strengthen European firms and the role of the CER in northern Manchuria. The three firms controlled the European soybean trade, with Mitsui mainly serving the British ports of Liverpool and Hull and the Danish firms serving Copenhagen.[29] From there, beans were shipped onward within Europe, mainly to Hamburg, Bremen, Rotterdam, Amsterdam, Szczecin, and Gothenburg. Mitsui maintained its strong foothold in the southern part of Manchuria and shipped mainly from Dalian, while the two Danish firms used the CER to transport beans from northern Manchuria to Vladivostok, helping the international harbor and associated businesses to recover after the turbulent years of the early 1920s.[30]

As a matter of course, German diplomats and some oil millers were well aware of the strong position Japanese and Danish merchants held in this trade and tried to gain more control to lower transaction costs. A notable German actor in the Far East was Otto Witte, who in the mid-1920s held no official position as consul or diplomat but nevertheless had close ties to the German foreign service. Witte obtained a formal commission from the German Foreign Office in January 1924 to approach the Chinese warlord Zhang Zoulin. Backed by Japan, Zhang Zoulin controlled large parts of Northeast China at the time, and Witte became a private employee working on behalf of the warlord. In doing so, he combined private and national interests as he laid the ground for the arms trade, mainly from the German firm Krupp, into this region, without officially offending Germany, China, or Japan. Since Witte lived in Shenyang (then Mukden), he obtained insights into the soybean trade as well and aimed to provide German trading companies with a stronger position within it. On October 30, 1924, he informed the secretary of state *(Staatssekretär)* of the Foreign Office, Adolf Georg von Maltzan, about his efforts "to bring the Manchurian soybean trade with Germany entirely into German hands."[31] His plan was to establish a cartel and he had apparently gained the support of a few actors, including Zhang Zoulin himself, for such an endeavor. Where Witte failed, however, was in acquiring the necessary capital and winning over a well-established German trading company. He had envisioned industrialist and politician Hugo Stinnes at the crux of his plan, but Stinnes had made commitments to the Japanese trading firm Kawasaki Kisen Kaisha at Dalian, which was an obstacle to his involvement in Witte's plan. From then on, Witte's scheme came to a halt.

Meanwhile, some Hamburg-based oil millers tried to push matters further. In the spring of 1925, they asked the Hanseatic minister in Berlin, Justus Strandes, to request an investigation into the possibility of German participation in the Manchurian soybean trade.[32] The resulting consular report, however, was as clear as it was disappointing. As most parts of the soybean trade, including transportation and price negotiations, lay in the hand of the Japanese and thus in the city of Dalian, the consul strongly advised against any attempts to build up a German trading presence there. A set-up in the north, in Harbin, was according to the report only slightly more promising, if at all. The report also recommended the formation of a cartel consisting of several robust trading companies, trustworthy ship brokers, and a set of German oil mills to secure the sales. As all this would also be capital-intensive, the report questioned whether it would be possible to find companies financially capable of engaging in such a venture.[33] Germany's economic situation in the 1920s was still weak, and besides one adventurous oil miller, none seemed willing to further entertain the idea. The soybean trade thus remained in the hands of Japanese and Danish trading companies.

There was yet another area in which Germany was less independent than some observers might have preferred: the oil milling industry itself. Some of the oil mills specializing in the margarine industry and with a large capacity were part of foreign trusts. By 1925, the Dutch group Antoon Jurgens and the German-Dutch van den Bergh controlled about ten German oil mills, and as such about 40 percent of all milling capacity lay in their hands. In 1927, they and others formed the principally Dutch company Margarine-Unie, which, after a merger with the British soap manufacturer Lever brothers in 1929, became the multinational Unilever. With a capital of 100 million British pounds, this new company was not only a giant in the fats and oils business but also the largest company of any in Europe at the time.[34] In other words, on the eve of Hitler's rise to power the Anglo-Dutch multinational dominated the German edible fats industry.

Soft and Creamy: Technological Advances

So far, this chapter has explored the correlation between a persistent demand for fat in Germany, political measures to serve this need, and the global fat business of the period. A generally high demand for fat imports, which had grown even more acute after the First World War, led to the Germans turning to soybeans to solve their supply problems. Soybeans, on the other hand, continued to become a globalized crop due to the highly specific German situation in the aftermath of the First World War. This next section continues by showing that the rising focus on soybeans as a fat resource in the production of margarine and, to a lesser extent, soap, resulted in more than a growth in import figures. The focus on soybeans offered a niche for specializing in processing technologies. In due course, soybeans became even more attractive on the entire European market, which in turn resulted in the globalization of soybeans again being driven by technical improvements.

A prerequisite for this was for soy to be imported as dried but otherwise whole beans, which thanks to new policies was increasingly the case from 1925 onward. Germany was not the only country exercising such a trading policy, and oilseeds were by far not the only commodity group to which this applied. A typical economic practice of the 1920s was for industrialized nations to impose import tariffs on manufactured goods and support the purchase of raw materials to protect their own industries.[35] Conversely, however, such trading policies meant that processing industries in the raw materials' countries or regions of origin suffered a decline. The soybean trade in these years fit into this global economic structure. While the Manchurian soybean oil industry and oil export figures steadily weakened, the processing of soybeans shifted more and more to European countries, particularly Germany, where the industry secured jobs, technological advances, and access to national and international markets.[36]

In Germany, the actor who flourished the most was Hermann Bollmann, a Hamburg-based entrepreneur who succeeded in initiating two fundamental developments. The first was a chemical extraction process that enabled considerably more oil to be extracted from the beans than had previously been possible; the second was the production of lecithin, a substance used as a softener in food processing. Bound up with these developments was the increasing use of soybean meal as fodder in agriculture.

When Bollmann founded his oil mill in 1916, three different methods were available for milling oilseeds: hydraulic presses, expeller or screw presses, and chemical extractions. While the Americans mainly relied on hydraulic presses, German millers preferred expeller or screw presses and chemical treatments. Through chemical extraction with benzine, alcohol, or benzene it was possible to obtain almost all oil in any given oilseed, but the use of solvents often caused new problems. Depending on the specific composition of the solvent, the chemicals used were either expensive, easily flammable, caused damage to the machinery, or affected the quality of the residue, which would then be less suitable as fodder.[37]

Hermann Bollmann was most interested in improving chemical processes and set to work on all sorts of oilseeds as long as they were available. It was only after the war that he specialized in soybeans, and in two different directions. He offered soybean flour, which was intended to enrich bread with fat and protein during the continuing food shortages the Germans were experiencing, and he worked on chemical extractions to serve the high demand for fat and fodder. He had to be adventurous as the milling of oilseeds was a competitive business, but despite his ambitions, Bollmann soon ran into financial difficulties. The solution was to reorganize the company's business structure. In 1923, Hanseatische Mühlenwerke AG was founded as a joint stock company with funds to embark on the new venture obtained from a group of Hamburg bankers, who held most of the stock in the company until after the First World War.[38] Bollmann's original oil mill, Hansa-Mühle, became a full subsidiary. Being more a businessman than a chemical expert, he left the job of further specialization in oil processing to his chemists.

In 1924, Bruno Rewald was particularly successful with a benzene-alcohol mixture, as the solvent neither attacked the machinery nor affected the taste and quality of the oil and meal. However, the oil extracted by this method had a slight flaw: it tended to be cloudy. When Rewald and his colleagues isolated and extracted the natural mucilage, it turned out to be lecithin, a then sought-after softener.[39]

Lecithin is the generic term for a group of substances that belong to the family of lipids. Besides a yellow-brownish color, they share a characteristic known as being amphiphilic, meaning they attract both water and fatty substances. Normally, fat and water do not mix, but with the help of lecithin, they form an emulsion. This quality is useful for smoothing textures, such as in butter, of which lecithin is a natural component, or margarine, where the addition of lecithin is beneficial to its texture and spreading properties.

Lecithin is part of every plant and animal cell, but it was not before the mid-nineteenth century that Théodore Gobley, a French chemist and pharmacist, was able to isolate the substance. As he succeeded in isolating it from raw egg yolk, Gobley named his finding *lécithine,* which referred to the Ancient Greek *lekithos*, meaning egg yolk. Gobley and other European chemists kept working on lecithin, but throughout the nineteenth century its main source remained egg yolk, where its concentration of eight to ten percent was highest.[40] It was mainly used as a pharmaceutic. Containing organically bound phosphor, it was hoped that it would remedy ailments including tuberculosis, anemia, and carcinomas.

Among chemists, other uses were known as well, but as egg-based lecithin was expensive its use in food and nonfood items remained limited. Nevertheless, one area it was used was in the production of margarine, as the addition of only small amounts helped make the spread more butter-like. Another was in the manufacture of extra-fine leather, since lecithin made skins particularly soft and smooth to the touch. The egg yolk was mainly imported from China, either dried or preserved in liquid form, but either way it perished easily. In addition, lecithin from egg yolk often contained other substances from the egg, which in turn limited its shelf life. In

1927, lecithin extracted from egg yolk cost between 40 and 60 Reichsmark per kilogram depending on the degree of purity.

Rewald's discovery of soybean-based lecithin revolutionized the entire market. Suddenly, lecithin was available in much larger quantities, was purer, and had a much longer shelf life. Prices dropped so dramatically that soy-based lecithin cost only one-twentieth of that from egg yolk.[41] With lecithin's price essentially plummeting overnight, margarine became even more affordable, and its quality improved further. In addition, other markets quickly opened up. Pasta and pastries were among the first food items to which lecithin was now also added. As for nonfood uses, the textile industry discovered that lecithin improved the vividness of colors. In a review of the uses of lecithin in 1929, Rewald also highlighted potential future markets where the substance could have beneficial effects, although research into these products was ongoing.[42] Among the products he mentioned were chocolate, cocoa powder, and jam, but also lotions and creams for personal hygiene. Rewald was correct in his assumptions. Only a few years later, lecithin became and would remain an almost universal ingredient in many a food item and cosmetic product. Lecithin makes mayonnaise as soft and creamy as chocolate and confectionaries, and it renders ointment and moisturizer emollient without making them feel greasy.

In addition to having found a way of isolating lecithin, Bollmann's team further refined the entire workflow for processing soybeans. They pursued automatic and continuous work practices which allowed them to process ever more soybeans. Apparently, it was soon known as the "Ford system among the oil mills."[43] Bollman's procedure for extracting soybeans was in fact so successful that it was before long in wide use in most German oil mills. In addition, the processing of soybeans in the Hansa plant increased tremendously. The company was reported as handling approximately 6,300 tons of soybeans in 1924 but more than doubled its processing to 14,500 tons the following year. By 1926 the plant was processing 17,400 tons and had reached capacity. By that time, the mill had an output of 12,000 kilograms of soybean oil and 250 kilograms of lecithin per day.[44]

Domestically Produced Fodder

The figures for oil production at the Hansa-Mühle sound impressive but considering the many tons of soybeans the plant processed, the output seems somewhat underwhelming. In fact, the numbers reflect that the soybean was not an oil crop per se but had been turned into one by industrial demand and eventually political economy. To enable the tariff-free or nearly tariff-free import of whole soybeans for use in oil processing, in the early 1910s, one European country after the other recategorized the beans from vegetables to oilseeds in their tariff regulations. Needless to say, that this had little effect on the bean's oil content. Depending on the variety, soybeans contained less than one-fifth and often only one-sixth of oil by mass, and it was only after Bollmann's chemists' invention that the majority of it could be extracted. In terms of quantity, the protein-rich byproduct bean cake, or bean meal, constituted the lion's share of the end products of soybean processing.

While the sales market for soybean oil and lecithin was secured early on, Bollmann needed to do some marketing to sell the residue from oil extraction. It was sold as a protein-rich concentrate feed under the brand name Vita and was accompanied by feeding instructions for a variety of farm animals. In addition, Bollmann came out with a number of publications to argue for the use of oil meal and particularly soybean meal in German agriculture. In an extensive, 50-page-long publication from 1927, the positive effects soy meal as a feed would have on German agriculture and the entire economy was given emphasis. Using data from official statistics, Bollmann and his team documented Germany's trade deficit regarding fatty resources such as butter, cheese, lard, eggs, margarine, and oilseeds. According to this publication, it was obvious that the country's agriculture was not able to produce enough fat domestically, and it concluded that "neither now nor in the future" would it be possible for Germany to become self-sufficient. Even increased domestic agricultural production would not be able to fulfill the country's demand for fats and protein. The soybean could be one solution for extricating the nation from this dilemma. It was proposed that a sophisticated German processing industry with a strong focus on soybeans would bolster the country's agriculture sector in its ambition to produce more fat. Soybean meal, went the argument, was a protein-rich concentrate that fed cows so well that they would produce more milk and, with that, fat for human consumption.[45]

The publication was doubtlessly promotional in its nature and Bollmann and his people were arguing for their own interests; nevertheless, the analysis was clear regarding the impossibility of the country becoming agriculturally autarchic. The Nazis tried to achieve this, as will be shown in the next section, but promptly encountered severe problems in providing enough fat and protein to the people, just as had been forecast.

To underpin their argument, the German situation was compared to that of Denmark, which also had a strong milling industry and where soybean residues were used in animal husbandry. According to the brochure, it was due to the Danes' major import of oilseed that the country had no need to import dairy products, and was able to export surpluses.[46] Danish agriculture was indeed specialized in animal husbandry and, as a result, was Europe's leading exporter of butter and cheese. Their agriculture relied on the import of oilseeds, with the obtained oil being used in the production of margarine and the residue serving as fodder. By contrast, most other European countries, including Germany, preferred a mixed-agriculture approach between animal and plant husbandry.[47] Bollmann suggested a more Danish-like agriculture would result in a better trade balance, as importing oilseeds from overseas was cheaper than importing dairy products from other European countries. Concluding his findings, he demanded that the German government facilitate the use of soybean meal among farmers and called for "the active support of the authorities in propagating the widest possible use of domestically produced concentrated feed in livestock farming." By "domestically produced" he was referring to bringing the processing of oils to Germany, not to using oilseeds cultivated on German farms, which grew far too sparsely.[48]

Considering that Bollmann was an oil miller, there is no doubt that he was trying to shore up his own business interests by presenting them as a national economic necessity. That Bollmann looked to Denmark as an industrial and agricultural role model for Germany came as no surprise, given the company's own ties to the country. The Aarhus Oliefabrik and the Dansk Soyakage-Fabrik also processed soybeans into oil and lecithin, and the three of them joined forces to dominate the European market for lecithin.[49]

In most of his publications regarding soy-based feed, however, Bollmann was careful to avoid the association of *fat* with soybeans. He claimed his feed would improve dairy products, and he associated vegetable feed with animal fats, but he made hardly any references to the rising demand for soybean oil and margarine. He was thus also cautious to avoid any reference to the competition between butter and margarine, perhaps demonstrating that he neither wished nor needed to enter this discussion. The sales market for margarine was secured and it was not necessary to put it at risk by entering into a discussion on domestic butter versus foreign margarine. What Bollmann needed was to convince farmers to buy the residues from the milling process.

It is difficult to estimate how big Bollmann's role in establishing soybean meal as feed actually was. After all, the feed caught on among farmers relatively quickly and by the late 1920s already led all oilseed-based feeds in German husbandry. This finding is based on the work of an economist, Erich Stietz, who in 1931 aimed to present the beans' role in the global economy. Stietz calculated that in 1926 about 20 percent of the feed generally used in Germany consisted of soybean meal; two years later, he figured, it had already reached about 33 percent.[50]

The product's good value for money ratio probably convinced farmers more than Bollmann's arguments did. Among all feeds available in Germany at the time, soybean meal contained most protein for the price. Protein-rich fodder, also called concentrate feed, produced good muscle tissue and was preferred in meat and milk production. In 1929, 100 kilograms (220.5 pounds) of soybean meal contained about 38 percent protein and cost 20.6 Reichsmarks. Only peanut meal contained more protein (45 percent), but at 24.80 Reichsmarks was more expensive. Meal from cottonseeds (38 percent) and sesame seeds (35.5 percent) had protein contents comparable to soybean meal, but at 24.80 and 22.70 Reichsmarks, respectively, both were also less competitive. Forage crops grown in German fields contained considerably less protein—bran from rye and wheat was at ten percent, feed from oats and barley less still.[51] They were nevertheless good feed, rich in other beneficial content, but did not have the same meat and milk-producing capacity as concentrates.

While soybean meal displaced a few other feeds, it nevertheless enabled German agriculture and industry to expand meat production. The increase in the use of soybean meal was paralleled by declining numbers in in the use of meal from processing sunflower, coconut, and palm kernels, all of which containing less protein than soybean-based fodder. It seems that farmers saved their expenditure on feed from these crops in order to focus on purchasing more soybean meal instead. The concentrate enabled them to produce a greater quantity and a better quality of meat without spending more on fodder, and it was this link that made the product attractive to farmers. German agricultural production, particularly for hogs and cattle, lagged behind in international comparisons and using cheap soybean meal offered an opportunity for farmers to increase their capacity.[52]

Beyond Fat and Feed

In addition to supporting the sale of soybean meal as animal fodder, Bollmann made efforts in further processing the residues from the milling process into flour and then marketing it for human consumption. His first known attempt at gaining approval for such a product from the German authorities dates to October 1920, and he promoted the use of soybean flour as a foodstuff in the years to come. Among the various regulations issued in the young Weimar Republic was one which determined the composition of bread.[53] As grains, just as other staples, were in short supply in the German market for food, it essentially prescribed a certain amount of grain flour to ensure a quality standard for bread offered for sale. In addition, the regulation permitted some ingredients such as cornmeal with which to bulk out or enrich bread, depending on one's point of view. It was here that Bollmann first found a niche for soybean flour. After various baking tests, positive evaluations, and a few letters of support, soybean flour was approved as an additional ingredient in bread making.[54]

Even though Bollmann remained a soy enthusiast in years to come, he did not further pursue the use and sales of soybean flour in his own company. The particular process his chemists developed in 1924 for extracting soybean oil was excellent only in so far as it extracted almost all oil out of the beans; processing them for flour, however, required a different method. When milling flour from residues of soybeans from which the oil had been chemically extracted, as in Bollmann's process, the end product was bitter and not suitable for human consumption. With alternative methods, the flour often turned rancid rather quickly as a result of its high fat content. To seek a solution, Bollmann backed the establishment of a new company, Deback, which specialized in processing soybeans more gently and offering flour for human consumption. The product was sold under the brand name Farinette.

In one of Bollmann's own publications from 1929, Curt Brüning, managing director at Hansa-Mühle, wrote about the benefits of adding Farinette to bread mixes to enrich the bread's nutritional value.[55] He provided an overview of prices for various proteins, according to which a kilogram (2.20 pounds) of protein from eggs cost 21.80 Reichsmarks while that derived from beef and cheese cost 15.40 and 16.19 Reichsmarks, respectively. In comparison, the equivalent from soybean flour cost 0.83 Reichsmarks. Brüning tried to convince his readers to eat more soybean proteins on the basis of such rational findings that soybean flour was the cheapest protein resource available, and called to add up to 20 percent soybean flour to the total flour mix in bread. This, claimed Brüning, would first and foremost provide Germans with more protein but also had the additional benefit of improving German breads in general and averting further strain on the German economy. His rationale was that German farmers' fields yielded less wheat, of lower quality, compared to imported wheat grown in Russia and the United States. Adding soybean flour to bread would thus enrich the poor German wheat and would enable the German economy to save on wheat imports, since soybean imports were much cheaper.

Bollmann and his team were not alone in their efforts to market soybean flour; in fact, the product was often mentioned in contemporary publications. Nutritionists, medical practitioners, and biologists tried to promote soybean flour as a protein food, pointing to its price and benefits for both agriculture and nutrition compared to animal proteins. Among the prominent actors engaging in promoting the use of soybean flour was physiologist and hygienist Max Rubner, a coryphaeus of the age, still remembered for his research on the human metabolism. Another prominent figure supporting the use of soybean flour was medical practitioner and politician Julius Moses. From 1920 to 1932, Moses was a member of the German Reichstag for the Social Democratic Party, and it was in the party's newspaper *Vorwärts* that he called on his compatriots to eat more soybeans.[56] The eagerness of people like Rubner and Moses, however, is not to be confused with enthusiasm for the product among the *Volk*, for beyond expert circles, soybean flour played a rather marginal role.

Other companies also embarked the sales of soybean flour, even though the sales opportunities remained comparatively small. By 1923 the Hungarian food physiologist Ladislaus Berczeller had developed a promising process that was gentle enough on the beans while guaranteeing the final product a longer shelf life. However, with Germans feeling disinclined to be reminded of the food shortages of the First World War, when soybeans, as far as they were available, served as an all-round substitute, it took time for Berczeller's method to gain recognition. It was not until the Great Depression had reached the country that a Berlin firm began producing this type of flour.

It was branded Edelsoja, suggestive of its supposedly precious and noble characteristics.[57] Despite catchy names like this as well as other marketing tricks, soybean flour barely entered German households.

Neither did other soybean-based foods. An advertising brochure published by Hansa-Mühle stated that the "form in which East Asians consume their soy food" would not correspond to European tastes. The argument may seem convincing at first glance but loses some of its truth when one considers that Asian foods made of soy were usually based on the whole bean, not its isolated ingredients. In other words, Asian-style foods were a product line that would have rendered oil mills redundant. In yet another publication, Hansa-Mühle declared the fermentation process necessary to produce some Asian-style foods such as tofu and soy sauce to be "cumbersome" and "extremely time-consuming" and the final product altogether less attractive to German customers.[58] Again, the mill was arguing its own case, since fermenting soybeans required both oil and protein. What oil mills like Hansa-Mühle were thus ultimately promoting was the use of a protein-rich plant in the fattening of animals in order to produce nothing else but protein. In this way, they carved the way for the evolution of Western industrialized agriculture as we know it today.

Thanks to developments like those at Hansa-Mühle and others, the German Reich became not only the leading importer of whole soybeans from northeastern China throughout Europe, but as a result also the largest European exporter of refined soybean oil. Exports, which were destined mainly for the Scandinavian countries as well as to the Netherlands, underwent a particular boom between 1928 and 1933, a time of general decline in which butter became too expensive for many people.[59]

While Hanseatische Mühlenwerke AG and its subsidiary Hansa-Mühle remained successful in the years to come, Bollmann's personal fortune faded. The bankers who helped founding corporation were severely affected by the Wall Street Crash and so was the company itself. Bollmann lost his position as managing director in 1930. His former role was not taken into account in the organization of a new company under the same name in the way he would have preferred, and, unable to cope with the situation, he left the reorganized company in an attempt to make a new start. He lost the patents to his own inventions, which by 1933 amounted to 65 worldwide, and died the year after.[60] By that time, what had become known as the Bollmann method for extracting oil had been proved valuable not only for soybeans but for other crops such as cottonseed, peanuts, and rapeseed as well. As the system was so widely successful, it was sold in Europe and beyond, among others to milling companies in Belgium, France, Hungary, Italy, and the United States.[61] In the latter, a then rather regional oil mill named Archer Daniels in Minneapolis was most interested in Bollmann's method. In the years to come this company became one of the most successful milling companies worldwide and is nowadays known as Archer Daniels Midland (ADM).

Autarky and Shortages in Nazi Germany

In November 1934, economist Willi Tomberg for the Reichs-Kredit-Gesellschaft (State Credit Agency) surveyed what was called the German "fat problem." In his report, Tomberg wrote that it was "economically impossible" to move toward self-sufficiency in regard to fat supplies and, rather, that the current agricultural and political ambition was a significant reduction in imports of fatty resources such as oilseeds in order to maintain the trade balance. He pointed to three major domestic commodities whose production would have to be increased to reach this goal: dairy cows, extra fatty hogs, and oilseeds. A surge in dairy cow numbers would lead to more milk and with that a greater supply of butter. What he called *Fettschweine* were breeds of pigs with a significant amount of fat to increase the domestic reserve of lard. The oils from seeds cultivated on German land, such as rape and flax, were to support the margarine sector and serve technical needs, such as paints.[62]

Tomberg was not outlining a specific German agricultural policy he envisioned but a summary of steps discussed and already partly taken since the National Socialists had gained power. The bank he worked for was government owned and specialized in financing international commerce and thus also involved in trading fatty resources. Tomberg's report was thus important for gaining an overview of current agricultural policy and for planning the bank's future transactions.

The Nazis' agricultural policy indeed aimed to achieve self-sufficiency, with agricultural minister Richard Walther Darré grounding the objective within the Nazi ideology of blood and soil. Despite all ideological aspirations, the real ambition was to save on imports and use the foreign exchange reserves to prepare for war. However, when it came to self-sufficiency in the food sector, the supply of fat proved most difficult, and Nazi Germany remained as dependent on importing fat resources to serve domestic demand as the Weimar Republic. The Nazis feverishly tried to find a solution for providing the people with enough fat and nevertheless achieve greater economic self-sufficiency. But raising animal fat production, as Tomberg outlined, caused another problem, namely that of sufficient fodder. After all, along with poultry and cattle, the fatty pigs he described had to be fed, and fodder for animal husbandry was in just as short supply as fat for the *Volk*.

Here, soybeans were a good fit, even though they had to be purchased abroad and their oil was used to produce margarine, a product that would ideally be replaced with German butter. From 1936–1937 onward, Nazi nutritionists concluded that using soybeans for human nutrition was more effective in terms of providing people with fat and proteins than having livestock process them first. This explains why after a short period of falling imports in the mid-1930s, which paralleled severe fat shortages in the Reich, soybean imports rose once again. In addition, industrialists, party officials, and agriculturalists were quite concerned with growing soybeans in Germany, or at least in regions Germany had better control of than faraway Manchukuo.

Even though the aim of (greater) self-sufficiency was new to this period, the focus on soybeans and attempts at limiting oilseed imports were not. There were certainly continuities regarding the importation, processing, and consumption of oilseeds between the Weimar Republic and the Nazi period. While this chapter mainly focuses on developments in the Nazi era, one aim of it is to include these continuities rather than understand the year 1933 as a break with former attempts at regulating the market for fat. Another is to understand German policies in the Far East from an economic perspective that pays attention to the allocation of raw materials.

The "Fat and Protein Gap"

The Wall Street Crash of 1929 and the subsequent depression shook the world profoundly. People around the world were hit by unemployment and faced bitter hardship. During this time, affordable food was in greater demand than ever—demand that created a growing market for soybeans. They were generally not eaten as beans, although certain circles promoting alternative lifestyles did precisely that. As in years previously, their oil proved valuable in the production of margarine, while the residue from the milling process was fed to livestock. One consequence of the depression was that prices for oil crops dropped, making soybeans even more attractive to notoriously strained Germany. The German Reich depended heavily on soybeans and continued to procure soybeans even after 1931, when the former three northeastern provinces of China were first occupied by Japanese troops and then became the Japanese puppet state of Manchukuo. Germany was a member of the League of Nations, which disapproved of events in the Far East, but it maintained its good relations with Japan not solely due to, but also precisely because of, its reliance on cheap resources of oilseed.

In 1932, for example, fat and oil consumption for food was estimated at 1.7 million tons compared to 320,000 tons for technical or industrial purposes, mainly soap production. Over half of these amounts were imported, and most of what was imported went toward the production of food. All imported oilseeds summed up to 200 to 250 million Reichsmarks annually between 1928 and 1934.[63]

Germany's high dependency on fat imports, and thus the country's trade balance dilemma, had already preoccupied administrations in the Weimar Republic. Another problem with fat was that imported oilseed and the foodstuffs derived from it were much cheaper than butter, lard, and all other animal fats from domestic livestock. Farmers feared for their sales of milk, and with that butter, and their pressure group Deutscher Landwirtschaftsrat (German agricultural council) urged measures to keep cheap margarine at bay and increase butter consumption. In December 1932, their efforts resulted in regulations that were already familiar from previous years: a tax on margarine and the enforcement of a blending quota for butter in margarine. However, as the annual amount spent on oilseed imports remained steady, this was of little help. Thus, from the very beginning of National Socialist rule, fat was among the most heavily regulated foodstuff. Although certain fats such as butter, lard, bacon, and whale oil were sourced from European neighbors on the basis of offsetting and/or compensatory agreements, imports of oilseeds, which were sourced from South Africa and Asia in exchange for cash currency, were a thorn in the side of National Socialist economic strategists. The aim was to reduce these expenditures and to avoid dependence on raw materials, the supply of which, due to the long access routes, would be cut off in the event of war.

For the average German the issue was coined as a "fat gap" or "fat-and-protein gap," and Nazi propaganda declared saving on fats as one of the major economic goals for the German *Volk*. It was followed by a complex package of measures designed to regulate the population's fat consumption.[64] In the spring of 1933, the German government increased import duties on raw materials and introduced the levying of a so-called fat tax on margarine and restrictions on advertising. Margarine production was generally restricted, and producers were to make 50 percent of their total goods available as "household margarine." Margarine labeled as such was available only against ration coupons. In addition, the fat plan contained an elaborate system of regulations for saving imported fats and oils. These included measures that had been common practice since the rise of margarine and farmers' fear about the commercial competition it posed to butter and lard. One of them was the introduced reduction in margarine production to only 50 percent of the previous year. This, however, was withdrawn rather quickly as the resulting amount was too low to serve needs.

A central element in implementing the goal and monitoring whether the regulations were observed was the creation of the Reichsstelle für Fette und Öle (State agency for fats and oils) in March 1933 under the Ministry of Food and Agriculture, with extensive powers to control the fats market. The Reichsstelle handled all import and export transactions involving raw materials and finished products and, in addition, controlled processing methods, end products, and eventually also the books of German margarine factories and oil mills. This was to make sure that the new measures were being observed.[65]

The "fat plan" package was supplemented by cultivation subsidies for domestic oil plants, the payment of compensation to oil mills for the processing of domestic raw materials, the compulsory use of domestic lard in the production of margarine, collection campaigns for beechnuts, and the cultivation of sunflowers along highways and railroad embankments. Last but not least, bakeries were urged to use other recipes and to offer fatty goods such as doughnuts only two days a week.[66]

German farmers did not have the capacity to supply the German population with domestically grown or produced fats and proteins, but the tax on oilseeds was clearly not helping either. The residue from the milling of various oilseeds served as valuable fodder, urgently needed to increase the production of animal fats and proteins. Soybean cake was particularly valuable as it contained high amounts of protein, but with import limitations, domestic fat production also declined. Harvests of domestic oilseed remained moderate, and shortages became apparent as early as 1934.

In April 1935, contrary to the previous policy of curbing imports, oilseed had to be sourced abroad, and again six months later. At the beginning of October of the same year, the unforeseen foreign exchange of three million Reichsmarks had to be made available for additional butter imports.[67] Despite these measures, there was not enough fat available for private consumption, especially in urban centers. On the basis of the Germany reports of the Social Democratic Party of Germany (Sopade) as well as the secret situation reports of the Security Service (SS), historian Reinhold Reith paints a bleak picture regarding the situation of supplying the German population with fat. At the turn of the year 1935–1936, 12.4 million Reichsmarks were again made available for the import of oilseed, which was not at all in line with National Socialist economic policy. The discord arose not least because nutrition experts like Hans Adalbert Schweigart, who was an early Nazi supporter, still fantasized about the possibility of reducing imports by up to two-thirds, even though the shortages in previous years had proven this to be too unrealistic.[68]

Against this background it is not surprising that the fat problem also reached high-ranking Nazi officials. In November 1935, Joseph Goebbels noted in his diary that the long lines in front of dairy stores were "breeding grounds" for sabotage and that something had to be done about it. In January 1936 he addressed the topic in a speech and called on the Germans to save on butter: "If necessary, we will manage without butter, but never without cannons." Hermann Göring, who gained more and more power over the German economy and was responsible for the Four-Year Plan, also called on the Germans' sense of duty. In 1936, he suggested a voluntary reduction of 25 percent in fat consumption. And in the same year, Rudolf Hess, deputy führer and minister without portfolio, famously coined the catchphrase "cannons instead of butter." The tone was set, and Germans had to accept shortages to enable rearmament and eventual war.[69]

What lay behind these measures, however, was not only the need to feed the people but also considerations regarding the production of war materials. The oils of oil palms and copra contain a high proportion of glycerol, which was needed in the production of explosives and synthetic rubber (for car tires, for example).[70] They had a high war-relevant value and their resources had to be conserved. The same applied for oils useful in the manufacture of paints and varnishes, such as linseed. For this reason, crops containing oils with no special properties, such as soybeans, rapeseed, and sunflowers, were directed into the food sector. As the production of technical and industrial appliances and matériel had to be secured at all costs due to Hitler's political ambitions and a corresponding policy of forced rearmament, the savings measures contained within the fat plan mainly affected crops necessary for private consumption.

In addition to curtailing private consumption, the new government encouraged alternative methods of sourcing fat such as the domestic cultivation of oil-bearing seed crops and experiments with less familiar oilseeds. In this context, IG Farben experimented with the cultivation of soybeans in southeastern Europe from 1934 onward. In 1936, the country's first whaling fleet left for Antarctica. In the years to come, the German whaling fleet would grow to seven factory ships and 54 catchers that harvested up to 90,000 tons of whale oil per season. Most of it went into margarine, which by that time was composed of up to 50 percent whale oil. Despite these efforts, the country's self-sufficiency gains regarding fats and oils were rather insignificant.[71] Shortages became more severe, and regulations for the production and composition of margarine were reintroduced. Fat was rationed in 1937, with only registered people being allowed to purchase butter, lard, margarine, or other fatty foodstuffs. German fat rationing came much earlier than other food quotas, which began in August 1939. The whaling mission ended in 1939 when the approaching war made oil transports too dangerous and unprofitable; in turn, this led to a complete shutdown of margarine production in July of the following year. In September 1940, only 31 factories, divided according to supply areas, were allowed to resume production.[72]

Soybean Imports and Usage

All measures accomplished under the label "fat gap" or "fat plan" illustrate that the Nazis were keeping an eye on the problem of sufficient food supply years before the country assumed a war footing. During the war, people suffered many shortages, but historical research has depicted the civilian fat supply for food as particularly dire.[73] In fact, the shortage of fats and oils was Germany's biggest supply problem, affecting both the human diet and war-related industries. Despite all measures outline above, Germany could not abandon the import of foreign fats and oils crops altogether, and the soybean, as one of the most affordable oil crops on the world market, was attributed a decisive role in solving the problem since it served as fat resource and fodder. Imports from Manchukuo only came to a halt with the attack on the Soviet Union in 1941, when the Trans-Siberian Railway could no longer serve as an alternative means of transportation to sea freight.

A comparison of worldwide soybean imports in the 1920s and 1930s shows the continuity in German dependence on soybeans from the Weimar Republic to the Nazi era. After 1933, however, German imports fluctuated more significantly than demand in Britain or Denmark, both of whom continued to be strong importing countries in Europe during this period. While Germany initially remained the leading importer of whole soybeans, imports slowed significantly in the mid-1930s and dipped below Japanese demand, before rising again toward the end of the decade (see Figure 3.3).

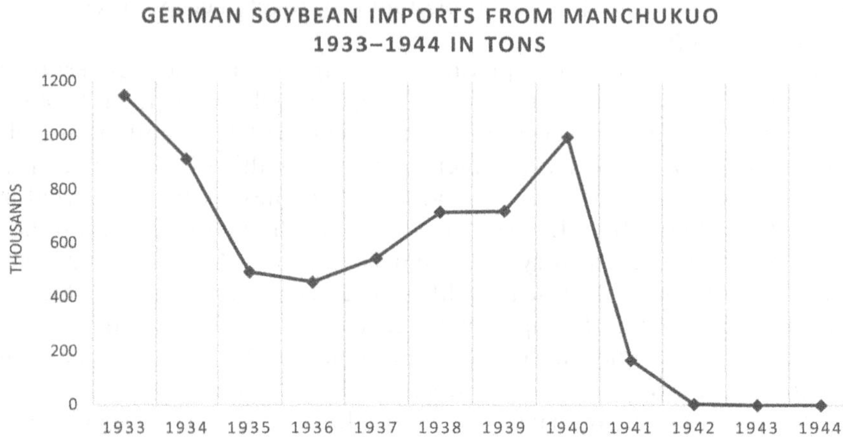

Figure 3.3 German imports of whole soybeans from Manchukuo in tons, 1933–1944.

© Author. Based on information from *Monatliche Nachweise über den auswärtigen Handel Deutschlands* (January 1933–June 1939), *Der Außenhandel Deutschlands. Monatliche Nachweise* (July 1939), and *Sondernachweis: Der Außenhandel Deutschlands* (August 1939–July 1944).

This finding confirms Germany's agricultural approach to self-sufficiency, which stemmed from both the economic necessity of readying the country for war and the blood and soil ideology proclaimed by leading agricultural politicians. Soybeans were classified as an oilseed and fell under the regulations curtailing the import of vegetable and animal fats and their resources; thus, limitations and higher duties explain the significant decline in soybean imports in and after 1934, and the failure of this policy in supplying the people with enough fat is reflected in the rising import figures from 1937 onward.

Back in the 1920s the production of soybeans from regions beyond Northeast China was immaterial, but this changed in the 1930s, and supplies from the United States and various southeastern European countries, mainly Romania, gradually entered the market.

To be sure, most of the soybeans obtained under National Socialist rule were grown by Chinese farmers and not those in southeastern Europe. The years 1938 and 1939 were the peak in terms of harvests and imports from Romania, lifting the total sum for European supplies to Germany to about 65,000 tons in each of the two years. However, in the overall picture, Romania's success was rather marginal as all European supplies were nevertheless one-tenth of what Manchukuo delivered—more than 700,000 tons a year in 1938 and 1939 (see Figures 3.3 and 3.4). The United States also supplied Germany with soybeans, and while the supply reached a peak of nearly 100,000 tons in 1936, it ceased completely in the years thereafter.[74]

In November 1936, the Hamburg-based Hansa-Mühle, one of the largest German oil mills of the period, made an overview of what it could obtain

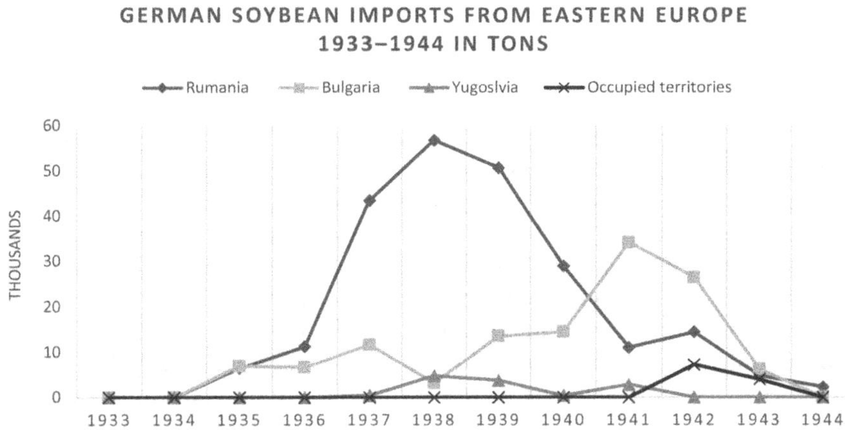

Figure 3.4 German imports of whole soybeans from Eastern Europe in tons, 1933–1944. Occupied territories refer to regions in Eastern Europe occu- pied by Germany, including Ukraine.

© Author. Based on information from *Monatliche Nachweise über den auswärtigen Handel Deutschlands* (January 1933–June 1939), *Der Außenhandel Deutschlands. Monatliche Nachweise* (July 1939), and *Sondernachweis: Der Außenhandel Deutschlands* (August 1939–July 1944).

from various oilseeds and how their products contributed to feeding livestock and eventually producing animal proteins relative to prices. Out of one ton of soybeans the company was able to obtain 160 kilograms of oil and 820 kilograms of soybean meal. The oil went into foodstuff while the soybean meal served as fodder. If fed to hogs, the overview estimated, the obtained soybean meal resulted in 118 kilograms of pork. In other words, a hog needed seven times as much protein-rich fodder to make one kilogram of its own protein. When fed to milk cows, the ratio was hardly any better as the amount of soybean meal obtained from one ton of beans resulted in a mere 176 kilograms of butter. With that, the survey concluded, soybeans had by far the best ratio, as all other oilseeds were more expensive and produced much less meat or milk.[75] By pointing to the advantage of soybean meal over all other feeds, Hansa-Mühle was promoting its own case here. The message was clearly that none of the other feeds were as efficient as soybean concentrates. However, nutritional experts and Nazi officials busy preparing for war read information like this differently. Soybeans, and particularly soybean flour, would now enter the human diet directly.

Nutritional experts highlighted the benefits of using soybean flour, for instance by contrasting prices and protein contents of various foods rich in it. One of those who was not only preoccupied with food and nutrition but also deeply engaged with Nazi policies was Wilhelm Ziegelmayer, who worked administering the Wehrmacht's food supply *(Heeresverwaltung)* in preparation for war and then also during wartime. In 1936, Ziegelmayer pointed out that beef and soybean proteins were each digestible to 93 percent, but while soybean flour contained up to 52 percent protein, the same amount of beef provided only 20 percent. Worse still, beef cost nearly 20 times as much. He made similar calculations for eggs, cheese, milk, wheat flour, and peas, with soybeans clearly providing the highest amount of protein while being the most affordable.[76] Analyses like this carved the way for the adoption of soybean flour in German households. Recipe books promoting its addition to breads, cakes, soups, and sauces were printed, cooking courses offered, and other measures taken to make its consumption more appealing. Yet, as Jürgen Drews has shown, soybean flour hardly made it into the average German diet, economic needs and promotions notwithstanding. Drews analyzed the production and consumption of soybean flour in the German citizenry in the 1930s and concluded that even though Nazi officials were highly engaged in promoting its use, ordinary people maintained a dislike of it.[77]

As a result of these developments, German planners made yet another turn and, with the beginning of the war, banned the production and distribution of soybean flour for private consumption altogether. This was not because the Nazis had lost interest in—let alone a need for—soybeans, but because they found a more effective way of channeling it, and one which required less effort. From the fall of 1939 onward, soybean flour was reserved for mass catering either in factory canteens or as Wehrmacht rations. For the period after 1941, when the vast supplies of Manchurian soybeans dried up, it is uncertain whether soybeans in Germany were even processed in the once-established way into fat and fodder. Given that the quantities on hand were very small now, it is more than doubtful. When the Americans investigated the Hansa-Mühle in August 1945 they learned that it had been "several years" since the plant had processed soybeans.[78] In wartime, it processed whatever was available, but soybeans were no longer destined for the production of margarine, butter, or schnitzel.

Soya, Manchukuo, and Japanese–German Relations, 1931–1941

In May 1938, the German Reich formally recognized Manchukuo as an independent state; of the European states, only Spain and Italy had previously done so. The League of Nations had not approved Japan's actions in Northeast China and subsequently states worldwide were reluctant to endorse them. Generations of later historians saw the German recognition of Manchukuo as an expression that Nazi ideologues had won out at the Foreign Office, which had preferred a policy of neutrality in the Sino-Japanese conflict if not one of outright sympathy with China. In a nutshell, the common narrative goes that when Japan initiated military aggression in Manchukuo in 1931 and founded the puppet state in June in the following year, the German Foreign Office defended traditional German commitments in China by maintaining a diplomatic balance between nationalist

China and imperialist Japan. Nazi ideologues, on the other hand—most notably Hitler himself—are in the literature often pictured as holding sympathies for Japan, which made them work toward closer relations and not least the recognition of Manchukuo from an early stage. According to this narrative, the recognition of Manchukuo and the shift to Japan in 1938 constituted a break with traditional diplomacy, because it was inspired by ideological persuasion and instituted by party operatives.[79] This perspective was strengthened by the fact that Germany and Japan had already signed the Anti-Comintern Pact against the Soviet Union a year and a half earlier, in November 1936. Among other outcomes, the agreement formed the basis for the formation of the Axis between Germany, Italy, and Japan.

My findings on the soybean trade between Germany and the Japanese puppet state of Manchukuo suggest that the shift toward Japan had an economic prelude two years prior to the official recognition—a prelude that the Foreign Office was deeply engaged in orchestrating. In April 1936, Germany, Manchukuo, and Japan signed a trade agreement regarding Manchurian-grown soybeans and German industrial products. Besides the fact that it treated Manchukuo and Japan as a single economic entity, it formally accepted Manchukuo as a partner in international trade. Interestingly enough, German official statistics also changed the registration of the beans' origin from then on. Beginning in 1937, the monthly reviews of Germany's foreign trade *(Monatliche Nachweise über den auswärtigen Handel Deutschlands)* listed "Manchukuo" as the beans' region of origin, whereas hitherto they had been registered as coming from China. As these statistics were published and widely available, this change surely also acted as a signal to international observers. Wasn't a trade agreement and with that economic recognition very close to de facto political ratification? Didn't economic cooperation proceed with political collaboration in this case? Besides the Sinophile ambassador to China, none in the Foreign Office opposed this agreement; on the contrary, it was worked out by their representatives. Why would they do so if their policy was one of maintaining an impartial attitude? Yet another question is why the Foreign Office would work out a trade agreement for a commodity in which hardly any other country had an interest, meaning the Germans did not have to fear someone else would purchase them, in the knowledge that such an arrangement could seriously offend China?

In his 1994 doctoral thesis, Robert Fahs suggested a re-interpretation of the events around 1938 and due consideration for developments in German relations with Russia, China, and Japan reaching further back in time than the National Socialists' seizure of power. He argued that German diplomacy in Northeast Asia followed a consistent pattern from the Weimar Republic to Nazi Germany, one driven by Germany's economic interests in the Far East and defined by commodity acquisitions. Starting in the 1920s, German diplomacy in that region was preoccupied with accumulating raw materials, first and foremost soybeans, to serve the country's urgent need for fat. These efforts continued throughout the 1930s, as the trade agreement of 1936 and subsequent arrangements prove. Thus, according to Fahs, the formal recognition of Manchukuo was an extension and continuation of diplomatic efforts established earlier on the grounds of economic demand rather than a change of course.[80]

Though neatly composed, Fahs has never published his work and it has thus received barely any scholarly attention. However, as interesting as the relation between the Foreign Office and Nazi officials is, it is less relevant for my endeavor of analyzing how and why soybeans entered the Western world. As for the trade agreement, actors from both sides worked in the same direction and not against each other. With a shift toward Japan for economic reasons, Germany risked losing access to tungsten from China, the only leverage China had against it. That did not happen at the time the agreement was concluded, but there was a certain risk. Tungsten was needed in the production of shells, grenades, and missiles, and Germany took 60–70 percent of what Chinese mines had on offer. With that, the country consumed 40–50 percent of the world supply of tungsten.[81] However, in deicing to nevertheless purchase soybeans, German officials put the feeding of young soldiers above the production of these weapons. In *The Taste of War*, Lizzie Collingham convincingly argued for the significance of food in wartime and the vast efforts all belligerent countries put into allocating supplies of it in order to advance their military aims.[82] My findings on soybeans as well as on other efforts at procuring fat resources seem to point in the same direction: that the allocation of soybeans was deemed vital to the German provision of basic foodstuffs.

Concluding from the sources presented in this chapter, I do not necessarily see the barter agreement as well as the recognition of Manchukuo as an expression of a break between the Nazis and the German Foreign Office. They seem, rather, to be examples of the inconsistent German diplomatic position toward China and Japan in general, as both the Weimar Republic and the Nazi era failed to establish a steadfast East Asian policy. Contemporary observers and later historians can agree on that.[83]

Ferdinand Heye

Part of the impression that the National Socialists were leaning toward positioning Germany on the side of the Japanese while the country's diplomats instead focused on neutrality in the struggle between China and Japan, is due to an episode surrounding the figure of Ferdinand H. Heye. In 1934, loyal Nazi Party (NSDAP) member Heye, who sometimes went by the pseudonym Fischer, tried to broker a deal for Manchurian soybeans against German industrial goods and made serious attempts to become an official negotiator of the German government. The proposal provided for Manchukuo to receive Germany's official recognition, while Heye wanted to become the special trade commissioner in Manchukuo with an appointment as consul-general there. The plan failed to achieve any of this but laid the ground for events in the following years, when a trade deal was eventually agreed upon in 1936 and then renewed in subsequent years.

In the 1920s, Heye became known to the German Foreign Office as a proprietor of the trading firm Eisenträger, Heye & Co., which was founded and registered in Berlin but located in Harbin. According to information in the Foreign Office, the company dealt with guns and opiates, but, apparently, was not as successful as their owners had hoped. At some point, Eisenträger committed suicide; meanwhile, Heye made attempts to change his business activities. He became a member of the NSDAP and came into contact with high-ranking officials. In the spring of 1933, he developed the idea of founding a German bank in newly established Manchukuo, a plan for which he was supported by Herman Göring, head of the Ministry of Aviation. Göring was probably involved because the German Lufthansa had business engagements in the Far East, and a financing institution may have benefitted its setup.[84] The Foreign Office did not completely oppose Heye's proposal—it had in fact earlier sounded out such a possibility—but objected on the grounds that given the desperate financial situation the government was dealing with, it would not have the means to fund such an institution abroad, and expressed doubts about the willingness of private investors to enter such a venture.[85]

Encouraged by industrialist Fritz Thyssen, who at this time still supported Hitler and the NSDAP, Heye reconsidered his options once more, and it was on assignment from Thyssen that Heye traveled to Manchukuo in the summer of 1933 to scour the market for potential economic opportunities, mainly regarding trade. Shortly after his return, he founded the Deutsch-Mandschurische Export und Import GmbH and, by the end of the year, approached the Foreign Office again. This time he requested official support to negotiate a trade deal for Manchurian soybeans in exchange for German industrial products.[86]

Only the Ministry of Food and Agriculture opposed this plan, as soybean oil was still considered the bean's main value and a trade agreement would support the margarine industry but not German farmers in their attempts to sell more lard and butter. The Foreign Office, however, did not object to a trade agreement in principle but protested Ferdinand Heye's appointment as German trade commissioner and that the plan included the official recognition of Manchukuo. Foreign Minister Konstantin von Neurath pointed out that formal recognition was the single and strongest leverage Germany had toward Japan and warned against playing this card at this stage, it being of greater benefit to Japan than to Germany. Most diplomats involved agreed that Germany could take advantage of the region without formally recognizing it since Germany was its biggest trade partner. In other words, the sheer volume of German soybean orders ought to be reason enough to enter into a trade agreement without any further commitment from the German side. The recognition would also offend China, and even though the Chinese were struggling internally with a civil war, a Chinese trade boycott ought not to be risked.[87]

On the basis of these considerations, Neurath made a few diplomatic decisions. In early February 1934, he ordered economic advisor and vice-consul Karl Knoll to Manchukuo to probe economic relations with the civil administration in Manchukuo, but he would not allow ambassador Herbert von Dirksen to pay an official visit to the region as that risked raising Japanese hopes too far while it also risked being interpreted as a snub by the Chinese. Neurath further instructed the embassy in Tokyo to be friendly toward Heye and generally support his endeavors to negotiate a trade agreement, but purely as a private businessman with no formal authority and certainly not regarding the recognition of Manchukuo.[88]

A mere ten days later, Neurath was forced to change course. Heye, who at that time was in Dalian, had been acting as though he held formal authority and had approached the Japanese military—not the civil administration as the Foreign Office preferred. He had promised official recognition in return for a favorable trade agreement regarding soybeans. For support he relied on his powerful contacts within the NSDAP. Besides Thyssen, Heye received the backing of Alfred Rosenberg, head of the party's Office of Foreign Affairs, and Werner Daitz, who oversaw the office's foreign trade division. Daitz, it seems, was Heye's main sponsor within the party. They joined forces and sought out Hitler's endorsement, and as a result Heye obtained official status as the German negotiator for potential trade deals in Manchukuo, although he was not authorized to deal with any issues regarding German recognition of Manchukuo. All Neurath, together with Walter Darré, minister for food and agriculture, could achieve beyond this point was stipulating a condition under which the final deal had to be approved by German authorities before it was signed.[89]

In subsequent months, the Foreign Office was content to gather complaints about Heye, a task which did not seem to be overly difficult. Heye had no talent for cautious negotiation and diplomatic sensitivity, and he repeatedly blended his position as head of a private company with that as an official German negotiator. In Tokyo, Karl Knoll kept complaining about Heye's clumsy negotiating skills while Heye protested Knoll's interference. Ambassador Dirksen cabled Berlin: "The state of affairs in which he [Heye] has been conducting negotiations with Japanese government agencies for weeks, with nothing being revealed about their content or progress, is untenable in the long run."[90] When Heye kept protesting about diplomats putting obstacles in his way, a formal investigation under the supervision of Rudolf Hess was initiated.

Complaints from third parties began to emerge. German businessmen engaged in East Asian trade were opposed to Heye's activities as he positioned himself as the main beneficiary of the envisioned deal and would not inform other merchants about his mission, never mind include them in talks and negotiations. At some point, the Japanese military negotiators also became suspicious of Heye, as ambassador Dirksen reported to his superior Neurath. Eventually, international newspapers began reporting on the upcoming bartering of soybeans against military equipment. In October, the *Daily Herald* reported on a deal involving weapons, munition, and chemicals as well as military pilots and engineers in exchange for soybeans, an article which deeply alarmed the Chinese.[91]

As a result, the Foreign Office was soon able to convince Thyssen and the involved NSDAP officials that Heye's attempts were not as promising as first envisioned. Although Heye managed to negotiate some sort of deal, his mission was eventually canceled in February 1935 since he had signed it without informing German authorities.[92] This was the condition Neurath had insisted on when installing Heye as the official negotiator, the very move that eventually brought him down.

The First Trade Agreement

The Heye episode is rarely missing in any historical account on Germany's ambiguous policies in the Far East. It is usually presented as an example of the frictions between the Foreign Office, which refused to recognize Manchukuo at this time, and Nazi ideologues making a strong push for it. Something of the same friction can be seen in the understanding of German ambassador in Tokyo, Herbert von Dirksen, that his job was to negotiate the recognition in return for economic advantages from Japan; in this, though, he was outmaneuvered by Neurath and his powerful *Staatssekretär* (secretary of state) Bernhard von Bülow. In contrast to the attention these frictions receive, in many studies the actual trade agreement, which was finalized in April 1936, is barely touched upon. Furthermore, scholars usually fail to interpret the agreement, which was worked out by diplomatic staff and not Nazi officials, as the first shift in German foreign policy toward Japan. Gerhard Weinberg, who wrote masterfully about German foreign policy under Hitler, devoted more than five pages to Heye but just a single paragraph to the eventually concluded agreement without attributing it much political significance.[93] John P. Fox, on the other hand, acknowledged that German-Manchukuoan economic relations had "a history of their own," meaning they were an area to test Germany's general position in the Far East and that the Foreign Office was the decisive body to handle such questions. In his book on *Germany and the Far Eastern Crisis,* Fox argues strongly that German Far Eastern policy under the Nazis "saw the triumph of ideology over diplomacy."[94] Contrary to that, I rather identify economic interests on both sides, and not ideological questions or concerns about international relations, as the most significant driving force behind the trade agreement of 1936. Germany depended on imports of cheap soybeans, which was a continuity from the Weimar Republic to the Nazi period.

Despite the humiliating outcome of Heye's attempts, the Foreign Office continued working on the trade agreement and none involved did so under duress or uttered negative expressions about it, which demonstrates that the frictions between the various agencies were not caused by the notion of concluding a trade agreement. It seems rather that the Foreign Office felt overlooked by party agencies meddling in state affairs. Neurath and his colleagues in the Foreign Office opposed Heye because he was an amateur and his mission would not come under their supervision. To be sure, Heye was a duplicitous and shady character, but because the affair was characterized by rivalries and intrigues among German and Japanese authorities, it rather looks as though he was a pawn in the hands of the powerful.

As the Germans relied heavily on soybeans from the Japanese puppet state, the matter at hand was no contrivance, but Manchukuo was a poor region with no demand for the industrialized and technically advanced products Germany was offering in return. Japan did have the need, but not the means. However, in the preceding years, Germany had become a lender to Japan, which was otherwise internationally isolated due to its activities in Northeast China. The solution was a triangular barter trade agreement between Germany, Japan, and Manchukuo from which all three benefitted. As early as December 1933, the powerful East Asian association in Hamburg suggested to the Foreign Office and the Ministry of Economy that when considering Japan and Manchukuo as one economic unit, German trade with it would be balanced.[95] In fact, trade agreements based on compensation, or clearing, were vital to the National Socialists' foreign trade policy at the time, which featured a passive trade balance and aimed to increase exports. Issues decreed under the *Neue Plan* (New Plan), which was adopted in September 1934, laid the ground for state control of all foreign trade. Its main features were to focus on bilateral contracts, import limitations, and compensation agreements. In fact, by 1935 around 80 percent of Germany's foreign trade was conducted via clearing accounts.[96]

After all, Germany could not afford to abandon all soybean imports but needed to balance its trade and save on foreign exchange. In April 1935, only two months after Heye had been turned down, Karl Ritter, director of the Economic Department in the Foreign Office, carefully analyzed the question of German-Manchukuoan trade relations and suggested sending a commission to Changchun to negotiate with Manchukuoan and Japanese authorities.[97] Within the Foreign Office, only Oskar Trautmann, the German ambassador to China, opposed the idea of a trade agreement with Manchukuo. Trautmann warned against offending the Chinese and risking German access to the country's market. The disturbance Heye had caused deeply alarmed them, Trautmann reported, as they feared deliveries of industrial goods to Japan would further strengthen it in its involvement and activities on the East Asian mainland.[98] Apart from Trautmann, nobody seriously opposed the idea of such a deal, and it was consequently pushed ahead. From the German side, there were only two differences: negotiations were not bound to the recognition of Manchukuo, and Heye was no longer involved. Instead, his former antagonist, vice-consul Karl Knoll, would play a major role in working out the deal.

At the second attempt the Foreign Office got its way and experienced diplomats were sent to negotiate with the Japanese. Head of the mission was Otto Kiep, former consul-general in New York. He became a member of the Nazi Party in 1937, but later participated in the assassination plot against Hitler. The fact that he was not as faithful to the National Socialists as some other Nazis, alongside Neurath and others' agreement on working out a deal, proves that the Foreign Office did not generally oppose negotiations with Manchukuo as long as they were conducted under their direction and oversight.

On his mission, Kiep was accompanied by Knoll and Gustav Rosenbruch from the Reichsbank. The party arrived in Tokyo on October 30, 1935. In December it made a three-week visit to Manchukuo, conferring with SMR and Manchukuo officials, but thereafter returned to Japan, where it spent most of its time. In the actual negotiations, Manchukuo was represented by officials from the Ministry of Industry. As the agreement provoked a protest from the Chinese government, Kiep made an official visit to China to reassure the authorities in Nanjing in February and March of the following year. On this trip, Kiep denied that his visit to Manchukuo and Japan would have any political implications but rather was of a purely economic nature. Bernhard von Bülow, the undersecretary in the Foreign Office and as such Neurath's deputy, gave the Chinese ambassador who protested the envisioned agreement a similar response. Bülow declared it was just a technical agreement about payment for their trade.[99] Other than that, negotiations went smoothly, and on April 30, 1936, the conclusion of a trade agreement was announced. Given the commotion Heye had caused on all sides, Kiep's efforts passed smoothly indeed.

The agreement, which was for a one-year period subject to renewal, provided for German purchases of Manchurian commodities to the amount of 100 million Manchurian yen, with one-fourth payable in what was called ASKI marks. These were Reichsmarks paid to special accounts at foreign banks in Germany, in this case the Hamburg branch of the Yokohama Specie Bank. The agreement established that Manchukuo would use the Reichsmark receipts to procure German goods. The remaining 75 percent was to be paid from the foreign exchange proceeds accruing to Germany from its export surplus in German-Japanese trade. Furthermore, if the balance of German-Japanese trade in favor of Germany exceeded a certain sum, Germany would increase its purchases by that amount.[100] Just as envisioned by the East Asian association a few years earlier, the conditions of this agreement identified Japan and Manchukuo as a single economic bloc, and Germany made its shipments to Japan while it received soybeans from Manchukuo.

Up to 1934, Manchurian soybeans had satisfied 30 percent of German demand for oilseed, which demonstrates an enormous dependency on this commodity. On the other hand, Germany had been the main destination for soybeans, and Chinese farmers alongside Japanese traders relied on the trade with Germany just as the Germans depended on the product. In this constellation, Germany would not need a trade agreement if it were not for the money involved to pay for the purchases. Thus, the fact that Germany was allowed to pay for up to one-fourth of its supply in Reichsmarks while the rest was left for clearing was a success for German diplomats.

To put the 100 million Manchurian yen as the value of Manchurian commodities Germany agreed on importing into context, it might help to know that in 1933 the country purchased Manchurian soybeans worth 66.5 million yen and that this figure had fallen to 32.6 million yen in 1935. As Manchuria did not have many other commodities of interest to Germany, the 100 million yen were spent almost entirely on soybeans. However, the agreement did not provide for fluctuations in soybean prices and the fixed sum spurred an immediate rise in the price of soybeans. As early as 1936, the year the treaty was signed, the price for whole soybeans rose by 49 percent over those of 1935.[101]

The sources I analyzed identify Thyssen as the driver behind Heye's activities in the Far East and with that an actor interested in vitalizing the trade in industrial goods to Manchukuo. The forces and motifs behind the second attempt at concluding a trade agreement are less obvious, but they seem rather driven by officials more concerned with the German fat and feed situation. The British Ambassador to Berlin observed that the German negotiations were less preoccupied with the stimulation of German exports to Manchukuo/Japan than that of Manchukuoan exports to Germany. He noted that "the Commercial Counsellor at Berlin stated that a shortage of fats was the Achilles heel of German economic autarchy; perhaps the new arrangement is designed to strengthen that heel."[102] Indeed, it was, and import numbers rose significantly from 1936 onward (see Figure 3.3).

Despite fears within diplomatic circles, China did not terminate trade relations with Germany as a result of the German-Manchurian-Japanese agreement. Chinese newspapers published negative reports about it, but in an official memorandum from the Chinese Foreign Ministry, the agreement was only regretted, not condemned. Historian Bernd Martin assumes that the Chinese reaction was an attempt at averting further damage to the already complicated situation between China, Japan, and Germany. An official German statement declared that the trade agreement was merely an arrangement for barter trade along the same lines as those that already applied between China and Germany. To further quell Chinese doubts, the Germans also sent Walter von Reichenau, a high-ranking army officer, to ratify new loans to China, but these were not of much help to the Chinese. The Second Japanese War began in July 1937, and contemporary observers knew full well that it was principally financed by German support.[103]

Japanese Interests

Japan's motivations behind the agreement were of an obvious economic and political nature. The country relied on German industrial products but did not have much to offer in return, and Manchukuo, as Japan's modernizing project, relied on the soybean trade with Germany. From the onset of Japanese rule in Manchuria in 1931, the region's agricultural sector experienced a heavy downturn which eventually reached a nadir in 1934. A triangular trade agreement with Germany promised to ease an otherwise very unstable economic situation.

The Japanese occupation of China's Northeast in 1931 led, among other things, to a devaluation of the local Chinese currency, which in turn triggered a sharp downturn in imports and numerous bankruptcies among Chinese merchants. In addition, the invasion was followed by political and military chaos. Chinese resistance caused transport interruptions, while the situation also invited banditry. Unsettled conditions, especially in the northern region, led to farmers burying their soybeans in the ground instead of taking them to market. When Manchuria's border with China was closed upon the proclamation of the new state in 1932, millions of migrant workers who had previously come each season to assist with the growing and harvesting of soybeans were shut out. Local farmhands left for work in the industrial sectors, where Japanese-owned firms were fostering urban development and general infrastructure. Finally, heavy rainfall caused recurring floods and crop damage, with 1932 and 1934 being the worst years. Combined, this disorder had a deleterious effect on soybean cultivation. Output of soybeans dropped from a peak of 5.3 million tons in 1930 to a low of 3.4 million tons in 1934, a decline of 37 percent over four years.[104]

The soybean trade was declining not only because of deteriorating production but also because demand was shrinking. China boycotted products from Manchukuo and the erection of customs barriers between the two only hindered trade further. Japan's soybean cake needs (see Chapters 1 and 2) were declining as artificial fertilizers replaced natural ones. Exacerbating the situation further was Germany's curtailment of soybean imports during these years. In result, the entire economy was in turmoil by the early 1930s. The 1933–1934 export trade was 31 percent below the average for the six-year period 1926–1931. Due to the Great Depression global trade shrank even further than that, but given that Manchurian trade relations depended so heavily on the soybeans as a cash crop, these developments did not work out well for the new rulers. Besides, there was not much hope in sight to boost trade. Declining trade led prices to slump as well. The export of whole soybeans dropped in value by 33 percent between 1931 and 1934, while total exports of bean products, including whole beans, bean cake, and bean oil, fell by 46 percent.[105]

The Japanese and Manchukuo governments sought to stabilize the region's economy by investigating the cultivation of alternative crops, such as wheat in the north and cotton in the south; nevertheless, in the mid-1930s, soybeans still accounted for around 24–26 percent of grain output by value.[106] In 1936, John R. Stewart for the American Institute of Pacific Relations concluded: "The political structure has been changed, but the new Manchu Empire of Emperor Kangteh [Puyi] continues to be economically dependent on soya beans as the staple export crop."[107] For the Japanese, a motivation behind the trade agreement with Germany was thus the stabilization of the soybean trade by any means.

Besides an economic upspring, however, equally important to the Japanese was the political outcome. The agreement provided Manchukuo with more formal strength and was a first step toward recognition by Germany. As the strongest economic actor in the region, the state-like SMR published a variety of English-language promotional materials, distributed worldwide, about the "progress" in Manchuria. Among them was a bi-monthly magazine, *Contemporary Manchuria*, which was printed on glossy paper and meant to inform about the company's—and thus Japan's—latest achievements in the region. When the trade agreement came up for renewal in the spring of 1937, the magazine published a detailed report with glossy photos showing Karl Knoll, who signed the agreement for the German side, and Zhang Jinghui, the premier of the puppet state, toasting each other while standing in front of the swastika symbol. The article reported that the signing was the "most important event in the history of Manchukuo's foreign relations" since the acquisition of the railway that had once belonged to Russia. It even went a step further and stated: "The conclusion of this pact signified Germany's *de facto* recognition of Manchukuo as an independent state."[108]

The wording was carefully chosen and contained a sideswipe at the Western powers, as it repeated the League of Nations' resolution against recognizing Manchukuo four years earlier. The League had initially advised against any "treaty or agreement" with what had been declared the independent state of Manchukuo and, in February 1933, adopted what became known as the Lytton Report. This was the finding of an official commission the League had sent to investigate the situation in the region. On this basis, the League's assembly passed a resolution "not to recognize" the existing regime "either *de jure* or *de facto*."[109] By the time the trade agreement was concluded, neither Germany nor Japan were members of the League of Nations any longer, but the mode of expression chosen in *Contemporary Manchuria* made clear to whom the text was directed. For the time being, Japanese imperial rulers seemed pleased with what they had achieved.

Karl Knoll, who served as the first German trade commissioner to Manchukuo, found more careful words in regard to the question of recognition, but they were nevertheless promising. Assuming the pretense of an official state representative speaking as a private man, he said in a speech addressing Prime Minister Zhang Jinghui:

> Germany and Manchukuo, as well as our mutual friend Japan, will have to face great difficulties in the future while carrying out their task to secure to their people what living space they need in order to exist. [...] In such labor, mutual understanding and cooperation will increase. [...] I feel sure that the friendship between Manchukuo, Japan and Germany is an element of world peace, and according to my ability I shall try to foster their friendship.[110]

Surely enough, the old guard in the Foreign Office was involved in the steps taken prior to the formal recognition of Manchukuo. Considering these developments, the negotiations for formal economic cooperation appear to have paved the way for political convergence, even though this would take more time. Knoll's speech dates from June 1937, and in a Reichstag address eight months later Hitler announced that Germany would recognize Manchukuo. He declared China too weak to resist communism and stated that a Japanese victory would be less dangerous than a victory for Bolshevism. The *de jure* recognition then came in May 1938.

Continuing German Interests but Changing Personnel

Around the time Hitler officially recognized Manchukuo, the Foreign Office's personnel changed significantly. Those who had initially worked out the German rapprochement with Japan and Manchukuo through trade agreements in the years prior were now replaced with personnel more faithful to the party's principles. In February 1938, Foreign Minister Konstantin von Neurath was sacked and replaced by Joachim von Ribbentrop, the mastermind behind the Anti-Comintern Pact that Germany and Japan had signed in November 1936.[111] Despite the timely coincidence, the barter trade agreement was not a forerunner of the pact, as the latter was worked out by officials other than those surrounding Neurath, Dirksen, Kiep, and Knoll.

With Ribbentrop becoming foreign minister, Herbert von Dirksen, hitherto ambassador in Tokyo, changed posts and became ambassador in London until the German attack on Poland. Thereafter, he never held a major post again. Knoll had built a career in the diplomatic service since his consular examination in 1924. In the intervening years, he served at various postings in Beijing, Berlin, and Tokyo before joining Kiep on his soybean mission in 1935–1936. The position of the official trade commissioner to Manchukuo was initially assigned to a colleague with more experience in soybeans than with Manchurian matters. Moscow embassy agricultural attaché Otto Schiller was involved in German agricultural ventures with soybeans in the Caucasus region in the 1920s but was soon replaced, with Knoll eventually being appointed permanent trade commissioner in early 1937. From then on, he was given promotion after promotion, among other things for negotiating the treaty of amity by which Germany officially recognized Manchukuo in 1938, before Nazi officials also found him ideologically unreliable.

In 1940 Knoll was rejected for the post of Germany's first envoy *(Gesandter)* to Manchukuo and his career began a downward trend. Considering that all these personnel changes occurred after the trade agreement and the recognition of Manchukuo, it seems there was rather a shift in personnel than in policies that marked a break within the Foreign Office.[112]

As for the trade in soybeans, German policies toward Japan and Manchukuo persisted. With the second agreement, signed in May 1937, the terms were extended for three more years, to May 1940. The extension stipulated that either Germany or Manchukuo might initiate negotiations for revision after January 1, 1938, and indeed, official negotiations for new trading terms began as early as July 1938, possibly because the agreement had stipulated a fixed sum, not the quantity of soybeans to be delivered. As prices for soybeans had risen due to the previous agreements, the new term stipulated that Germany would buy two million tons of soybeans annually at a cost of 200 million Manchurian yen.[113] As Knoll was still in office at the time, he was again charged with negotiating the terms. The new agreement included a few other products such as corn, peanuts, and hemp seeds, and it was still in force when war broke out in Europe in September 1939, remaining so until it expired in May 1940.

From then on, German-Japanese trade relations became more complex, which was mainly due to the war on both continents. The 1940 agreement between the Soviet Union and Nazi Germany allowed for the use of the Trans-Siberian Railway for transshipments, but it was not until September that a new trade agreement with Manchukuo was in place. In June 1940, Emil Wiehl, head of the economic policy division within the Foreign Office, was outraged that Germany had hitherto been Manchukuo's largest customer but that it had served German interests to the tune of only 70,000 tons that year, and according to his sources the decline was not due to transportation issues on the Trans-Siberian Railway.[114] In August the same year, the issue was taken up in an official meeting between the new German ambassador in Tokyo, former military attaché in Japan Eugen Ott, and the Japanese foreign minister Yōsuke Matsuoka. Matsuoka promised to find a remedy, and in fact, by the end of the year, Germany had received nearly one million tons.

It is apparent that there was a good deal of mutual mistrust involved, but German officials continued in their war-related trade efforts. Fresh negotiations were conducted in April 1941, this time by Helmuth Wohltat, who held a variety of positions in the Nazi era but was generally tasked with the procurement of foreign exchange. By that time the issue involved not only Manchurian soybeans but included rubber from Japanese-occupied Indochina, whale oil from Japan's own hauls, metals such as tungsten from China, and tin from Thailand and even Bolivia, which Japan was to procure on Germany's behalf. Under this plan, Germany in return would continue with the delivery of weapons, ammunition, machines, airplanes, stainless steel, and finally loans. The new, and final, agreement was signed on May 31,

1941.[115] Its termination came about only weeks later, when the German Wehrmacht began Operation Barbarossa and shipments by land became equally as impossible as by sea. By then, about 3,500 tons of Manchurian soybeans had found their way to the German Reich in this year.

Soya in Southeastern Europe

Attempts at growing soybeans closer to if not in Germany date back to a time before the Nazi period. Cultivation trials around 1900 were often inspired by Austrian botanists and the idea of overcoming the Malthusian crisis with the help of soybeans, as shown in Chapter 2 of this book. Even though these efforts did not meet much success, they never completely dried up. They were given fresh impetus after the First World War. Several agriculturalists and industrialists more or less escorted by the Foreign Office made efforts to grow soybeans on European soil and thereby become less dependent on Manchurian supplies. Research institutions in Bonn, Breslau, and Halle also picked up on the issue of cultivating soybeans in Europe and with that breeding varieties suited to the climate. In addition, private companies became interested in developing knowledge about soybeans.

As for growing the beans in Europe, two areas received greater attention: southern Russia and the regions beyond the river Leitha, formerly known as the Hungarian territories of what was once Austria-Hungary. German attempts at fostering soybean cultivation in the Kuban region of the Caucasus remained a short-lived and loss-making endeavor, but ventures in what had in the meantime become Romania, Bulgaria, Hungary, and Yugoslavia had better success. That was, however, only after Nazi Germany guaranteed the bean's sale and offered prices higher than on the world market, which in the long run also rendered this a losing game.[116]

By the late 1920s, the activities at Bollmann's Hansa-Mühle and that of its parent company, Hanseatische Mühlenwerke AG, reached far beyond milling beans for fat and fodder. Hansa-Mühle fostered soybean cultivation in Europe by distributing practical information on seeds and growing conditions and served as a hub for all matters soy. It was in contact with the U.S. Departure of Agriculture and its soybean enthusiasts, who at that time were working on cultivating beans in the South and the Midwest. While the Hamburg company sent information on milling and what kind of qualities it required for ideal results in oil, fodder, and lecithin, the Americans delivered samples of their newly bred varieties for cultivation trials in Europe. Bollmann distributed the American seeds further, together with some Manchurian beans. As a result, in 1929 the company was involved in cultivation trials to varying degrees in Yugoslavia and Austria, but also in German territories such as Hessen, Schlesien, and Schleswig-Holstein. The latter were of less interest for milling purposes because it remained unlikely that beans grown there would ripen. In Hansa-Mühle's eyes, the green plants would still serve as local fodder. The fact that the green soybean, known as *edamame*, could be served as a nutritious food fell outside the mill's interests.[117]

In short, the Hamburg milling plant had turned into a powerful and trustworthy corporation, and the chamber of trade in Hamburg relied on it when being addressed with questions regarding soy. That was the case when in May 1929 the Stuttgart-based Deutsch-Donauländische Warenaustausch GmbH, a trading company specializing in German exchange with the Danube countries, requested information about possible interest in Romanian-grown soybeans in Germany. Since the trading company was specialized in the Danube as a commercial route, shipments seemed not to be too challenging.

Hansa-Mühle was thrilled and immediately sent seed samples of various varieties, including those it had obtained from the United States. The suggestion was to foster cultivation in Romania and encourage farmers and local authorities to support the efforts in the promise that the beans would find an outlet in Germany. It further developed a plan to inform the trading company about the wider implications of trading and processing soybeans. According to this plan, deliveries of Manchurian soybeans were by no means satisfactory. The steadily growing volume of beans obtained from there notwithstanding, the milling company complained about the unreliable quality, rising prices, uncontrollable trading conditions, and an imbalance of power in favor of the Chinese government, which still controlled the region at this time. According to this account, it was using soybeans as a means to steer financial policies. Stating the reasons why action was necessary, the report concluded:

> Under such circumstances, the question of whether the total dependence of European consumers on Manchurian production, market and supply conditions is justified, unalterable and sustainable is becoming more and more obvious.[118]

The underlying idea for the strong reliance on soybeans in the first place was to push back German imports of meat through the production of home-reared livestock. As a concrete step to come closer to the goal of greater economic independence, the suggestion was to combine forces, including with the Hungarian food physiologist Laszlo Berczeller, to foster soybean cultivation all over southeastern Europe. As interesting as the plan seemed at the time, it never went far. While the prospect of growing soybeans was perhaps promising in the spring of 1929, the ensuing months and years of financial and economic crises turned them on their head.

The actual soybean project then came about by means of IG Farbenindustrie, Germany's biggest chemical and pharmaceutical trust at the time, better known simply as IG Farben. The conglomerate was not so much interested in the bean itself as in saving its own businesses. In the years prior to the Great Depression, IG Farben had sold its products for foreign exchange to Romania and Bulgaria, but when the crisis hit Europe, payments became impossible, and with Germany raising its import tariffs on grains, these countries had nothing to offer in return. Thus, starting in the summer of 1932, IG Farben sent representatives to Romania and neighboring states to investigate trade possibilities. Romania's economy, just as that of the other countries, revolved around agriculture but relied heavily on the import of more specialized articles such as chemical and pharmaceutical goods, and IG Farben worked out a plan to bring both countries' trade balance into line with its own interests. In these efforts, it was supported by the Foreign Office, but state actors were not yet formally involved. The focus lay first on wheat but shifted to soybeans in 1934 thanks to the personal engagement of Max Ilgner, deputy of the board at IG Farben.[119]

Since southeastern Europe was a contested space and France, Great Britain, and others also had economic interests in it, the story of Germany's influence in the region was not one of straightforward success. Nevertheless, between 1933 and 1939 Germany managed to build an "Informal Empire" there, as Hans-Jürgen Schröder has aptly coined it, and IG Farben had a fair share in this process.[120] After the National Socialists gained power, southeastern Europe became of greater interest to the German economy because the region matched the new regime's economic policy and its plans regarding a new war. Germany's extension eastwards went back to the idea of *Mitteleuropa* (Central Europe), a term which refers to the economic and political grouping of certain regions in Central Europe under leadership of Germany and Austria-Hungary. It was framed most prominently in 1915 by liberal politician Friedrich Naumann. Now, in the 1930s, the idea was to gain greater independence from the fluctuations of the world market by creating a more or less autarkic zone of a limited number of actors, but, of course, still under German leadership. In addition, the region was thought to be the Wehrmacht's entry point to Russia, thus, having more control over it made sense in various respects. The idea of clearing the imbalance in German trade, which suffered from import surpluses and indebtedness, while simultaneously expanding eastwards, formed the ideological and economic background for the cultivation of soybeans under German supervision in southeastern Europe. It was initiated by private actors, and they were supported by the state, but there was less activity on diplomatic grounds.[121]

IG Farben's idea of bringing soybean cultivation closer to the Reich became quite a prestigious project for all parties involved, as the plan foresaw saving on foreign exchange while simultaneously securing the supply of urgently needed fat resources. Hitler requested more information about the project's progress as early as June 1934, but it took another year to work out the details.[122] The resulting deal included the founding of on-site subsidiaries which would work with state and local administrations as well as farmers to foster the cultivation of soybeans. Farmers were guaranteed prices 20 percent higher than the world market level for their beans, while oil mills back in Germany would have to pay only world market prices, with the difference to be covered by the German government and IG Farben. As the latter was less interested in soybeans than in extending its own trade, it secured itself a share of 50 percent of all trade made possible through the import of soybeans. Such set-ups were implemented first in Romania and Bulgaria in April 1935, but in subsequent years also in Yugoslavia and Hungary.

In terms of rising soybean cultivation, the set-up initially thrived, as shown in Figure 3.4. Romania, where the project became particularly successful, exported an average of 50,000 tons to Germany in the peak years 1937–1939. Financially, however, it was a loss-making enterprise, if not for IG Farben then for the German government. IG Farben's burden of compensating for the 20 percent difference between what farmers received and oil millers paid decreased over the years. In addition, the trust made a large profit from its exports, which outweighed the compensation costs by far. Experts in the Foreign Office, on the other hand, acknowledged the progress in soybean cultivation but complained about its high costs.[123]

Compared to the vast amounts Germany continued to import from Manchukuo, the share of soybeans harvested in Europe remained rather small. Between the year Romania and Bulgaria made their first shipments, 1935, and the last full year of supplies from the Far East in 1940, supplies from the various European regions reached an average of merely five percent of what Germany obtained from the Far East. In the peak year of 1939, Germany imported a total of 68,000 tons of soybeans from the three largest growing areas—Romania, Bulgaria, and Yugoslavia—an eight-percent share of total imports, but far less in all other years.[124] When replenishments from the Far East dried up as a result of Operation Barbarossa, amounts harvested in southeastern Europe or captured in the occupied territories were much too insignificant to compensate for former sources. They totaled a mere 50,000 tons in 1941, which seems close to nothing compared to the one million tons from Manchukuo in the previous year (see Figures 3.3 and 3.4).

When plans for the invasion of the Soviet Union were underway, measures had to be taken to compensate for the foreseeable loss of access to supplies from the Far East. The war had cut the German Reich off from about half of its food imports, and by 1941 all food reserves had been used up. In addition, the loss of agricultural workers who had been drafted for the war had a negative impact on overall agricultural production, and finally, the situation came to a head due to the shortage of fertilizers, whose chemicals were now needed for the construction of bombs and explosives.[125] But Nazi Germany's military and economic leaders had already made different plans to secure those counted as Aryans urgently needed food: the plundering of the Soviet Union.

One of the key documents to put the brutality of the Nazis on record is a file memo from May 2, 1941, which details the economic goals of Operation Barbarossa. With frightening matter-of-factness, seven weeks before the

German invasion, the memo documents the Nazi leadership coolly calculating the starvation of the people of the Soviet Union. The first of five points in this memo states that the war could only continue if the entire Wehrmacht was fed from the Soviet Union by the third year of the war. The second point states that in this process "undoubtedly tens of millions of people" will have to starve to death in the territories to be occupied. These first two points were presented as evidence in the Nuremberg war crime trials, and historical research regards the entire memo as a central document for the war of extermination, exploitation, and starvation against the people of the Soviet Union. This kind of warfare was intended from the outset.[126]

These two points being so shocking in their brutality, historical research paid slightly less attention to the remaining three. While they do seem less extreme, the third is particularly relevant to the theme of this book—fat, feed, and food. It refers to the commodities which would need to be plundered in the Soviet Union and transported back to the Reich to secure domestic food supply. Most important, the memo states, was the finding and removal of "*Ölsaaten, Ölkuchen, dann erst Getreide*" ("oilseeds, oil cake, then grain"). In the memo's wording, the priority was on oilseeds and oil cake, even before grains, which again points to the relevance of this commodity in the German Reich. However, the allocation, distribution, and use of these particular commodities in wartime are still a research desideratum.

As for soybeans, almost 4,000 tons were plundered annually from Ukraine in 1942 and 1943. Thereafter the Germans were on the retreat, but agricultural production in the region was so low that nothing was left for either of the warring parties. Furthermore, in the early 1940s, few more tons were captured from other occupied regions in the East or otherwise located in Hungary, Croatia, Serbia, Slovakia, and even Turkey.

By 1944, many oil mills in Hamburg and Bremen, which were often situated by waterways to ease transport, had been destroyed by Allied bombs. One of the mills able to uphold production until November 1944 was the C.F. Hildebrandt company in Hamburg, which, according to an investigation by American intelligence, produced more than 50 percent of all soy flour in Germany during wartime, all of which was sold to the Wehrmacht. According to the same source, only two other plants produced significant supplies of soybean flour during wartime: the Vienna Edelsoja company, a subsidiary of IG Farben, and a Hamburg-based company named Neue Edelsoja.[127] IG Farben had in fact acquired the Berczeller patent in 1936, which allowed it first to pave the way for supplying a greater volume of soybean flour to German grocery stores, and, once that turned out to be an unsuccessful endeavor, to Wehrmacht provisions.

The Hansa-Mühle too was nearly completely destroyed by the end of the war. By the time it came under investigation in the summer of 1945, then director G. Kruse reported that soybeans had not been processed at the plant for several years; they had used whatever resources were available.[128] The plant was soon reconstructed, but it did not regain its former position as a leading soybean processer. The parent company, Hanseatische Mühlenwerke AG, ceased to exist in 1965; its former subsidiary, Hansa-Mühle, survived slightly longer but eventually shut down in 1971.

Conclusion

A combination of availability, price, and the illusion of economic independence, at least from other European empires, was initially decisive for the German preference for soy after the First World War. The result was that the German Reich specialized in a raw material that contained comparatively small amounts of fat and had to be shipped for about 60 days in jute sacks before it could even be processed. However, in Germany the import of whole soybeans offered opportunities for processing industries. Domestic oil mills had both the incentives and opportunities to optimize their production. This in turn gave urban centers, in this case Hamburg, technological boosts in oil extraction and processing, which paid off in particular in the production of margarine and lecithin, a plasticizer.

In the general decline during the Great Depression, most European countries and the United States stopped importing copra and palm nuts, yet the demand for fats and oils remained, with countries turning to less expensive sources. Germany had been importing cheap soybeans from Manchuria on a large scale since the mid-1920s, but between 1928 and 1933, Germany became the largest exporter of soy oil in Europe.[129]

When the National Socialists came to power, the goal of reducing Germany's dependency on foreign oilseed supplies was central to the new economic policy because importing them swallowed vast amounts of foreign currency. In addition, the German Reich would need to become independent of imports so that the population would be able to be self-sufficient in the event of war and the accompanying blockades. There were several commodity groups for which this goal was essentially doomed from the start; one of them was fats and oils. Within the Reich, the Nazi leadership propagandistically sold the dilemma of dependence on imports as the "fat gap." Customer lists were introduced to curb consumption as early as 1935. Only three years later the "fat card" was issued, which was the first phase of food rationing. Even though the import of soybeans was at first limited as well, they eventually continued to be an important resource in solving supply problems and saving on foreign exchange. Nazi Germany entered into several trade agreements with the Japanese puppet state of Manchukuo in the 1930s, each of which provided that Manchukuo would supply hundreds of thousands of tons of soybeans annually in exchange for German heavy industrial goods. This barter trade was maintained until the invasion of the Soviet Union in 1941. Yet again, soy was intertwined with international economic interests and international politics too.

While soybeans were at first processed in their established ways, as fat and fodder, from 1936–1937 onward they acquired a different value, namely as foodstuff. The beans were now processed into flour to be used as a protein-rich additive to bread and soups. However, when the flour's private consumption did not increase, all stocks were channeled into army rations. In addition to trade agreements and consumption controls, National Socialist leadership focused on the cultivation of oil crops, and soybeans were also given more attention. Initiated by the pharmaceutical conglomerate IG Farben, soy was cultivated in southeastern Europe, mainly in Romania and Bulgaria, from 1935 onward. The yields, which were nowhere near the imports from Asia, were then shipped almost entirely to Germany.

Notes

1 It was not before 1941 that Swedish botanist Sven Holmberg bred a variety that grew and ripened north of the 50th latitude. He named it after his hometown, Fiskeby.

2 Gustavo Corni and Horst Gies, *Brot, Butter, Kanonen: Die Ernährungswirtschaft in Deutschland unter der Diktatur Hitlers* (Berlin: Akademie Verlag, 1997); Tim Schanetzky, *"Kanonen statt Butter": Wirtschaft und Konsum im Dritten Reich* (München: C.H. Beck, 2015); Reinhold Reith, "'Hurrah die Butter ist alle!': 'Fettlücke' und 'Eiweisslücke' im Dritten Reich," in *Experience of Modernity. Festschrift für Roman Sandgruber zum 60. Geburtstag,* eds. Michael Pommer, Herta Neiß, and Michael John (Stuttgart: Franz Steiner Verlag, 2007), 403–26; Richard J. Overy, *War and Economy in the Third Reich* (Oxford: Clarendon Press, 1994), 259–314.

3 Jürgen Drews, *Die 'Nazi-Bohne': Anbau, Verwendung und Auswirkung der Sojabohne im Deutschen Reich und Südosteuropa, 1933–1945* (Münster: Lit Verlag, 2004); Robert G. Fahs, "German Economic Diplomacy in Northeast Asia, 1917–1936" (PhD diss., University of Hawai'i, 1996); Ernst Langthaler, "Gemüse oder Ölfrucht? Die Weltkarriere der Sojabohne im 20. Jahrhundert," in *Umkämpftes Essen: Produktion, Handel und Konsum von Lebensmitteln in globalen Kontexten,* eds. Cornelia Reiher, Sarah Ruth Sippel (Göttingen: Vandenhoeck & Ruprecht, 2015), 41–66; Ernst Langthaler, "Hitlers Ölfruchtanbauer: Avantgarde des Agrobusinesses?" *Rural History Working Papers* 30 (2014), https://www.ruralhistory.at/de/publikationen/rhwp/RHWP30.pdf.

4 Within Europe, the Netherlands, Italy, France, Norway, and Sweden also purchased soybeans in this period, but the respective volumes were significantly lower than that of the other three.

5 International Institute of Agriculture, ed., *Oleaginous Products and Vegetable Oils: Production and Trade* (Rome: International Institute of Agriculture, 1923); International Institute of Agriculture, ed., *Oils and Fats: Production and International Trade.* Part 1 (Studies of principal agricultural products on the world market, no. 4) (Rome: International Institute of Agriculture, 1939) and Part 2 (Studies of principal agricultural products on the world market, no. 5) (Rome: International Institute of Agriculture, 1939).

6 The German language does not differentiate between margarine and shortening but subsumes both under margarine. I use the term accordingly.

7 At about 360,000 tons on annual average between 1913 and 1936, industrial demand for fat, that is fat for non-food processing, accounted for only one-fifth of Germany's total fat requirements; see *Oils and fats*, part 2, 230.

8 *Oils and fats*, part 2, 227.

9 Birgit Pelzer, and Reinhold Reith, *Margarine: Die Karriere der Kunstbutter* (Berlin: Klaus Wagenbach, 2001), 34–35; Walter Bartram. *Die Rohstoffversorgung der inländischen und ausländischen Ölmühlen-Industrie* (Mannheim: Self-publishing, 1920), 8–9.

10 Bartram, *Rohstoffversorgung*, 9 (author's translation). After the Second World War, Bartram was the first minister president for the new state of Schleswig-Holstein.

11 Pelzer, Reith, *Margarine*, 58–62, 72.

12 Adam Tooze, *The Deluge: The Great War and the Remaking of Global Order* (London: Penguin Books, 2015), 464.

13 Werner Hille, *Der Weltmarkt der Ölfrüchte und Ölsaaten in seiner Bedeutung für die Rohstoffversorgung der deutschen Ölmühlen-Industrie* (Hamburg: Bertram, 1939), 35; H. Willemsen, "Aus Geschichte und Tätigkeit des Verbandes der Deutschen Oelmühlen," in *Die deutsche Oelmühlen-Industrie: Festschrift zum 25-jährigen Bestehen des Verbandes der deutschen Oelmühlen* (Berlin: Im Verlage des Verbandes, 1925), 16–20.

14 Erich Stietz, *Soja in der Weltwirtschaft: Ein Beitrag zur Ernährungs- und Rohstoffwirtschaft der Erde* (Bethel b. Bielefeld: Anst. Bethel, 1931), 31.

15 Bartram, *Rohstoffversorgung*, 14–23; Sarah Waltenberger, *Deutschlands Ölfelder: Eine Stoffgeschichte der Kulturpflanze Raps, 1897–2017* (Paderborn: Verlag Ferdinand Schöningh, 2020), 189–252.

16 *Oils and fats*, part 2, 223.

17 *Oils and fats*, part 2, 402. In the Nazi period, the share of whale oil in margarine rose to over 50 percent.

18 *Oils and fats*, part 2, 402.

19 Aleksandr V. Marakueff, "The Export of Soya Beans from Manchuria and Its Financing," *Chinese Economic Journal* 2, no. 6 (June 1928): 477.

20 Bartram, *Rohstoffversorgung*, 50, 76 (author's translation); *Oils and fats*, part 2, 227.

21 *Oils and fats*, part 1, 7.

22 On yearly average 1910–1914, Bartram, *Rohstoffversorgung*, 18.

23 Pelzer, Reith, *Margarine*, 60.

24 Lien-en Tsao, "The Marketing of Soya Beans and Bean Oil," *Chinese Economic Journal* 7, no. 3 (September 1930): 952.

25 Rudolf Fitzner, *Die Weltwirtschaft der Fettstoffe 11: China* (Berlin: Heymann, 1920), 5 (author's translation).

26 Bartram, *Rohstoffversorgung*, 83 (author's translation).

27 *Oils and fats*, part 1, 31, 71.

28 Stietz, *Soja in der Weltwirtschaft*, 30 (author's translation).

29 Deutsches Konsulat Harbin, "Mandschurische Ausfuhr von Sojabohnen nach Deutschland" (May 22, 1925), Handelskammer Hamburg. 11.B.135a.5.5 Einfuhr von Sojabohnen; *Soya Beans in Manchuria*, ed. South Manchurian Railway Co. (Dairen: Agricultural Office, South Manchurian Railway Co., 1926), 9.

30 For the changing Manchurian soybean trade of the 1920s, see Marakueff, "Export of Soya Beans," 567–89.

31 Otto Witte to Adolf Georg von Maltzan, October 30, 1924, cited in Fahs, "German Economic Diplomacy," 203.

32 Auswärtiges Amt Berlin to Julius Strandes (March 2, 1925), Handelskammer Hamburg. 11.B.135a.5.5 Einfuhr von Sojabohnen, 2.

33 Deutsches Konsulat Harbin, "Mandschurische Ausfuhr von Sojabohnen nach Deutschland," (May 22, 1925); Hermann Bollmann to Handelskammer Hamburg (August 8, 1925). Handelskammer Hamburg. 11.B.135a.5.5 Einfuhr von Sojabohnen.

34 Youssef Cassis, *Big Business: The European Experience in the Twentieth Century* (Oxford: University Press, 1997), 37; H. Willemsen, "Die Entwicklung der deutschen Oelmühlenindustrie in der neueren Zeit," in *Die deutsche Oelmühlen-Industrie: Festschrift zum 25-jährigen Bestehen des Verbandes der deutschen Oelmühlen* (Berlin: Im Verlage des Verbandes, 1925), 98. For the significant role of these groups and the development of their businesses, see Ben Wubs, *International Business and National War Interests: Unilever between Reich and Empire, 1939–1945* (London: Routledge, 2015), 11–35.

35 For this typical pattern of world economic relations at the time, see Jürgen Osterhammel, *Die Verwandlung der Welt: Eine Geschichte des 19. Jahrhunderts* (München: C.H. Beck, 2009), 1037; Reinhard Wendt, *Vom Kolonialismus zur Globalisierung: Europa und die Welt seit 1500* (Stuttgart: UTB Schöningh, 2012), 253–59.

36 While in 1919, 140,000 tons of soybean oil were exported from Dalian, ten years later the figure was only 118,000 tons. During the same period, exports of whole beans increased fourfold, from about 700 tons to 2.8 million tons. *Third Report on Progress in Manchuria, 1907–1932*, ed. South Manchurian Railway Co. (Dairen: South Manchurian Railway Co., 1932), 135; see also Stietz, *Soja in der Weltwirtschaft*, 24, 29.

37 Stietz, *Soja in der Weltwirtschaft*, 22; Edwin G. Strand, *Soybean Production in War and Peace* (Report, U.S. Department of Agriculture, Bureau of Agricultural Economics, Washington, DC, September 1945), 19.

38 Warren H. Goss, *The German Oilseed Industry* (Washington, DC: Hobart Publ. Co., 1947), 26.

39 Adolf Schneider, "Die Verarbeitung der Sojabohne in der Ölmühlenindustrie unter besonderer Berücksichtigung des Bollmannschen Verfahrens," in *Soja. Ein Beitrag zur Kenntnis des Wertes der Sojabohne und ihrer Produkte für die deutsche Wirtschaft*, ed. Hansa-Mühle Hamburg (Hamburg: Hansa-Mühle, 1929), 70. Stietz, *Soja in der Weltwirtschaft*, 22; Armin Wendel, "Lecithin: The First 150 Years. Part I: From Discovery to Early Commercialization," *Inform* 11 (2000): 885–92, here 889–90; *Die deutsche Oelmühlen-Industrie*, 134–35.

40 Wendel, "Lecithin," 885.

41 Stietz, *Soja in der Weltwirtschaft*, 43; *Die rationalisierte Ölsaatverarbeitung*, 35–38. Wendel, "Lecithin," 890, reports the price for soy-based lecithin was at 2–3 Reichsmark per kilogram in the mid-1920s.

42 Bruno Rewald, "Das Lecithin der Sojabohne," in *Soja. Ein Beitrag zur Kenntnis des Wertes der Sojabohne und ihrer Produkte für die deutsche Wirtschaft*, ed. Hansa-Mühle Hamburg (Hamburg: Hansa-Mühle, 1929), 59–62.

43 Schneider, "Die Verarbeitung," 69 (author's translation).

44 Wendel, "Lecithin," 890.

45 Hansa-Mühle Hamburg, *Die rationalisierte Ölsaatenverarbeitung als Wirtschaftsfaktor für Deutschland und besonderer Berücksichtigung der Sojabohne* (Hamburg: Hansa-Mühle, 1927), 26 (author's translation).

46 Hansa-Mühle, *Die rationalisierte Ölsaatenverarbeitung*, 12–14.

47 Osterhammel, *Verwandlung der Welt*, 320.

48 Hansa-Mühle, *Die rationalisierte Ölsaatenverarbeitung*, 43 (author's translation). Similar also Adolf Schneider, "Die Sojabohne und ihr wirtschaftlicher Wert in Asien und Europa," in *Soja. Ein Beitrag zur Kenntnis des Wertes der Sojabohne und ihrer Produkte für die deutsche Wirtschaft*, ed. Hansa-Mühle Hamburg (Hamburg: Hansa-Mühle, 1929), 53; for declining rapeseed cultivation in German fields in the interwar period see Waltenberger, *Deutschlands Ölfelder*, 49.

49 Wendel, "Lecithin," 890.

50 Stietz, *Soja in der Weltwirtschaft*, 39.
51 Stietz, *Soja in der Weltwirtschaft*, 37.
52 Stietz, *Soja in der Weltwirtschaft*, 39.
53 Verordnung über die Zubereitung von Backwaren, October 14, 1920, *Reichsgesetzblatt,* 1777.
54 Reichsminister für Ernährung und Landwirtschaft to Handelskammer Hamburg (January 18, 1921), Handelskammer Hamburg. 11.B.135a.1.1 Verwendung von Sojabohnen zur Streckung von Brotgetreide.
55 Carl Brüning, "Die Lösung ernährungswirtschaftlicher Probleme durch das Sojaeiweißmehl," in *Soja. Ein Beitrag zur Kenntnis des Wertes der Sojabohne und ihrer Produkte für die deutsche Wirtschaft,* edited by Hansa-Mühle Hamburg (Hamburg: Hansa-Mühle, 1929), 9–15.
56 Max Rubner, "Soja-Brot," in *Vossische Zeitung* (May 30, 1929), reprint in *Soja. Ein Beitrag zur Kenntnis des Wertes der Sojabohne und ihrer Produkte für die deutsche Volkswirtschaft,* ed. Hansa-Mühle Hamburg (Hamburg, 1929), 22–24; Julius Moses, "Eßt Soja!" *Der Abend: Spätausgabe des 'Vorwärts,'* no. 330/B164 (July 17, 1929): [no page numbers].
57 Drews, *Die 'Nazi-Bohne,'* 51.
58 Hansa-Mühle, Hamburg, *Die Soyabohne. Herkunft und Verwendung* (Hamburg: Hansa-Mühle [192?]); Hansa-Mühle, *Die rationalisierte Ölsaatenverarbeitung*, 21–22 (author's translation).
59 Lois B. Bacon, Friedrich C. Schloemer, and Henry C. Taylor, *World Trade in Agricultural Products: Its Growth, Its Crisis, and the New Trade Policies* (Rome: International Institute of Agriculture, 1940), 214–327, 1008–9.
60 Wendel, "Lecithin," 890.
61 Goss, *German Oilseed Industry*, 26.
62 "Das Fettproblem," Survey written by Willi Tomberg for Reichs-Kredit-Gesellschaft (Berlin, November 2, 1934), BA R/15/V, 429; similar Walther Hübner, "Neuorientierung der deutschen Öl- und Fettwirtschaft," *Die Deutsche Volkswirtschaft* 1, no. 4 (1933): 1–6; Wegener, "Deutschlands Fettversorgung," *Fette und Seifen* 44, no. 3 (1937): 86–95; historical research confirmed this approach, see Gustavo Corni, *Hitler and the Peasants: Agrarian Policy and the Third Reich 1930–1939* (New York, NY: Berg, 1990), 55–61, 309–14.
63 Wegener, "Deutschlands Fettversorgung," 87–88, 91.
64 Corni, *Hitler and the Peasants,* 53–62; Corni and Gies, *Brot, Butter, Kanonen*; Birgit Pelzer and Reinhold Reith, "Fett aus Kohle? Die Speisefettsynthese in Deutschland 1933–1945," *Technikgeschichte* 69 (2002): 173–206; Reith, "'Hurrah die Butter ist alle!,'" 403–26; Dieter Petzina, *Autarkiepolitik im Dritten Reich. Der nationalsozialistische Vierjahresplan* (Stuttgart: Deutsche Verlagsanstalt, 1968), 32. Wegener, "Deutschlands Fettversorgung," 87, 91.
65 It was renamed Reichsstelle für Milcherzeugnisse, Öle und Fette on January 1, 1934. The various regulations are printed in *Reichsgesetzblatt* Teil 1 (1933): 145; 166–67; 206; 376; 662; 1066. Ration coupons were again issued on margarine as of January 1, 1937.
66 Wegener, "Deutschlands Fettversorgung," 87; Pelzer-Reith and Reith, "Fett aus Kohle," 173–81.
67 Petzina, *Autarkiepolitik*, 32.
68 Petzina, *Autarkiepolitik*, 33; Hans Adalbert Schweigart, *Der Ernährungshaushalt des deutschen Volkes* (Berlin: Deutscher Verlag für Politik und Wirtschaft, 1937), 1.
69 Elke Fröhlich, ed. *Die Tagebücher von Joseph Goebbels*, part 1, 3/1 (München: K.G. Saur, 2005), 323–24; Kurt Bauer, *Nationalsozialismus: Ursprünge, Anfänge, Aufstieg und Fall* (Wien: Böhlau, 2008), 306; Reith, "Hurrah die Butter ist alle!," 408; Norbert Frei, *Der Führerstaat. Nationalsozialistische*

Herrschaft 1933 bis 1945 (München: C.H. Beck, 2013), 226–30 (author's translations).

70 Hille, *Weltmarkt*, 60.

71 Pelzer, Reith, *Margarine*, 87–89; see also Ole Sparenberg, *"Segen des Meeres": Hochseefischerei und Walfang im Rahmen der nationalsozialistischen Autarkiepolitik* (Berlin: Duncker & Humblot, 2010), 256–347; Corni, Gies, *Brot, Butter, Kanonen*, 309.

72 Reith, "'Hurrah die Butter ist alle,'" 415.

73 Corni and Gies, *Brot, Butter, Kanonen*, 309–18; Pelzer, Reith, *Margarine*, 555–73.

74 I am grateful to Sascha Brünig for assisting me in collecting the data given in Figures 3.3 and 3.4.

75 Wirtschaftlichkeit der Sojabohne im Vergleich zu anderen Ölsaaten und Ölfrüchten [November, 1936], Staatsarchiv Hamburg, 371-8 II_6, Vierjahresplan 1936. Thanks to Moritz von Brescius for pointing me to this file.

76 Wilhelm Ziegelmayer, *Rohstoff-Fragen der deutschen Volksernährung: Eine Darstellung der ernährungswirtschaftlichen und ernährungswissenschaftlichen Aufgaben unserer Zeit* (Dresden, Leipzig: Steinkopff, 1936), 91–92.

77 Drews, *Die 'Nazi-Bohne,'* 148–54.

78 Goss, *The German Oilseed Industry*, 32.

79 Gerhard L. Weinberg, *The Foreign Policy of Hitler's Germany [2]: Starting World War II 1937–1939* (Chicago: University of Chicago Press, 1980), 120–32, 337–48; John P. Fox, *Germany and the Far Eastern Crisis 1931–1938: A study in diplomacy and ideology* (Oxford: Clarendon Press, 1985), 8; Ernst L. Presseisen, *Germany and Japan: A Study in Totalitarian Diplomacy, 1933–1944* (The Hague: Marinus Nijhoff, 1958), 61; Bernd Martin, "Germany Between China and Japan – German Far Eastern Policy in the Interwar Period," in *Deutsch-chinesische Beziehungen, 1928–1937: 'Gleiche' Partner unter 'ungleichen' Bedingungen*, ed. Bernd Martin (Berlin: Akademie-Verlag, 2003), 433; Donald M. McKale, "The Nazi Party in the Far East, 1931–1945," *Journal of Contemporary History* 12 (1977), 297, 301; Che-Wei Chang, "Oskar Trautmann, ein deutscher Diplomat in Ostasien: Individuum, Nation und Diplomatie aus der Perspektive der Globalgeschichte, 1877–1950" (PhD diss., University of Bonn, 2021), 148–49.

80 Fahs, "German Economic Diplomacy."

81 Kurt Bloch, *German Interests and Policies in the Far East* (New York, NY: AMS Press, 1978, reprint of the 1940 edition published by International Secretariat, Institute of Pacific Relations, New York), 28.

82 Lizzie Collingham, *The Taste of War: World War Two and the Battle for Food* (London: Penguin Books, 2012).

83 Bloch, *German Interests*, 24; John R. Stewart, *Manchuria since 1931* (New York, NY: Institute of Pacific Relations, 1936); Martin, *Deutsch-Chinesische Beziehungen*, 424.

84 Bloch, *German Interests*, 21.

85 Aufzeichnung des Ministerialdirektors Meyer (Berlin, March 6, 1933), document no. 50 in *Akten zur deutschen auswärtigen Politik, 1918–1945: Aus dem Archiv des Auswärtigen Amtes* [hereafter: *ADAP*] (Göttingen, Vandenhoeck und Ruprecht, 1950–1995), series C 1,1: 103.

86 Das Auswärtige Amt an die Botschaft in Tokio (Berlin, December 2, 1933), document no. 97, in *ADAP*, series C 2, 1: 169.

87 Der Reichsminister des Auswärtigen Freiherr von Neurath and die Botschaft in Tokio (Berlin, January 18, 1934), document no. 198 in *ADAP*, series C 2,1: 376–78; Der Botschafter in Tokio von Dirksen an das Auswärtige Amt (Tokio, February 17, 1934), document no. 267 in *ADAP*, series C 2,2: 494–96.

88 Der Gesandte in Peping Trautmann an das Auswärtige Amt (Beijing, February 2, 1934), document no. 236, in *ADAP,* series C 2,2: 436–38; Der Reichsminister des Auswärtigen Freiherr von Neurath and die Botschaft in Tokio (Berlin, February 5, 1934), document no. 238, in *ADAP,* series C, 2,2: 440.

89 Aufzeichnun des Vortragenden Legationsrats Ulrich (Berlin, February 19, 1934), document no. 260 in *ADAP* series C, 2,2: 498.

90 Der Botschafter in Tokio von Dirksen an das Auswärtige Amt (Tokyo, March 14, 1934), document no. 326 in *ADAP* series C, 2,2: 595 (author's translation); Der Ostasiatische Verein Hamburg-Bremen e. V. an den Reichsminister des Auswärtigen Freiherrn von Neurath (Hamburg, March 13, 1934), document no. 324, in *ADAP,* series C, 2,2: 593–94.

91 Der Botschafter in Tokio von Dirksen an das Auswärtige Amt (Tokyo, March 14, 1934), document no. 326 in *ADAP,* series C, 2,2: 595; Der Ostasiatische Verein Hamburg-Bremen e. V. an den Reichsminister des Auswärtigen Freiherrn von Neurath (Hamburg, March 13, 1934), document no. 324 in *ADAP,* series C, 2, 2: 593–94; Der Botschafter in Tokio von Dirksen an das Auswärtige Amt (Tokio, May 7, 1934), document no. 438, in *ADAP,* series C, 2,2: 778–852; Aufzeichnung des Ministerialdirektors Meyer (Berlin, November 23, 1934), document no. 350 in *ADAP,* series C, 3,2: 648–49.

92 Aktenvermerk des Ministerialdirektors Ritter (Berlin, July 21, 1934), document no. 107, in *ADAP,* series C, 3,1: 204–5; Der Reichsminister des Auswärtigen Freiherr von Neurath an den Stellvertreter des Führers Reichsminister Heß (Berlin, February 4, 1935), document no. 478 in *ADAP,* series C, 3,2: 883.

93 Weinberg, *Foreign Policy,* 126–32, 340; similar Chang, *Oskar Trautmann,* 148–53, 193.

94 Fox, *Germany and the Far Eastern Crisis,* 8, 146.

95 Ostasiatischer Verein Hamburg-Bremen an die Handelskammer Hamburg (December 8, 1933), Handelskammer Hamburg. 11.B.135a.1.11. Austausch für das Mandschureigeschäft, Sojabohnen gegen Industrieerzeugnisse.

96 Eckart Teichert, *Autarkie und Großraumwirtschaft in Deutschland, 1930–1939: Außenwirtschaftspolitische Konzeptionen zwischen Wirtschaftskrise und Zweitem Weltkrieg* (München: Oldenbourg, 1984), 33.

97 Fox, *Germany and the Far Eastern Crisis,* 146–49.

98 Der Gesandte in Peping Trautmann an das Auswärtige Amt (Beijing, February 2, 1934), document no. 236, in *ADAP,* series C 2,2: 436–38.

99 Guo Bingwen to Wo Dingchang (Nanjing, February 6, 1936), in Martin, *Deutsch-Chinesische Beziehungen,* document number 124: 448–49; Aufzeichnung des Staatssekretärs Bernhard von Bülow (May 4, 1936), in Martin, *Deutsch-Chinesische Beziehungen,* document number 125: 449–51.

100 "Die deutsch-mandschurische Wirtschafts-Vereinbarung," *Ostasiatische Rundschau* 17, no. 11 (June 1, 1936): 281; Stewart, *Manchuria since 1931,* 52–53; Bloch, *German Interests,* 35.

101 Robert G. Fahs, "The Historical Background to German Trans-Siberian Transit Trade," (Master's thesis, University of Hawai'i, 1992), 72.

102 Sir Eric Philipps/Foreign Office, Berlin, June 5, 1936, cited in Fox, *Germany and the Far Eastern Crisis,* 170.

103 Bloch, *German Interests,* 37–42; Lawrence K. Rosinger, "Germany's Far Eastern Policy Under Hitler," *Pacific Affairs* 11 (1938): 426–27; Martin, *Deutsch-Chinesische Beziehungen,* 433.

104 Stewart, "Four Years of Manchukuo," *Far Eastern Survey* 5, no. 6 (March 12, 1936), 51–58, here 54; Tim Wright, "Manchurian Economy and the 1930s World Depression," *Modern Asian Studies* 41, no. 5 (September 2007): 1093–97.

105 Stewart, "Four Years of Manchukuo," 55; John R. Stewart, "Manchurian Import Boom Subsiding," *Far Eastern* Survey 5, no. 11 (May 1936): 114; *Foreign Crops and Markets* 32, issued by the Foreign Agricultural Service, Bureau of Agricultural Economics (January 20, 1936).
106 Wright, "Manchurian Economy," 1088.
107 John R. Stewart, "The Soya Bean and Manchuria," *Far Eastern Survey* 5, no. 21 (October 1936): 226.
108 "The Manchukuo-German Trade Agreement," 33 [highlighted in the original].
109 Cited in Manley O. Hudson, "The Report of the Assembly of the League of Nations on the Sino-Japanese Dispute," *The American Journal of International Law* 27, no. 2 (1933): 302, 304.
110 Cited in Bloch, *German Interests,* 32.
111 Wolfgang Michalka, "Das Auswärtige Amt und der Weg in den Krieg," in *Das Auswärtige Amt in der NS-Diktatur,* eds. Johannes Hürter and Michael Mayer (Berlin: Walter de Gruyter, 2014), 104.
112 Fahs, "German Economic Diplomacy," 220–22.
113 Rosinger, "Germany's Far Eastern Policy," 426; "The Manchukuo-German Trade Agreement," *Contemporary Manchuria* (September 1937), 46. "The New Manchukuo-Germany Trade Pact," *Contemporary Manchuria* (January 1939), 129–35.
114 Vermerk des Leiters der Wirtschaftspolitischen Abteilung (Berlin, June 20, 1940), document no. 502, in *ADAP*, series D, 9: 524–25; Der Botschafter in Tokio an das Auswärtige Amt (Tokyo, August 2, 1940), document no. 273, in *ADAP*, series D, 10: 322–24.
115 Aufzeichnung des Leiters der Wirtschaftspolitischen Abteilung [Berlin, November 15, 1940], document no. 341, in *ADAP*, series D, 12,1: 489–91; Aufzeichnung des Leiters der Handelspolitischen Abteilung (Berlin, August 20, 1941), document no. 216 in *ADAP,* series D, 13, 1: 279–81.
116 See Fahs, "German Economic Diplomacy," 170–95 on attempts in Russia.
117 Hanseatische Mühlenwerke AG to Deutsch-Donaländische Warenaustausch GmbH (May 15, 1929), Handelskammer Hamburg. 11.B.135a. 1.4 Anbauversuche von Sojabohnen in Europa (1929).
118 Projekt des Soya-Anbaus in Europa (March 21, 1929), Handelskammer Hamburg. 11.B.135a. 1.4 Anbauversuche von Sojabohnen in Europa (1929) (author's translation).
119 Hans Radandt, "Die Interessen der IG Farbenindustrie AG in Bulgarien bis 1944," *1999. Zeitschrift für Sozialgeschichte des 20. und 21. Jahrhunderts* 3, no. 4 (1988):14; Drews, *Die 'Nazi-Bohne,'* 231.
120 Hans-Jürgen Schröder, "Südosteuropa als 'Informal Empire' Deutschlands 1933–1939: Das Beispiel Jugoslawien," *Jahrbücher für Geschichte Osteuropas* NF 23, no. 1 (1975), 70–96; see also Ludolf Herbst, "Die nationalsozialistische Wirtschaftspolitik im internationalen Vergleich," in *Der Nationalsozialismus. Studien zu Ideologie und Herrschaft*, eds. Wolfgang Benz, Hans Buchheim, Hans Mommsen (Frankfurt am Main: Fischer Taschenbuchverlag, 1993), 153–76.
121 Hans Radandt, "Die IG Farbenindustrie und Südosteuropa bis 1938," *Jahrbuch für Wirtschaftsgeschichte* 7 (1966), 146–95.
122 Aufzeichnung des Ministerialrats Willuhn, Reichskanzlei (Berlin, June 7, 1934), document no. 484, in *ADAP*, series C 2,2: 859.
123 Drews, *Die 'Nazi-Bohne,'* 231–39; Aufzeichnungen des Gesandten Clodius, Wirtschaftspol. Abt. (Berlin, February 15, 1938), document no. 294, in *ADAP*, series D 5: 294.
124 Contrary to these numbers, Radandt, "Die Interessen der IG Farbenindustrie," 15, states that in 1939 Germany received a total of 140,000 tons of

soybeans from Romania, Bulgaria, and Yugoslavia, and that these countries combined held a share of 17.6 percent of total soybean imports. Radandt worked with Germany's annual statistics, which did not list soybeans separately but subsumed them under "oilseeds." He assumed that all oilseeds in this category were soybeans, which is not correct, as the *Monatliche Nachweise* I worked with show.

125 Gesine Gerhard. *Nazi Hunger Politics: A History of Food in the Third Reich* (Lanham, MD: Rowman & Littlefield, 2015), 87.

126 Wigbert Benz. "Aktennotiz über Ergebnis der heutigen Besprechung mit den Staatssekretären über Barbarossa, 2. Mai 1941," *100(0) Schlüsseldokumente zur Deutschen Geschichte im 20. Jahrhundert.* https://www.1000dokumente.de/pdf/dok_0227_hun_de.pdf; Alex J. Kay, "Germany's Staatssekretäre, Mass Starvation and the Meeting of 2 May 1941," *Journal of Contemporary History* 41, no. 4 (October 2006): 685–700.

127 Goss, *The German Oilseed Industry,* 68–69.

128 Goss, *The German Oilseed Industry,* 32.

129 Lois B. Bacon, Friedrich C. Schloemer, and Henry C. Taylor, *World Trade in Agricultural Products: Its Growth, Its Crisis, and the New Trade Policies* (Rome: International Institute of Agriculture, 1940), 214–327, 1008–9.

4 Americanizing Soy

In 1927, farmer William McArthur from Indiana reported in the agricultural magazine *Wallaces' Farmer* on his ten years of positive experience with the soybean as a field plant. He gave a detailed account, useful as a guide for others willing to try out soy. Although his text was so extensive that it had to be published across two successive issues of the magazine, he focused on growing and using soybeans as feed for his own animals only. He deviated from this perspective only once, when mentioning that surplus beans could be sold as seed. It seems as though the use of soybeans in the production of oils was beyond his knowledge, or he considered this possibility a negligible one and thus not worth mentioning, just as he failed to mention the use of soy as food.[1]

In the same year McArthur published his text in *Wallaces' Farmer*, the commercial interest in soybeans in Europe was skyrocketing. Germany had just surpassed Japan as the main purchaser of supplies from Manchuria, and in various European countries, the beans were sought after in the production of margarine, soap, paints, and many more consumer products. Nothing of the great interest in the crop in other parts of the world and thus the possibility of gaining an income from it was reflected in McArthur's account. He did not mention soy's advantages as an oil crop even once. In light of the flourishing and profitable soybean business in Europe and Asia, his perspective seems rather unusual; in fact, his view was common in the Corn Belt. Here, soy had gained some approval among farmers in the 1920s, but instead of providing oil, the crop promised to rejuvenate depleted Midwestern soils and serve as fodder. It was thus an alternative to corn, the cultivation in monoculture of which during the First World War had caused many agricultural problems. In the interwar period, soy's great promise to Midwestern farmers lay in it being an inexpensive feed in addition to a soil fertilizer. In this respect, soy served as a beacon of hope.

The rise of the soybean as a crop in the United States has been dramatic and is hardly comparable to any other crop in American agriculture. In the years 1907–1917, the farmland devoted to soybeans, either as a forage crop or for harvesting the beans, expanded from 50,000 to 460,000 acres. By 1924 the same figure exceeded 1.75 million acres, by 1934 it was over

DOI: 10.4324/9781003255222-5

6 million acres, and by 1943 almost 16 million acres.[2] Most of this acreage was planted in the Corn Belt in the American Midwest.

This chapter focuses on the advance of the soybean as a field crop mainly in Midwestern agriculture. By analyzing the connection between soy and land use change, it asks why farmers started to include the soybean in their crop rotation system and how the cultivation of soybeans developed in the 30 years around the two world wars. Besides analyzing structural reasons and driving forces, I will also focus on the actors involved in promoting soybeans among farmers. Which institutions participated in gathering knowledge about soybean cultivation? To which degree were the United States' government, colleges, and universities involved in circulating seeds and information on how to plant them? And how did local and regional businesses engage with the bean and its promises?

The rise in soybean cultivation in the United States relates back to developments during three distinct periods: the aftermath of the First World War, the Great Depression, and the Second World War. The chapter analyzes how the soybean served to solve economic problems tied to these events, and it explains that the rise of the soybean in U.S. agriculture was first and foremost a result of governmental interventions.

During the First World War, farmers in the South turned to the soybean to plug shortages in fats and oils. These efforts were neither significant nor persistent. It was not until after the war, during the agricultural crisis of the 1920s, that farmers in the Midwest tried out soybeans on a slightly larger scale. These efforts were accompanied and encouraged by scientists in the USDA and at local colleges, among others. The resulting rise, however, was rather related to depleted soils and overproduction in other crops than to soybeans as an oil crop, as farmer McArthur's testimony exemplifies. The breakthrough in soybean cultivation and thus the use of soybeans as an oil crop eventually occurred in the 1930s and 1940s. When, in 1934, the U.S. government enacted the Agricultural Adjustment Act (AAA) in an attempt to fight the Great Depression, soybeans were an indirect but significant beneficiary. Then, during the Second World War, soybean cultivation rose thanks to governmental support intended to avoid greater shortages in fats. Soybeans became a war crop, meaning that their cultivation rose tremendously during the war as a result of government intervention.

Interestingly, soybean production in the United States evolved rather independently from developments in the global soybean market. I was not able to find much evidence for direct links between American farmers trying out the soybean and European oil mills importing the beans from Asia. European oil mills were not entirely unaware of American farmers' successes in growing the soybean, and vice versa; nevertheless, there were hardly any scholarly exchanges or reports of future business opportunities. In fact, when in the 1930s Midwestern farmers significantly boosted soybean cultivation, they did so in response to an internal crisis, not to compete on the world market. Interest in beans as a commodity for sale remained rather low at first, and it was only after the Second World War that soybeans in the United States were traded on a global scale.

The Future Crop and the Department of Agriculture

In the spring of 1917, the *American Food Journal*, published by the Association of American Dairy, Food, and Drug Officials, reported on the merits of Dyer's Beans, a canned dish of pork, broad beans, and soybeans. The article emphasized the high protein content of soybeans, which were said to give extra strength. A few months later an advertisement in the same journal—which claimed to be the "national magazine of the food field"—touted the dish as a food that would win the war.[3] In light of the origin of these sources, an organization closely linked to the Department of Agriculture, the question arises as to whether soy was set to become an officially approved food.

Other sources, stemming from similar origins, indicate that soy was even available for purchase as flour and whole beans. Here, eating soy was also connected to patriotic duties and efforts to win the war. In 1918, the USDA published a brochure with recipes designed to teach American housewives how to use soybean flour. Besides scones and muffins, the recipe book included a "Victory Bread," which was apparently intended to provide strength and energy. It was a bread similar to those nowadays available as protein bread at some food stores and bakeries. Whether the Victory Bread was actually made and eaten is difficult to prove; what is more relevant for the American soybean story is that soy was explicitly seen as a substitute commodity in times of shortage.[4] Soybean flour and the beans themselves did not seem to have any value beyond accommodating wartime necessities at that time.

Another interesting observation with whole soybeans and soybean flour in the United States regards their general availability. As shown in Chapter 2, American statistics listed shipments of soybean oil imports at this time, but they did not register any other soy-based products and neither did Japanese statistics. How did various food products based on either whole soybeans or soy flour become available if neither one was being imported? Surprisingly, these products most likely stemmed from American-grown soybeans. The USDA had made efforts to convince farmers in the Cotton Belt to grow soybeans to meet wartime oil shortages, and the flour used in foodstuffs was probably one of the results of these efforts.

Beginning in the early 1910s, interest in cultivating soybeans in the United States was rising. Scientists working with the USDA conducted experiments and field trips, farmers in the Cotton and Corn Belts made efforts to grow them, and a few rather local companies tried to make use of the beans. Their efforts intensified during the war, but the volume of beans then harvested was still too insignificant to qualify for American statistics. That eventually happened in 1924, and the years leading up to it are particularly interesting for why soy found its way into American agriculture at all.

The Bureau of Plant Industry (BPI), a government agency under the Department of Agriculture, was crucial for researching foreign plants. It was founded in 1900 in a merger of several USDA divisions that had dealt sporadically with aspects regarding lesser-known crops and commodities. While the BPI generally pooled this work, sub-divisions were assigned with examining the potential use of various plants in the American agriculture and economy.[5] Within the BPI's Office of Forage Crop Investigations, Charles V. Piper and William J. Morse were particularly enthusiastic about soybeans. They investigated soy's potential as a field crop in American agriculture, as a commodity for trade, and as an ingredient in various food and nonfood goods. Their work in the 1910s and 1920s was pioneering and influential for generations to come.

Piper and Morse started researching soybeans in the early 1910s by planting some beans at the USDA experimental farm in Arlington, V.A., and publishing a few brochures on their findings. They also kept in touch with other soybean enthusiasts in the country and supported their work by helping to spread and exchange information. In 1916, there was even a short publication with special focus on the use of soy as an oil crop.[6] Despite the significance of the year, however, the authors were not concerned with the potential of using soybeans in the war. It seemed too distant for them, and they barely mentioned a few substitutes containing soybeans in use in the warring countries in Europe. The brochure thus had a rather general approach when focusing on soybean oil. Piper and Morse's goal was to make soy generally known in the U.S., promote its cultivation, boost imports from Manchuria, and accelerate the use of soy oil in the manufacture of margarine, lard substitute, and soap, and eventually also spread the beans as a foodstuff in their own right. Already at this time, they portrayed soy as a "crop of importance" in the United States, which was an overstatement given that soybean cultivation in the U.S. itself was still too small to be recorded.

The pamphlet even included a map identifying, according to them, where soy was especially adapted for cultivating for oil.[7] They envisioned both the Corn and Cotton Belts as the main future growing regions for soybeans in the United States. Climatic conditions were favorable in both regions, but the early focus on the Cotton Belt took soybeans' potential as an oil crop into account. Contrary to the American Midwest, the South, through years of growing cotton and flaxseed, possessed the technical prerequisites as well as the expertise to process oilseeds. Thus, Morse and Piper's bulletin on soybean oil was explicitly intended for "general distribution in the Southern States, where it will be of special interests to farmers and cotton-oil millmen."[8]

At first, interest among farmers remained low, largely due to the foreign nature of the plant and its characteristics. Contemporary sources indicate that soybeans were grown and processed by local oil mills in the late 1910s in various southern states, including Maryland, North Carolina, Virginia, Alabama, Tennessee, Kentucky, and Louisiana.[9] Most of the soybean fields at that time were in North Carolina; however, the total outcome remained rather small.

Nevertheless, USDA, and in particular the BPI, kept working toward soy. Between 1907 and 1917 the acreage for soybeans increased from an estimated 50,000 acres to around 500,000 acres. Even though this was a significant increase, the area seems all the smaller when considered that at the time more than 300 million acres were being tilled annually in the United States. Of that, 30 million acres went to cotton alone.[10] Thus, despite the confidence that Morse and his colleagues spread about the use of locally grown soybeans in general, the crop's actual share in agriculture and thus consumption remained relatively low. As for soybean oil, domestic supplies were estimated to account for only one to two percent of total U.S. fat consumption during the First World War.[11]

The BPI provided an interface for the transfer of knowledge among farmers, oil mills, agriculturalists, and others interested in soy. In addition, the agency's commitment to gaining new knowledge extended far beyond national borders, as evidenced by several expedition trips. Botanical research trips had a long tradition in American history. In the early twentieth century, Asia and especially China came into focus, which was related to the founding of the BPI and the personal interests of its staff. At around the same time as Morse and Piper were working toward establishing soybeans in the United States, David Fairchild and Frank N. Meyer from the BPI's Office of Foreign Seed and Plant Introduction were working toward researching plants in China, Japan, and Asian Russia. With such geographical focus, their work naturally included soybeans. While Fairchild headed the office from 1904 to 1928 and set the research agenda, Meyer made the actual research trips. Between 1905 and 1918, he traveled to Asia four times on behalf of the USDA. From his trip, he sent back seeds of 25,000 new plants or varieties, including walnuts, pistachios, apricots, grapes, apples, pears, lychees, winter wheat, and millet, and gathered local knowledge on cultivation and processing, among others regarding soybeans.

In the fall of 1916, Meyer's last trip took him to southern China. A travel journal of over two hundred pages compiled back in Washington, DC, by his supervisor provides information about the purpose and circumstances of the trip in addition to notes and letters from and to Meyer, as well as the packing lists of boxes sent back home. Soy was only one of many crops Meyer explored on this trip, but it was explicitly mentioned as a main research object. According to the letters kept in the journal, his work encompassed botanical and agriculturally relevant findings as well as questions of further processing and the use of various products containing soy. While Meyer was compiling local knowledge in China and sending it to his supervisor, Fairchild, the latter disseminated Meyer's research to other USDA staff. In turn, it was through Fairchild that Meyer knew about the work of other scientists. In early 1917, Meyer sent cans of tofu to Washington to be explicitly passed on to Morse, his colleague in the BPI's

Office of Forage Crop Investigations.[12] He also took numerous high-quality pictures, which besides illustrating plants and seeds documented Chinese cultivation and processing methods. Interestingly, all his shipments were declared as diplomatic mail, a protection that ensured that the letters and parcels reached their destination, especially during the war. This measure signals how important his research must have been, even when the world was in turmoil. Sadly, despite being a successful and valued collector, he must have felt rather lonely on his trips to Asia. He never returned from this last trip—he drowned in the Yangtze River in June 1918.[13]

The travel journal kept by Fairchild back at the USDA provides insight into an entire network of U.S. agricultural experts working on soybeans at that time. Among others, the correspondence mentions Kin Yamei, a cosmopolitan physician who had grown up with American missionaries and in 1885 was one of the first women of Chinese origin to earn a medical doctorate in the United States. Yamei was a colorful personality who was able to travel and mediate between Asia and America. In China, she worked to establish American medicine, and in the United States, she promoted the benefits of Chinese food. In 1918, the Bureau of Chemistry, another agency in the USDA with responsibility for food and drug controls, sent Yamei to China. She was to find out more about the production of tofu, soy milk, and other edible soy products, given the wartime deprivations, especially in food.

Contrary to Meyer, who investigated soy as a potential crop in U.S. agriculture, Yamei's mission was to get Americans to eat foods with soy proteins and cut back on animal proteins, which were costly to produce. As another contemporary observer put it:

> It has been calculated that, roughly speaking, it takes 100 pounds of foodstuffs to produce 3 pounds of beef and that a given acreage of land can support five times the population if the necessary protein can be derived directly from vegetable sources rather than going through the roundabout way of an animal form.[14]

Yamei was thus considered a food and nutrition mediator who was to bring the joy of eating soybeans to the United States. However, her efforts, like those of Meyer, Morse, and others, met with little success as soy was soon forgotten in American agriculture and society after the end of the war.

It was not only soy food that found little interest after 1918. Soybean oil imports dropped, and, in addition, farmers lost interest in soybeans again, despite the efforts of Morse and Piper. During the war, the USDA stepped in as a breeder and helped to grow soybean seeds for distribution among farmers. The samples Meyer had sent helped to improve this effort. In the spring of 1918, the department planted 300 acres of land with soybeans to hand the yield to farmers for sowing in the following year. The measure was justified in light of growing food shortages.[15] However, in 1919, when farmers for the first time planted and harvested soybeans to a larger extent than ever before,

Americans had no more use for them. With the end of the war, the time of fat shortages was over, at least in the United States and the beans were thus of no use. Instead, most of the beans were pressed and the oil shipped to Europe. In 1919, 13,000 tons of soybean oil worth six million U.S. dollars were exported, more than half of which went to Great Britain alone. In the following year, Europeans received 34,000 tons valued at nearly 15 million U.S. dollars.[16]

At around the same time as scientists in the USDA were busy collecting information on the soybean and its potential as a domestic crop, officials in the Departments of Commerce and State were watching trade in Manchuria closely, including the trade in soybeans. They generally feared Japanese competition on the world market and gathered information on the soybean as a resource for fat and fodder in Europe, as shown in Chapter 2. Despite this coincidence, the soybean trade between Europe and Asia and the cultivation of soybeans in the United States do not seem to be connected. There is no evidence that the Departments of Commerce and State knew about the efforts of the Department of Agriculture to establish homegrown soybeans, or, likewise, that agriculturalists knew about the powerful Japanese commercial interest in trading soybeans. The question remains whether they ought to have known about each other's efforts. In light of the sources provided here, it seems obvious that Americans had at least some interest in soy and the disconnection or noncommunication between the three departments might reveal a dysfunctional administration. On the other hand, what linked their work was a plant which at that time was so insignificant to the American economy that sources beyond publications from soybean enthusiasts within the USDA are hard to find. The plant was simply not yet considered as having much relationship to the United States.

In the early 1920s the southern states quickly returned to cotton monoculture, even though the boll weevil plagued the region's farmers and their main crop. In his monograph on soybeans in the United States, Matthew Roth provides a reason for why the crop was not met with sustained interest at that time despite the challenges farmers faced in continuing to plant cotton in monoculture. He argues that the "soybean's habit was an advantage mainly for mechanized farms, the sort that could emerge in the South only by pushing tenants off the land."[17] Indeed, the use of harvesters was beneficial for soybeans, and farmers in the South usually lacked access to them since picking cotton was labor-intensive and done by hand. On the other side of the ocean, though, Manchurian farmers did not have access to harvesters either. They relied on farm animals and their own hands and were nevertheless highly successful in producing soybeans. I suggest that the waning interest in soy had several causes, with the lack of know-how and general unfamiliarity with the plant being central. While the USDA conducted research, it lacked the resources to promote the cultivation of soybeans further. All they had to offer were a few enthusiastic employees who shared their knowledge in some pamphlets. The soybean did not succeed at that time because it was a plant promoted by officials who did not have the means to really help it come through. This was not only about convincing farmers but finding a market with processing businesses and customers willing to buy products made of soy. Farmers were unfamiliar with the plant and in addition did not see a market for soybeans at that time; consequently, they lost interest again.

Nevertheless, the First World War helped raise the profile of soybeans in the United States more than ever before. Whereas soybeans had been known mainly to specialists and immigrants until then, they reached at least some southern farmers, entrepreneurs, and maybe even few housewives in wartime. In this respect, the war increased the awareness of soybeans, and it was the beginning of what would become an enduring relationship with soy. The following section in this chapter shows that the breakthrough of soybean cultivation in the United States was ultimately set in motion by a different and incomparably greater crisis than the distant European war: that of American agriculture in the aftermath of the war.

The Midwestern Dilemma

While interest in soybeans among farmers and oil mills in the southern states waned after the war, it increased among ranchers in the Midwest. Indeed, farmers in both regions faced almost the same challenges—depleted soils and pest infestations partly as a result of increased crop production during the war. In the Midwest, farmers' reliance on corn in monoculture during the war and the devastating effect of the corn borer led to a decline in their yields. When they started cultivating soybeans, it was not only for lack of alternatives, but they could also make use of the harvested beans by feeding them to their livestock. That the beans contained oil, useful for whatever purpose, played a secondary role to them. USDA staff and scientists from local universities took on an accompanying and advisory role in this process of switching from corn to soybeans, thereby tirelessly pointing to the fact that growing soybeans would also fertilize and recover the soil.

In the early 1910s, agriculture in the Midwest had enjoyed considerable prosperity. In retrospect, the years leading up to the war are even considered the "golden age of American agriculture," as historian Douglas R. Hurt put it.[18] During the war, this upward trend continued as the federal government encouraged farmers to support the war effort. Midwestern farmers were asked to grow as much grain and feed as possible, while those in the south were requested to do the same with cotton. Prices also rose; however, they fell quickly after the war because any anticipated food shortages, especially in Europe, did not materialize. There, the recovery, and with it the domestic production of food, began rapidly. In addition, American farmers now competed with wheat and meat from Argentina, Australia, and Canada. Finally, the purchasing power of the American population declined, especially in and after the depression of 1920–1921. For U.S. agriculture, this meant overproduction and falling prices, especially for wheat, feed, and meat.

The sudden downward trend resulted in many farmers barely being able to make a living from their products. Contemporary experts such as economic geographer Oliver E. Baker estimated that, except for Georgia and South Carolina, probably no other part of America was as severely affected by the economic downturn of the early 1920s as the Corn Belt.[19]

The post-First World War depression hit Corn Belt farmers especially hard because consumption of meat, which was the region's primary product along with forage, plummeted dramatically. Geographically, the Corn Belt was made up of large portions of Iowa, Indiana, Illinois, Minnesota, South Dakota, Nebraska, Kansas, and Missouri, with boundaries that were fluid but still determined by climate, topography, and soil fertility. Nearly half of all hogs produced nationwide were fattened in the Corn Belt. Besides hogs, the region also produced poultry, horses, and, to an increasing degree, cattle. The Corn Belt comprised only eight percent of the land mass of the United States, but in terms of financial value, it produced 25 percent of all farm products in 1919. The region was thus of enormous importance to the entire economy, and it depended on the eating habits and purchasing power of the American people. With globalizing markets and meat imports from overseas, the pressure to produce affordable foods only grew. When meat consumption dropped sharply after the war, farm incomes declined dramatically as well.[20]

What made matters worse was that the production of meat depended on that of fodder, which stemmed from the same region. Corn was a particularly valuable fodder, especially for hogs, and in 1919, this comparatively small region accounted for about one-third of the world's corn production. Besides corn, which accounted for about half of the arable land, oats, wheat, and hay were each grown in roughly equal proportions. With these crops, the Corn Belt produced primarily forage and, as a result, meat. No one expressed the connection between corn and meat better than Alonzo E. Taylor, director of the renowned Stanford Food Research Institute. He aptly summed up that "broadly considered, hogs are condensed corn [...] condensing corn into hogs is essentially conversion of corn starch into hog fat."[21] With corn and meat being so closely related, it is obvious that the cycle was vulnerable, and problems with one commodity would usually affect the other.

Ranchers were troubled by the consequences of years of corn monoculture. They had typically followed a four-year rotation of corn, oats, wheat, and hay, but broke this cycle in the wake of increased demand for feed. Clover, used as hay, was a crop normally planted in the fourth year, and it served a twofold purpose, as it fertilized the soil naturally while growing, and was turned into hay and with that fodder. Just as the soybean, clover belongs to the legume family, which means that the root's nodules form a symbiosis with so-called nodule bacteria through which the roots can enrich the soil with nitrogen. Such a plant was crucial on a farm. Nitrogen-enriched soil was necessary for the successful cultivation of corn, the crop with which the next rotation cycle would begin the following year. From 1915 onward, however, farmers grew corn on the same land for two or more years, and this practice removed too many nutrients from the soil and modified it so much so that it became too acidic. It was clover that suffered the most from over-acidified soils and would not grow as usual. Less clover meant less fertile soil, which in turn resulted in declining corn yields.[22]

Theoretically, farmers could have used artificial nitrogen fertilizer to maintain or even increase their yields. Since 1911, it was possible to produce artificial fertilizer, thanks to the so-called Haber-Bosch process. In Germany, factories provided nitrogen on a large scale and at reasonable prices since 1913, but the United States lagged heavily behind. Despite government subsidies and numerous efforts to produce artificial fertilizer on an industrial scale, it was not before 1925 that prices for fixed nitrogen significantly fell.[23] Until then, and even thereafter as the case of the soybean shows, farmers relied on natural methods to fertilize their soil.

Declining meat consumption and depleted soils were critical, and still farmers in the Corn Belt faced yet more challenges to deal with. They were plagued by the corn borer, a butterfly caterpillar that ate through corn cobs and destroyed entire crops. The pest had been introduced from Europe around 1917 and had been spreading rapidly ever since. One simple solution may have solved the problems relating to corn. Growing less of it would have given the soil a chance to recover and deprived the corn borer of its food base. However, that would have lost ranchers their income from selling meat, and they sowed more corn, not less, to keep yields even. The attempt succeeded despite the challenges, but this approach further depleted their soils, and the corn borer also spread easily.

The practice was paradoxical, but a combination of ignorance and the lack of alternative crops left farmers with few choices. Outlets for hops, barley, and rye had diminished with Prohibition in 1920, and the cultivation of them was no longer profitable to the same extent as before.[24] With oats, farmers faced also declining sales, although for a different reason. Demand decreased nationwide as Americans and their farms became more motorized and mechanized. Farmers gradually replaced horses and mules with cars, streetcars, trucks, and tractors.[25] Between 1920 and 1946, the stock of horses and mules decreased by 15 million animals. For American farms, this meant a significant switch from producing draft animals and providing feed for them to breeding animals for human consumption. And while grazing animals such as mules and horses required oats, hay, and grains, hogs and chicken required feed rich in protein and fat.[26] The gradual shift to greater meat production stimulated the planting of soy.

Finally, Midwesterners found themselves in trouble because they were unable to pay their debts. Farmers often paid for new equipment such as tractors and harvesters on credit but were unable to make their repayments due to the declining income caused by the mixture of crop failure and overproduction. A vicious cycle was set in motion. It was hardly possible to find a single remedy to solve the farmers' desperate situation, as the structural problems with American agriculture were too all-encompassing. However, finding a crop other than corn and trying to make a living from it implied facing the situation and taking action. Interestingly, the tractor eventually enabled farmers to tend more acres than they could with draft animals. Land previously used as pasture could be sown with crops. With all crops being in trouble, the internal combustion engine was eventually a vital factor in opening the land to the mass production of the soybean.[27]

Growing Soybeans to Get Along

In the spring of 1920, some farmers and agronomists met in Indiana to share their experiences with soy. At this time, neither the mechanization of American farms nor its consequences for the shift to producing more hogs and chicken, and with that soybeans, were in sight. Nevertheless, the gathered farmers were united by a general interest in this foreign plant that they hoped would solve some of their manifold problems. Someone had even written an ode to the soybean that was performed by a quartet of local farmers.[28] The title alone, "Growing Soybeans to Get Along," is telling regarding their hopes of making a living out of soy as a new crop. There was no long-standing, traditional experience such as with corn or wheat upon which farmers or interested industries could draw, which explains these early meetings. Anyone interested in learning more about soy had to connect with like-minded people. Thus, the first meetings were quite informal, as reported some years later, by which time the participants had formed a growers' association:

> The Association in its early history had no registered membership and no dues. Anyone who felt sufficiently interested in soybeans to attend these meetings was entitled to a voice in whatever business was transacted.[29]

Since 1925 the growers' association has been known as the American Soybean Association (ASA), but for the meetings in the early 1920s no minutes or other transcripts are available. Later recollections show that the gatherings were characterized by so-called field meetings, which took place at farms in Indiana, Illinois, Missouri, Wisconsin, or Iowa. On these occasions, the assembled farmers and scientists presented their experiences with soybeans to each other, visited their fields, and examined the benefits of using harvesting machinery. Although their wives often offered homemade soy dishes, no one seriously talked about growing or using soy as food. Rather, soy would be grown to supply depleted soils with nitrogen, to fatten pigs and poultry, and to help farmers earn an income. According to the association's 1925 constitution, its goal was:

> To encourage the rational use of the soybean as a crop for soil building, forage, grazing, as a money crop, especially on lands too poor or too poorly drained to be profitable for other crops, and as a smother crop for bad, low-growing grasses.[30]

In the 1920s, American farmers began to cultivate soybeans, even if the amount was still rather small. The potential of soybeans for improving the soil as well as serving as feed and fertilizer was so promising that farmers in fact moved ahead and included the crop in their rotation system, as reflected in the annual statistics (see Figure 4.1).[31] Illinois was by far the state with most soybean farmers, followed by Indiana.[32] Most of the beans were planted for hay or without harvesting them at all, while the prevalence of planting beans as a cash crop either as a resource for oil or as seed was low. Usually, this purpose did not even reach one-third of the total acreage.

The plant's potential to serve as fertilizer simply by growing it in the fields was a key factor in attracting the interest of farmers. Even contemporary observers noted, however, that there was probably too much talk about the plant's benefits as fertilizer, because the matter was complicated, and the fertilizing effect was achieved only under certain conditions. In the late nineteenth century, scientists in Europe had made the observation that legumes can convert molecular nitrogen from the air into ammonium, which is

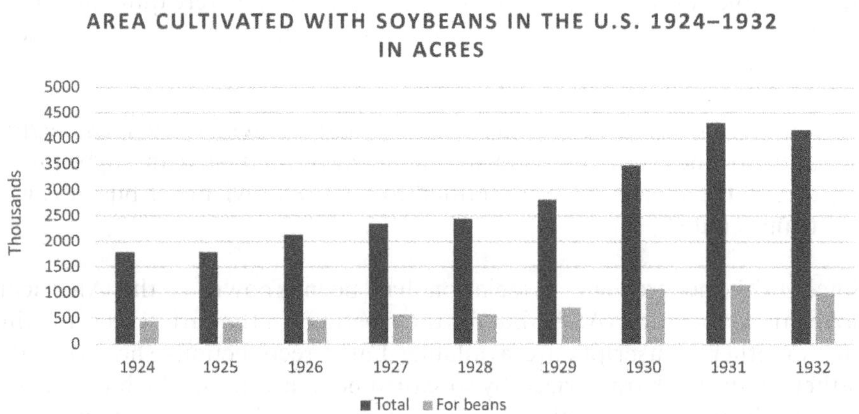

Figure 4.1 Acreage planted with soybeans in the United States, 1924–1932. The dark column indicates acreage for total soybean cultivation, whereas the column in light gray shows acres planted with soybeans for sale.

© Author. Based on information from the U.S. Department of Agriculture, Crop Reporting Board, *Soybeans, Cowpeas, and Velvetbeans, by States, 1924–1953. Acreage, yield, production, price* (Washington, DC: USDA, 1957), 2.

a compound of nitrogen and hydrogen. That process is called nitrogen fixation. One of their findings was that each legume needed to form a symbiotic relationship with a specific rhizobia, or bacteria, to fix nitrogen.[33] Soybeans required *Bradyrhizobium japonicum*, a species not native to North American soils. To use soybeans as a fertilizer, it was therefore necessary to bring the soybean seeds into contact with this rhizome before sowing, a process that experts call inoculation. Today, inoculation is common practice, because if the bacterium is not added to the seed or soil, soybeans remove nitrogen from the soil, with fatal consequences. Back in the 1920s, agronomists in the USDA as well as at the University of Illinois and other educational institutions were familiar with the difficult interaction between plants, bacteria, and soil. However, this knowledge was still in its infancy, as the University of Illinois' Jay Hackleman, who was just as much a soy enthusiast as Morse and Piper from the USDA, explained in an article for the *Agronomy Journal*. He doubted that these insights had made it to the farmers and to which degree they embraced the need for inoculation at that time.[34]

The USDA offered to send the rhizobia to interested farmers upon request and provided instructions on how to successfully grow soybeans but making the bacterium native to the soil was a matter of time and good soil management.[35] Farmers could also mix the seed with soil from such fields where inoculated plants had grown earlier. They then applied the mixture of mud, rhizomes, and seeds to a new field and obtained good yields. The issue of to which degree farmers followed the instructions remains an open one, but regardless of all these challenges of using soy for soil improvement, farmers in the Midwest found the idea of using soy for this purpose the most convincing argument for growing it. Notably, "soil building" was also the most prominent keyword mentioned in the ASA's constitution of 1925.

A second reason for soy's success in the Corn Belt was its use as feedstuff. Soybeans are well suited as what is called concentrated feed, a protein-rich fodder that made good, muscular meat. Farmers in the Midwest typically purchased protein-rich concentrates from the southern states, as this was a byproduct of the extraction of vegetable oils, most notably from cottonseed and to a lesser degree from flaxseed. Soybeans offered farmers who did not have much purchasing power the prospect of saving on these expenditures. In these early years, they simply used the entire plant as feed by letting their livestock graze the fields.[36] If farmers harvested the crops at all, it was not to sell the beans but rather to make silage for winter months or to save seeds for the coming year. It is reported that they only gave beans that they could not use themselves to the few existing oil mills, and it was only hesitantly that they agreed to grow soybeans as an oil crop and to take the byproduct back from the mills as feed. In a retrospect to the early years, a brochure from the 1950s stated that "hundreds of thousands of individual farmers who 'home-mixed' their feeds, were completely unfamiliar with—and in some cases actually hostile toward—this newcomer in the protein field—soybean meal."[37]

As early as 1923, experts in the USDA predicted a more profitable future for soybeans than oats in the Midwest.[38] Looking at Midwestern agriculture over the past hundred years, they were undoubtedly correct. The soybean succeeded there because it fit well into the crop rotation system and, in the long term, replaced low-value oats. In addition, the soybean supplemented corn, a crop to which farmers still clung. In an ideal crop rotation cycle, farmers would grow corn in the first year, then followed by soybeans instead of oats. To grow soybeans, they added lime to the soil, which neutralized it and caused soybean yields to increase. The practice was less important for wheat, which then usually came in the third year but vital for clover in the fourth year. On less acidic soils, clover grew again and enriched the soil with nitrogen, thus preparing it for the next cycle, which started over with corn.

In reality, matters were not as easy as that. While soybeans are generally easy to grow and are resistant to most pests and diseases, they are sensitive to the length of the day. The phenomenon is called photoperiodism, and it was not before 1920 that scientists gained sufficient insights to breed varieties that suit Midwestern conditions.[39] Nevertheless, the early 1920s saw the beginning of the transformation of the Corn Belt into a Corn-Soy Belt. While the transformation was completed by the 1950s, the term, as accurate as it is, has never left agricultural circles.[40] Caught in the dilemma of infertile soils and declining yields for their favored crop—corn—farmers embraced the Asian stranger out of necessity, not in loving devotion. Maybe herein lies the reason why soy, contrary to corn, has made hardly any inroads into American popular culture.

In any case, farmers themselves were only partly responsible for the orientation toward soy at that time. Rather, a complex interplay of governmental and academic actors alongside farmers led to the spread of soybeans throughout the Corn Belt. First, better structures for the dissemination of agricultural knowledge significantly promoted soy's success among farmers. In the 1910s, federal law laid the ground for improved cooperation between governmental institutions and farmers, from which soybean cultivation benefitted as a secondary effect. The Smith-Lever Act of 1914 increased funding for farmers willing to operate demonstration fields and act as regional multipliers for the conveying of agricultural knowledge. It established a system of cooperative extension services that were connected to some universities and colleges and intended to inform citizens about agricultural developments, but also home economics and related subjects. Only three years later came the Smith-Hughes Act, which promoted vocational agricultural education for farmers. It also helped to spread information on new crops and techniques to plant them.

Also, the role of the BPI changed at that time. Originally, the main task of this agency was to systematically research plants, which meant verifying whether they were suitable for cultivation in the United States and determining any economic benefits. The agricultural downturn of the late 1910s required more than that—specifically, answers to how farmers could find ways out of the crisis. Thus, the BPI's scope and responsibilities were broadened. Now it was supposed to also help implement its findings. In addition, it focused not only on researching foreign plants but also on hybridization to help them adjust to American climates. The agency encouraged trials on the newly established crop extension farms, worked more closely with interested farmers, and continually published and communicated its findings.[41]

None of these measures was directed toward promoting specific crops, but rather toward improving American agriculture and the economy in general. Soybeans benefitted indirectly as the federal steps laid the ground for the dissemination of scientific knowledge and the crop was among those in which some agriculturalists were highly interested at the time. In 1923, for example, Morse and Piper published a compendium on the agricultural and commercial advantages of the beans that intended to inform farmers and entrepreneurs alike. They focused on soy not because any governmental program instructed them to do so or because farmers were demanding more information but did so out of personal interest and the firm belief that it was the country's most promising future crop. Indeed, they stated that there was "a wide and growing belief that the soybean is destined to become one of the leading farm crops of the United States." In reality, however, it was rather a small circle of agronomists and farmers who praised soybeans as a solution to the manifold problems in American agriculture at this time.[42]

Another key figure in the promotion of soy was agronomist Jay C. Hackleman, who in 1919 became head of the newly established Crops Extension Office at the University of Illinois. Hackleman was in close contact with his colleagues from the BPI; in fact, he and Morse worked hand in hand to establish soy in the Corn Belt.[43] Both actively participated in the early field meetings of soybean farmers in various Midwestern states and reported on the work of the BPI and the Crop Extension Office at the University of Illinois, respectively.

In the early 1920s, the ASA was headed not only by farmers but also by agronomists who either worked for the USDA or at universities and colleges which participated in the cooperative extension service. Their experimental stations were in Indiana, Iowa, Ohio, and elsewhere, and they all fundamentally streamlined the organizational structure of the ASA. In 1924 and 1925, for example, Morse was president of the ASA while Hackleman served on various special committees. It was around this time that the association acquired bylaws, the board of directors was expanded, and various committees worked out specific aspects of nomenclature and varietal diversity. The ASA took on tasks of networking, distributing information, and interacting with government and private actors at the regional, national, and international levels.[44] Their work resulted in the recording of soybeans in annual agricultural statistics in 1924, the establishment of quality standards and classifications two years later, and the admission of soybean farmers to local agricultural events. In 1925, ASA members met in Washington, DC, to raise the hardships of Corn Belt farmers before Congress and request more support for growing soybeans. In response, the USDA supported so-called Soybean Days and produced films about the gatherings so that they could later be used to distribute knowledge and information about growing, harvesting, processing, and marketing the crop.[45]

Eventually the USDA authorized three research expeditions to Asia with a special focus on alternative crops for the crisis-ridden American agriculture. The scientists sent abroad were to study the cultivation and processing methods of various foreign plants, and the soybean was just one of many, but thanks to the growing interest in it, the crop received increasing attention in these trips over the years.[46] All three journeys took place in the 1920s, and the most important in terms of gaining new knowledge on soybeans was the last one, the so-called Oriental Agricultural Exploration Expedition. For this nearly two-year trip, agronomists P. Howard Dorsett and William J. Morse set out with their families in February 1929. The trip was specifically justified by the economic downturn in the South and the Midwest, and hopes were raised that soy, next to cotton and corn, would soon become a crop of high significance:

> Although grown primarily for forage in the United States, many sections are looking forward to the production of soybean as a cash grain crop for oil and oil meal, and for human food, and industrial uses. It is quite generally predicted that the soybean will become one of our major crops, particularly in the South of the boll weevil sections and in the Corn Belt states through the menace of the corn borer.

Dorsett and Morse aimed at not only gathering strictly agricultural knowledge, such as on soybean varieties, their growing and harvesting as well as how to fight diseases, but also on ways of processing and marketing them. The search for methods of utilization of the soybean was particularly important on this trip.[47]

Given the strong Japanese presence in Manchuria at the time, which is outlaid in Chapter 2 of this book, it is hardly surprising that the two almost exclusively studied Japanese networks and facilities. They stopped at the experimental fields that the SMR operated along its tracks and reported on processing industries and further transportation facilities in Dalian. They took photographs of the production of tofu, soy sauce, miso paste, and candy, and studied the use of soybean cake as fertilizer or the processing of soybean oil into various industrial products. Dorsett and Morse brought or sent back home a total of 9,000 different seed samples, of which about 4,500 were soybean varieties; the remaining samples were other plants of potential value to American agriculture.

The work of farmers and scholars alike, either at their farms, through this journey, or the activities of the ASA, was crucial for further pushing the soybean into American agriculture. What was needed to establish the soybean in the Corn Belt were governmental actors and institutions, such as soy enthusiasts in the USDA, as well structures for communicating with farmers and scientists such as through the crop extension service and the ASA. In fact, it was not least thanks to the activities of the USDA that soybeans received more attention in the 1920s. However, while farmers began to grow soybeans to serve their own needs, a sales market for them still had to be found.

Marketing Soy: The Example of Illinois

In the 1920s, the ability to market soybeans from the Midwest was somewhat a vision of the future and an opportunity seen by only a few. Those in favor of marketing soy were not necessarily farmers, who preferred to keep the beans as seeds and feed, but by some institutions and companies focusing on the entire economic development of the region—among them the Illinois Central railroad company, the University of Illinois, the USDA, and several regional companies specialized in feed. In the spring of 1927, they joined forces to use a train for a rolling soybean exhibition and toured it around Illinois. The 35,000 visitors to the Soil and Soy Bean Special were given access to a wide range of information on soybeans, including illustrative materials, lectures, and film screenings. The aim of this was clear: As the train toured at the peak of the sowing season, farmers were to be convinced to try out soybeans. It is evident from the name of this special train that the focus still lay on the relationship between soy and soil, but that was only part of the story. The train exhibited numerous products made from soybean oil and also drew attention to how to market the soybean rather than using it merely as fertilizer and feed. It presented soybeans as a cash crop meant to be sold and processed.[48]

On board the train were exhibits and employees of the A.E. Staley Company, an oil mill from Decatur, Illinois. The company showcased over 30 consumer products it had made from soybean oil, including salad oils, glycerin, soap, glue, linoleum, paints, printing ink, and lubricating oil, all of which were touted as innovations in soy processing. The company had a firm interest in obtaining beans from the farmers for further processing—into oil for industrial purposes on the one side, and fodder to be sold back to the farmers on the other.

The head of the company, Augustus Eugene Staley, was a businessman who had started a flour mill specializing in corn and wheat processing in 1912. Ten years later he added an oil mill for soybeans but had hardly used it as soybeans were in short supply.[49] He was not necessarily the first entrepreneur to operate an oil mill in the Midwest, but he was one of the most successful over the long term. A later unreferenced business history claims that Staley continually promoted the growing of soybeans among farmers in the region in the 1920s in order to keep his oil mill running. Apparently, when farmers brought their wheat to him complaining about depleted soils, and poor harvests, he suggested an alternative in the form of soybeans as a cash crop. He presented them with outlets and distributed bulletins and other information issued by the USDA and the University of Illinois that provided them with the knowledge needed to grow the beans.[50]

Compared to other states, Illinois was very well developed in terms of transportation. A functioning infrastructure was generally important for the economic exploitation of any region, and, because they depended on it, railroad companies in turn had an interest in keeping trade flowing. Like the SMR in China, American railroad companies also participated in the regional development. They could secure business by committing to a region and it was in this context that what became known as "colleges on wheels" emerged.[51] Beginning in the early 1900s, railroads such as Illinois Central furnished special trains with displays, informational materials, and personnel to lecture on various agricultural issues. On the Illinois Central's network ran educational trains featuring corn farming, soil management, dairy farming, calf raising, or poultry farming. Staff from the company's own agriculture department worked closely with the College of Agriculture at the University of Illinois; they were involved in disseminating knowledge to farmers by holding events, demonstrations, and exhibits on various technical topics. So using a train for educational purposes was quite common, and equipping a train with material on soybeans fit well into this concept.[52]

H.J. Schwietert, who was employed as a developer at Illinois Central, supervised the Soil and Soy Bean Special. According to a contemporary newspaper clipping, Schwietert put forward the urgent need to revive American agriculture as the main reason for establishing the train. In an interview with the *Decatur Review* he emphasized that the United State's prosperity depended on the state of agriculture and therefore the problems of farmers affected businessmen, bankers, preachers, lawyers, politicians, and "above all, the American home." Referring to Illinois Central's commitment, he added ambiguously that the railroad was deeply interested in "in building up our agriculture along constructive lines."[53]

The University of Illinois and USDA promoted the train as well as other innovative forms of education against the backdrop of farmers often being reluctant to attend colleges or learn their trade from books. Enabled by the Smith-Lever Act, the USDA established regional model farms, opened extension services at state colleges and universities, hosted folk festivals and fairs on specific topics, and promoted some demonstration trains.[54] For the Soil and Soybean Special, various USDA staff members and agronomists from the University of Illinois rode along to lecture on their experiences with soybeans at the countless stops. Together with experts from the railroad company, they met with local farmers already familiar with the crop in order to demonstrate successes, discuss challenges, and convince those less inclined toward soy.[55]

Finally, the local press was also involved in this venture. The region's newspapers not only carried announcements about the specific stops but reported extensively on the potential of the "lowly bean," as several articles framed the crop.[56] The *Daily Free Press* of Carbondale was only one of many which commented on the connection between ailing agriculture and the economic future of the Midwest:

> In deciding to operate this train the Illinois Central has hit upon a most constructive program and especially one at this time when the farmer needs constructive suggestions in making his farming preparations more profitable than they have been during the past few years.[57]

In reference to the famous King Cotton in the southern United States, the *Dixon Evening Telegraph* even expressed hope the soybean one day would be king in the Corn Belt.[58] In retrospect, this hope sounds like a prophecy.

The Soil and Soy Bean Special once again illustrates the complex relationship between farmers, entrepreneurs, government officials, and academics that took on the task of advancing Midwestern agriculture and thus the entire American economy. Judging by the steady increase in crop production, the train, and the various other activities, were highly successful. By 1930, acreage devoted to soybean cultivation had more than doubled from 1.8 million acres in 1924 to 3 million acres. Likewise, there was a steady increase in acreage from which the crop was harvested rather than being left for grazing by cattle and later being plowed under. Whereas in 1924 the crop was being harvested from about a quarter of all cultivated areas, this proportion had grown to one-third in 1930.[59]

Gene Staley's calculations also paid off. By 1927, the company was dealing with 39 percent of all soybeans processed into oil in the United States, making it the largest soybean mill in the nation. Impressive as this sounds, Staley's success must nevertheless be put into perspective. For one, A.E. Staley was comparatively unrivaled because there were few other oil mills specialized in processing soybeans. For another, in the late 1920s farmers sent less than ten percent of their harvested beans to oil mills. They held back the greater part as silage for the winter months and seed for the coming year.[60] Considering soy's low use as an oil crop and thus a cash crop, the beans contributed only to negligible amounts to the nominal income of farmers. In 1924, soybean sales in Illinois accounted for only 0.2 percent of farmers' gross income. The figure increased only marginally in subsequent years, to 0.7 percent. Thus, soy had not truly yet become a cash crop.[61] In light of these numbers, it is no wonder that in 1927 William McArthur, the farmer I cited at the beginning of this chapter, does not even mention soybean processing.

There are three main reasons why Americans in the Midwest had comparatively little interest in soybean oil despite the combined efforts of governmental, private, and state actors. First, after the end of the war the demand for additional oil resources was low. Cheap domestic and imported oils were available to manufacturers of paints and varnishes, soaps, and margarine. These fat resources were mainly cottonseed and linseed. While in 1927, for example, only seven percent of all harvested soybeans went into oil production, 80 percent of all harvested cottonseed was destined for the same. Next to vegetable fats, the processing industries made use of lard and beef tallow and eventually had duty-free access to coconuts and copra from the Philippines.[62] There was insufficient demand to trigger the processing of soybeans into oil.

Another reason behind the initial reluctance to use soybeans as a resource for cheap vegetable oil was the poor state of processing industries in the Midwest. The southern states, with their long tradition of growing and processing cottonseed, were much better equipped and could have easily handled soybeans, but the Midwest was the wrong region to exploit soy as an oil crop. A.E. Staley remained the most important and largest soybean processing company in the United States until the 1950s because he had been unrivaled for so long. That also meant that there hardly was an interest group for the exchange of information and technology to push common interests further. The National Soybean Oil Manufacturers Association was only formed in 1930.[63] Other firms active in processing soybeans included Cargill, ADM, Allied Mills, and Spencer Kellogg & Sons, but in the 1920s they were yet to become business tycoons and soybeans were not yet among their key businesses.

The third reason for the narrow focus on soybeans as a feed and fertilizer crop was due to the initial difficulty of marketing soybean cake, the residue from the oil extraction process. Feed producers were reluctant to introduce new blends containing soy due to the cost of the approval process. Various states required proof of successful experiments with cattle, hogs, and poultry, which slowed the process and, more importantly, made it more expensive.[64] And while farmers were quite comfortable to feed their livestock silage made from homegrown soybeans or let them graze the fields, they were hesitant about using soybean cake. From their perspective, it seemed more economical to feed the beans directly to their livestock rather than buy back the residue from oil extraction as feed.

Agricultural and Industrial Change: New Deal and Chemurgy

When the Wall Street Crash of 1929 turned from a national financial crisis into a global economic downturn, U.S. President Herbert Hoover started a series of economic and social reforms which became commonly known as the New Deal. Agriculture, among many other policy areas, was also affected by these reforms. The best known in this respect is the Agricultural Adjustment Act (AAA) of 1933, a federal law designed to reduce surpluses. The aim of the resulting AAA program was to subsidize the cultivation of certain crops by bolstering prices, offering advantageous credits to farmers, and buying directly from the farms. It also imposed production controls to raise the value of those crops available in abundance. Although soybeans were not among the commodities explicitly addressed by the program, their cultivation expanded as a side effect of the limits on cotton, corn, wheat, and tobacco.

In the Midwest, regulations for corn were crucial for stimulating the expansion of soybean cultivation. The AAA program set limitations and allotments for the acreage of corn and so increased the farmland available to other crops. Soybeans competed effectively for a part in this acreage, with Illinois, Indiana, and Missouri being the states in which this measure was most effective.[65] Other states with similar developments were Tennessee and North Carolina, where restrictions on wheat and tobacco, respectively, opened up for more soybean cultivation.

Besides the AAA program, an important factor for increased acreage of soybeans particularly in and after 1934 was a severe drought that struck almost all regions in the northern United States. In the Midwest, it ruined large acreages of corn, small grains, and grass for hay production in the spring of 1934. In addition, a chinch bug infestation destroyed large parts of the wheat, oat, and corn harvests at around the same time. It was too late in the year to start over with the same crops, and farmers faced a severe downturn at a time long before the harvesting season.

Soybeans were not affected by the drought or the destructive insect, and the beans could still be sowed in this region after the summer solstice. In the South, the drought affected flax and cotton, making increased demand for affordable oil crops likely. In this situation, Midwestern farmers tried out soybeans as an emergency crop. The soybean network established in the 1920s in this region surely helped push soybeans into this situation. Many built on the positive experiences from earlier years or were able to connect with those who did have such experiences. In the years to come they would be encouraged to expand soybean cultivation by the regulations set in motion for other crops by the AAA program, and many decided to stick to devoting larger proportions of arable farmland to soybean production.[66] As a result, soy cultivation in the United States rose steadily from three million acres in 1930 to more than 11 million in 1940. Most of the beans were grown in the three Midwestern states of Illinois, Indiana, and Missouri.

In the mid-1930s, when the effects of the AAA program became more and more visible, not all soybeans planted were also harvested for their beans. In fact, harvesting the beans was partly not even intendet by the program's advisors. Just as in the decade before, many farmers in the 1930s cultivated soybeans purely to fortify the soil. The actual crop was then used for forage, either preserved as hay or silage, or cut and fed as green silage. Another option was to not harvest anything but have fields barely pastured with hogs and sheep, which on the one hand provided them with plentiful protein-rich fodder and on the other ensured the soil was in any case fertilized.[67] These practices explain why by 1939 not even half of all acreage planted with the crop was harvested for beans. Those beans that were harvested were then either kept as seed or sold on for further processing.[68]

While soil management was an important issue on any given farm, not all actors concerned with soybeans agreed on growing soybeans merely for soil improvement and as a forage crop. Those who tried to get more out of the crop were oil mills such as Staley of Illinois. Chemists working in various industrial and academic environments also pointed to the many possibilities of using soybean oil and proteins for chemical synthesis. In 1934, when the spring drought had already destroyed the prospects for harvesting the long-established crops, the Staley Company offered farmers a large discount on soybean seeds to solve their problems. Staley made this generous offer only under one condition, namely that the farmers subsequently harvested and sold the beans and did not feed them directly or keep them as hay.[69] It is doubtful to which degree Staley's efforts changed the farmers' habits of keeping the beans, but the company surely played a part in rising soybean cultivation in general. In any case, compared with other regions, in the years to come in the Midwest more soybeans were harvested for their beans, and with that for the production of oil and fodder. In 1939 the share was already at 55 percent of all farmland planted with soybeans, and this rose further in subsequent years. By the time the United States entered the Second World War, about 82 percent of all acreage planted with the soybean in the Midwest was also harvested and sold on.[70]

Once harvested and sold, soybeans were first and foremost crushed into their main components. The oil was mainly used to make margarine, shortening, soap, and paints, while the residue served as fodder. Compared to Germany, this pattern was established slightly later, though. As shown in Chapter 3, German oil millers obtained large quantities of Manchurian-grown soybeans in the interwar period, particularly from 1925 onward, and processed them to serve the country's demand in vegetable oils and fodder. In the U.S., on the other hand, it was only the AAA program and the severe drought of 1934 and again in 1936 that led to increased soy cultivation and with that also increased efforts to extract oil from the beans. Oil mills, which mushroomed in the Midwest as a result of these developments, fostered soybean cultivation further, and once farmers had been convinced to market their beans the pattern of crushing the beans first and then distributing them as intermediate products was not reversed.

In the early 1930s, most soybean oil went into the drying industry—that is, the production of paints—followed by the manufacture of soap. However, from 1935 onward and in response to the Depression and the drought, which also affected the production of cottonseed, there was a large increase in the proportions used for food purposes. While at the beginning of the decade less than 4,500 tons of soybean oil found use in food products, by 1935 this had increased to over 27,000 tons, and 68,000 tons the year thereafter. From then on, most soybean oil was used in the production of shortening and margarine, and other food items made of it were salad dressings and mayonnaise, and eventually also lecithin.[71] The increased demand particularly for shortening and margarine came about through shortages in other domestic commodities such as lard and cottonseed oil, which were affected by the regulations of the AAA. In other words, on the American market soybean oil became a product for human nutrition by means of governmental responses to agricultural and economic challenges in the early 1930s.

As interesting as this insight might be, soybean oil still played a comparatively small part in the total domestic industry in fats and oils. Cottonseed oil continued to dominate the edible-oil market despite all measures on the national level to curtail cotton production. Even in 1936, when consumption of soybean oil reached a peak, more than half of all factory-made food items based on fat stemmed from cottonseed oil, while only 6.5 percent was from soybean oil. The reason for this was also that soybean oil had its shortcomings, as it had a tendency to acquire an unpleasant flavor over time. Thus, even by the end of the decade, soybean oil was still considered a substitute, and shortening and margarine based on it were more affordable compared to others and were considered lower-grade products. American oil mills solved this problem only after the Second World War.[72]

Finally, soybean oil was also used for the production of various other consumer goods. The only thing that united this group of products was that they were not food. Candles, celluloid, glycerin, organic fuels, linoleum, lubricants, oilcloth, printing ink, rubber substitutes, and many others required fat for their production, but they did not rely specifically on soybean oil. In turn, the amount of soybean oil used in their manufacture varied widely but was nowhere near the figures for the production of shortening, margarine, paint, or soap.[73]

Just as in Germany, the residue from the milling process served as feed for livestock. Sure enough, also American farmers were first concerned about the quality of the meat and feared effects on the color and taste of milk and butter when feeding soybeans to their cattle. However, this uncertainty in handling the novel feed disappeared soon after experiments initiated by the USDA, which resulted in differentiated feeding instructions.[74] It did not take long to convince farmers that soybean cake—or meal, as it was now called due to different processing methods—had an excellent capacity for producing muscle tissue. Contemporary sources estimated that in the immediate pre-war years, nearly all of the product, about 90–98 percent, was used as fodder.

The remaining, comparatively small percentage gained uses in three other areas—industrial products, mixed fertilizer, and edible soybean flour. Even though the latter received some public attention in the form of recipe books and advertisements, this sector remained rather insignificant. No more than one percent of all soybean meal was processed to flour and destined for human consumption. Even during the war it never climbed over three percent.[75] In mixed fertilizers, soybeans were used to ensure farmers were able to conduct good soil management. Eventually, soybean meal was used in industrial products, a sector which encompassed specialized commodities such as certain glues, molding compounds, plastics, paper coatings, and foam solutions, among others. The industrial uses of soybean meal in these novel ways have attracted much attention, both contemporarily and in historical writing, but in terms of the actual use of soybean meal, this field remained comparatively small.[76]

The interest in soybean meal for a variety of industrial uses came about by what was then called chemurgy, a term referring to the chemical and industrial use of domestically produced agricultural raw materials. As a consequence of the agricultural downturn and the economic crisis the United States was facing, some agriculturalists, chemists, farmers, industrialists, and policy makers became interested in transforming the country's agriculture into a source for more chemical components for consumer commodities instead of as a source for food alone. In this context, chemurgy became a magic word at the time.[77] Guided by the aspiration to make the American economy more autarchic from imports of certain crucial raw materials such as rubber, chemurgy's advocates campaigned for more chemical research on domestic agricultural products and their possible uses in industry. The Chemurgic Council, founded in 1935, had the protectionist ambition to revive U.S. agriculture and reduce the country's dependence upon foreign sources of industrial raw materials. The movement encouraged industrial and governmental interest not only in new uses of various plants with which Americans have long been familiar but also in those less familiar to the country. Soybeans were among the plants that it found promising.[78]

Despite being quite influential, chemurgy was rather an expression of a certain *zeitgeist* and never became more than a loose network of people sharing the same idea of making the country more independent from imports by using domestic crops and their waste products more effectively. However, the spirit of chemurgy had an influence on various research institutions and their agenda, particularly in Illinois. In 1938 the USDA established four so-called Regional Research Laboratories, which conducted little research on agriculture and chemistry themselves but instead awarded research contracts to companies. Together with several private firms, the northern laboratory in Peoria, Illinois explored the uses of soybean oil and soybean meal for industrial uses.[79] Less than a hundred miles away, in Urbana, a Regional Soybean Industrial Laboratory had been founded in 1936. It was set up in cooperation with Urbana's State Experiment Station, which also fostered research on soybeans.

One of the best-known representatives of the chemurgic movement was Henry Ford. He developed his own agricultural trials and laboratories, attempting to ascertain the potential of converting botanical oils into plastic and rubber for applications in the automobile industry. The most conspicuous outcome of his experiments was the presentation of a soy car in 1942, the body of which was comprised entirely of plant-based derivatives.[80] These visionary plans were purely speculative, though, as their further development was prohibited when the U.S. entered into the war.

While Ford worked on various domestically grown crops, the Glidden Company of Illinois invested in more direct research on soybeans. The company got its start in the nineteenth century with linseed milling and the production of paints. In 1920, Glidden also created a food processing branch, and it was in this context that the company invested heavily in research on soybeans. In 1934 it opened a soybean oil extraction plant in Chicago which also manufactured lecithin. For that purpose, it had obtained a patent from the Hamburg-based Hansa-Mühle. A few years later, and inspired by the chemurgy movement, the company claimed to be the "pacemaker in soya research." It pioneered the isolation of the proteins found in soybean meal. These "servants of industry," as a marketing brochure called them, were sold under the brand name Alpha Protein, the main use of which was in the coating of printing paper and wallpaper, among other applications.[81]

Finally, a poem dedicated to the soybean is telling for the spirit of chemurgy. In 1944, Mrs. J.W. Hayward presented the readers of the *Chemurgic Digest,* a specialized periodical for experts on questions of how to obtain more than food from agricultural products, a piece of poetry entitled "Little soybean who are you?" The following rhymes answered the question by pointing to key aspects in the most recent history of the soybean and the many products potentially resulting from them. Besides the obvious—foodstuffs, soaps, paints, and fodder—she listed rubber substitutes, early plastics, glue, and many others. She offered no explanation for her intention in writing and publishing the little poem, but the piece's obvious purpose was to foster a greater understanding and knowledge about soybeans beyond strictly scientific circles.[82] As such, she was supporting the efforts and work of her husband, who was director of the nutritional research division at ADM from Minnesota. ADM had also once started out in linseed milling and the production of paints and varnishes, but became specialized in food processing over time and, by the 1930s, was investing heavily in research on soybeans.

As spectacular as the findings of Ford, Glidden, ADM, and other research regarding soy were, they remained rather marginal in the overall soybean picture. The growth in soy cultivation in the 1930s had certainly stimulated industrial research about soy derivatives, and this research may in turn have had some influence on pushing the cultivation rates even higher. Thus, this group of actors helped to promote the still rather unfamiliar plant, and their enthusiasm may have affected people beyond farmers and scientists. Nevertheless, the actual use of soybeans for industrial purposes remained minor. Instead, much of the increase in soybean acreage and harvests that occurred in U.S. agriculture in the 1930s was of an "emergency nature," as one contemporary analyst put it.[83] In fact, governmental programs such as the AAA and unusual weather conditions such as the droughts of 1934 and 1936 led to the increasing uptake of the crop. It was the challenge of providing people with enough fats that led to the American government keeping an eye on soybeans as a solution to meet these challenges and, as a result, expand the crop's cultivation further.

"Soybeans Are a War Crop": Developments in the Second World War

In 1947, Walter W. Wilcox, an agronomist at the University of Wisconsin, retrospectively evaluated U.S. soybean production during the Second World War and stated that "had it not been for our general knowledge and success in growing soybeans, [the] wartime increase in fats would have been largely limited to the expansion in lard production, and far more severe rationing of food fats would have been required." Similar accounts are to be found elsewhere too. In 1950, the Chicago Board of Trade wrote about soybeans:

> During the past decade, an almost unbelievable amount of research on soybeans has been conducted by various educational institutions and trade and industrial organizations. Their prime objective was the growing of better oil-producing soybeans and more of them per acre.

Missouri agricultural experts even considered soybeans a "war crop," relevant for winning the war.[84] Such statements about the importance of soybeans in wartime open for questions about the actual relevance, use, and consumption of the crop during the period.

In fact, the long-term success of the soybean in the U.S. is closely tied to the history of the war and that of official regulations. Increases in soybean cultivation and consumption were initiated by the Roosevelt Administration on the advice of agricultural experts in the USDA. Measures began in the summer of 1941 with the goal to secure sufficient food supplies in the event of war. After the Second World War, however, the soybean did not simply vanish from the fields. On the contrary, its cultivation was extended so much that today it is among the country's most important crops and is still primarily grown in the Midwest. By 1970, the soybean ranked second to corn in terms of agricultural production value in the country, and still holds this position today.[85] This development had its origin in wartime, when Americans faced shortages in fats and meat.

Food products constituted about two-thirds of all fat usage before the war. This included butter, which alone accounted for 20 percent of the total fat usage, and lard, which came to 16 percent, as well as margarine, salad oils, frying and baking fats, mayonnaise, and the like. The remaining third of total fat usage went into a rather heterogeneous group of consumer products and industrial goods. These included household articles such as soap or candles and various industrial products such as paints and varnishes, linoleum, waterproof materials, food tins, and dynamite.[86] Besides being non-food items, they did not share much in common apart from them requiring fat either as part of the final product or during the production process, and all being vital to both civilian and military needs. People needed to wash; paints and varnishes offered protection against erosion and weathering on all sorts of machines, including defense matériel; food cans also needed protection against erosion to keep provisions fresh. For all these purposes, vegetarian and animal raw materials were in great demand, and soy became an increasing focus of interest because it contained oil and was easy to grow. Although the products mentioned here are not necessarily based on fats of organic origin, petroleum had not yet become sufficiently accessible at that time and was also only available in limited quantities. For this reason, even wartime experiments to produce an alternative fuel during the Second World War were based on organic raw materials. Today, the result is better known as biodiesel, but it was already being researched at the time due to the scarcity of petroleum supplies.[87]

In the United States about half of all fats used in the 1930s for these various purposes were of animal origin, coming from cows, pigs, or, to a minor degree, whales. Another 35 percent came from vegetable sources, with cottonseed being the most important domestic oil crop, followed by flaxseed, peanuts, and also soybeans. About 15 percent of the required raw materials was imported, either from South America (about five percent) or from Asia (about ten percent). Fatty raw materials from the latter usually included copra from the Philippines and palm hearts from the Dutch East Indies and Malaysia.[88] It was from these tropical resources that the United States was cut off after the attack on Pearl Harbor in December 1941, and their loss weighed heavily since their excellent applicability in certain processing operations was vital to the war effort. Palm hearts, palm oil and copra contained comparatively large amounts of glycerin, which was needed for the production of nitroglycerine and thus dynamite. In addition, palm oil was particularly suitable as an anti-corrosion agent for food cans, which was central to providing the military with sufficient food rations.

Being at war in the Pacific meant not only that the United States was cut off from high-glycerin oils for the production of explosives but also from its main sources of natural rubber. Rubber served both military and civilian needs because it was vital to the production of tires for cars, bicycles, and airplanes, and was therefore also in high demand. There were experiments running worldwide regarding synthetic rubber, and American scientists were actively engaged in this research. Besides being of lower quality compared to natural rubber, however, synthetic rubber came with the disadvantage that it was based on fats, especially those from tropical regions.[89] Thus, taking the production of war materials into consideration, the shortage of vegetable oils from Southeast Asia was more serious than the aforementioned 10 percent might initially suggest.

Among foodstuffs, sugar and meat were particularly affected, closely followed by fats. Other commodities with limited availability included petroleum and rubber, making gasoline and automobile tires scarce and expensive. These shortages were by no means comparable to those in other countries. No other warring country, for example, had more meat available per capita than the United States during the war, but the public's fear of potential shortages, as well as the resultant hoarding, on the one hand played a major role in ensuring that the shortages actually occurred and on the other that prices for the goods in question skyrocketed.[90] Prices for fats in the United States had risen by an average of 40 percent during the year of 1940, which exceeded the average price increases many times over.[91]

Thus, from the summer of 1941 onward, measures were taken to avert dependencies on imports. These actions affected many more commodities than fat, as the war disrupted international trading routes and limited the supply of raw materials and manufactured goods worldwide. However, management of the supplies of fat for civilian and military needs was pivotal for the soybean becoming a crop of major significance in the United States. In June 1941, the Steagall Amendment to the AAA was passed. It required price supports for those agricultural products of which the supply was affected by the war at 85 percent of parity, and thus promoted their domestic production. The so-called Steagall crops essentially included commodities that contained fat and protein, including milk, butter, eggs, and hogs as animal-based foods, and peanuts, soybeans, and flaxseed as field crops. Besides these, a few other crops vital for human nutrition were supported, such as green beans and potatoes. The Stabilization Act, which followed two years later, expanded and extended the subsidies that had been introduced, and through this measure, the lucrative support prices ultimately remained in force until the end of 1948.[92]

These legislative changes cleared the way for the extensive cultivation of soybeans, and, compared with the other crops and commodities, it was the soybean that experienced the greatest and most enduring growth as a result. By the spring of 1941, the area planted with soybeans had reached about ten million acres. Thanks to the Steagall Amendment this rose to nearly 14 million acres in the following year, an increase of more than a third in just one year. The rise led to a tremendous difference in the supply of soybeans, and with that fat. In 1941, American farmers harvested a total of 2.9 million tons, and in the following year 5.1 million tons. This was the greatest annual increase in soybean cultivation since records for the acreage and harvesting of the crop had begun.

Even though a significant amount of the harvest had to be kept as seeds, the supply of soybeans in the United States was much higher than that Germans had at their disposal at the time. In 1941, the last year Germany received shipments from Manchuria, export figures were at just one million tons (see Chapter 3).

During the war and in the immediate postwar period, the acreage planted with soybeans in the United States remained constant or declined slightly due to adverse weather conditions. What continuously went up, however, were the figures for harvested beans, as more and more farmers marketed them as a result of government price subsidies. By 1944, three-fourths of all acreage planted with soybeans were eventually harvested, compared to not even half of the beans planted in 1939. The five Corn Belt states of Illinois, Iowa, Indiana, Ohio, and Missouri accounted for 70 percent of the total acreage planted and 84 percent of the acreage harvested for beans.[93] As a consequence, Americans had ever more soybeans at their disposal.

For processing companies, a deal with the government was equally appealing as for farmers. Oil mills were offered contracts with the Commodity Credit Corporation, a financing institution for the USDA's various programs for stabilizing, supporting, and protecting farm income and prices. The contracts provided that the corporation took in all soybean products and protected oil mills against price drops. In this way, companies like Staley were encouraged to purchase and process as many soybeans as possible. Although the company lamented that those governmental controls had "greatly restricted the exercise of ingenuity and business judgement," it admitted that the regulations had positively affected the company's profit: "It has assured us of reasonable profits and has eliminated a substantial amount of risk from the business."[94] With all these incentives in place, the soybean quickly gained a firm place in American agriculture and industry.

Besides the soybean, flax and peanuts were also oil crops whose cultivation was subsidized by the Steagall Amendment, with the increase in peanut acreage in the southern states of Virginia, North Carolina, Alabama, Georgia, and Florida being especially notable.[95] During wartime, peanuts were mainly used in their established ways as food. About 75 percent of the harvest was processed into peanut butter, salted peanuts, and confectionery, and as such played an important role in providing fat to soldiers and the civilian population alike.[96] In contrast to peanuts, however, attempts to expand the cultivation of flax were mostly unsuccessful, probably more due to ingrained consumer habits than to farmers. In contemporary sources, linseed oil was often described as an unpopular product due to its harsh taste, thus hardly any outlets were found for the product and the support program for the cultivation of flax was discontinued in 1943.

Managing Consumption

The Steagall Amendment was soon accompanied by detailed restrictions on the distribution of various raw materials, and they were followed by new administrative institutions. As fats were one of the United States' few more severe shortages during the war, almost the entire market was soon regulated. To counter inflationary price increases, the Office of Price Administration (OPA) was established in August 1941. It was the central government agency used to levy price controls on food, consumer goods, and rents. The OPA established a rationing system with ration books as early as May 1942, but it was not until the next year that fat was included.[97] In early 1943, the purchase of canned goods was curtailed due to the shortage of fatty raw materials which were central to the coating of cans and the need to make the remaining reserves available for food provisions at the front. Then, as of April 1, 1943, meat, cheese, and fats, including butter and lard, were added to the rationing system and could now only be obtained through food stamps.[98]

Beginning in late December 1941, the Office of Emergency Management for the first time issued quotas on fatty resources from the Pacific region, which were soon followed by additional so-called priority orders which regulated the market. The War Production Board (WPB), which took on planning for the American war economy in January 1942, henceforth also regulated fats.[99] The WPB obtained information from the USDA on all fats still available and evaluated the needs for civilian supplies, wartime production, and U.S. obligations to its Allies. The board relied heavily on the expertise of the USDA, which conducted analyses and made various recommendations regarding restrictions and channeling of available supplies.[100]

Combined, these institutions regulated the market for fats and oils with the main goal to save tropical oils for the technical and military sector. Simultaneously, they were to avoid shortages among private households by channeling domestic oil reserves into the civilian food sector. Coconut, palm, and palm kernel oil, for example, were no longer permitted in the production of margarine and shortening. Palm oil was only to be used in the production of tinplate for cans. Coconut oil extracted from copra, on the other hand, went into the production of soap because it produced glycerin as a byproduct, which was further processed into nitroglycerin. Interestingly, the fact that glycerin was obtained as a byproduct in the manufacture of beauty products such as soaps, creams, and lipsticks may explain why American women hardly ever had to do without cosmetics during the war. As an expression of their patriotism, they were even encouraged to wear makeup, as Geoffrey Jones has shown. That, however, was only possible with adequate supplies of resources, which usually meant fat.[101]

Even though food shortages in the United States were by no means as severe as in other parts of the world such as the plundered regions of Eastern Europe, even the Americans experienced some war-related shortfalls. In the summer of 1942, city dwellers were called upon to make an active contribution to solving the supply problem of fat. Initiated by the USDA, a campaign was launched in numerous major cities such as Chicago, Atlanta, New York, Baltimore, and Washington, DC, to encourage private households to save old frying and baking fats so that they could be reused in the manufacture of dynamite. "Save waste fats for explosives" was a major campaign in which an active contribution by private households to solving the supply problem was also seen as an expression of civilian patriotism. Its success is doubtful, but the campaign, which lasted until 1945, likely helped to anchor the problem in the public's mind.[102]

The domestically produced oils from soybeans, peanuts, and flax were largely directed to the civilian food sector. They were intended to alleviate shortages resulting from tropical commodity restrictions and scarcities in butter, which was reserved in large quantities for the military. Thus, most soybeans obtained thanks to the government's appeal and program went into the production of shortening and margarine, which in turn meant that the amount of soybean oil in these products rose. During the war, shortening and margarine were made up by about 40 percent by weight of soybean oil. While the use of soybean oil in food was supported, its use for industrial purposes was restricted. In 1943, 79 percent of the domestic production was used for edible products, mainly shortening and margarine.[103] Thus, also Ford's fantastic soy car, for example, became a casualty of restrictive practices as the governmental regulation of vegetable oils and fats as foodstuffs was prohibitive to the industrial designs on soy oil.

Such technological fallbacks notwithstanding, the soybean benefitted broadly from the governmental measures taken to attend to wartime needs. Contemporary sources speak of 100 million U.S. dollars in subsidies for this crop alone, which accounted for various subsidies regarding its cultivation and processing.[104] To ensure that enough beans could be processed, new mills had to be built and existing ones extended or converted. Support for this ensured that by early 1944 about 100 oil mills had begun specializing in soybean processing, most of them located in the Midwest, and nearly 40 mills were still in the planning.[105]

Despite all these measures, the situation remained complex, and the problem only partly solved. Although the cultivation of soybeans had increased massively and there was potentially sufficient oil available, it flowed only slowly into the production of margarine or baking and frying fats. This was mainly due to the strong odor of soybean oil and an unpleasant aftertaste no company had yet been able to eliminate. Consumers were reluctant to buy products based on soybean oil, and food companies tried to avoid using it as well. Eventually, the oil was largely bought up by the government, which then channeled it into margarine production at large discounts. It was only as a result of this measure that, from 1943 onward, about 132 million gallons per year flowed into the production of margarine and other food fats compared with just under 80 million gallons the year before.[106] The harsh aftertaste of margarine and other products based on soybean oil remained and probably contributed to Americans' perception of soybean as an inferior substitute product.

The problem was only solved after the war. In the summer of 1945, chemist Warren H. Goss, who worked at USDA's Northern Regional Research Center in peacetime but was in the service of the U.S. Army during the war, was commissioned to investigate the state of the oilseed industry in Germany. It was here that Goss learned about how to eliminate the taint and happily made the process available in the United States as well.[107] It was, after all, an even more refined version of Bollmann's method.

Soybean Flour: War-related Necessity or Revolutionary Food?

Without soybean oil, Americans would undoubtedly have faced further food restrictions and rationing. However, a focus on fat ignores an essential aspect regarding soybeans, and that is the utilization of the residue of the milling process. An outcome of the increased production of soybean oil was the use of soybean meal as animal feed and rising livestock production. Thus, with increasing soybean cultivation, Americans automatically had more feed and with that meat at their disposal. In addition, just as in Germany, during the war the U.S. war administration discovered the benefits of using soybean flour for human nutrition. From the late 1930s onward,

USDA specialists, food companies, and nutritionists started to disseminate knowledge about the flour and other soy-based foods, but the various products were rarely seen as attractive as either a vegetable or meat substitute. Comprehensive compendiums, recipe books, and brochures on varieties suitable for human consumption were published to inform merchants, consumers, and farmers alike, but the public remained skeptical.[108] While soybean flour was considered healthy and nutritious, providing the human body with valuable and cheap proteins and solving war-related shortages in meats and fats, customers still would not buy it.

A governmental agency engaged in rising the consumption of soybean flour in private households was the War Food Administration (WFA), which the Roosevelt administration created in April 1943 under the USDA. In theory, it was to be the central agency where all aspects of war-related food issues previously dispersed among different offices, institutions, and commissions converged. In practice, however, the idea of pooling all food issues in wartime was only partially successful because two central areas were not under the control of the WFA. These were all aspects relating to the supply of food to the military, and issues of price controls and rationing which remained in the responsibility of the OPA, an independent agency within the Roosevelt Administration. While in collective American memory the WFA is best remembered for its work regarding the introduction of school lunches, it held quite a significant number of responsibilities, among others the settling of allocation issues among the Allies.[109] In addition, the WFA published on balanced diets in times of war-related shortages, offered training to American housewives on food preservation, and designed programs to adjust eating habits according to the strictures of the war economy. While the OPA rationed meat beginning in early April 1943, for instance, the WFA promoted the alternative use of soybean flour, which was intended to provide an adequate supply of protein for the population.

Besides promoting the consumption of soybean flour, the WFA was engaged in increasing the pure availability of the product. The agency called for an increase in its production to 680,000 tons per year. To ensure this, it assisted soy-processing companies to be classified by the War Department as essential to the war effort. Once they obtained that status, firms were eligible for subsidies which enabled them to expand or rebuild their plants to meet the needs of war. Staley's company from Decatur, Illinois, was one of those that took up the offer. Staley introduced soybean flour under the brand name Stoy in the summer of 1943. Supported by the WFA and subsidized by the War Department, Staley built a new processing plant, which began operations by producing Stoy in January 1944. As promising as the plan sounded, it was ultimately of limited success. Only three months later, Staley reported that the government had not yet requisitioned all the soy flour it had expected to purchase. Accordingly, it was doubtful to what extent the new plant would ever reach full utilization.

Nevertheless, Staley was confident about its new product. The company's house journal stated that Stoy was a largely unknown product and that its introduction would have to be accompanied by extensive marketing campaigns. Besides newspaper advertisements, the company had also contracted for a serial radio program appearing on 174 stations of the Blue Network, a radio network owned by the National Broadcasting Company. Thus, news about the product was spread throughout the Midwest and also to the large cities on the East Coast. Eventually, there was also a special booklet on soybeans and soy flour available. It held the bold subtitle *The Story of a Revolutionary and Important Development in the History of American Foods*, indicating that soy was the most adaptable foodstuff of the future. Besides recipes and photographs, the booklet included comparison tables designed to convince consumers of the equivalence of animal proteins to those of the soybean.[110]

While Staley tried to market soybean flour as a futuristic food item highly valuable to human nutrition due to its high content in fat and proteins, others were more skeptical about soybean flour as a savory foodstuff. In 1944, Demetria M. Taylor, author of several recipe and household books, wrote a 200-page *Soy Cook Book* that was explicitly labeled a "wartime book." In the preface she wrote, "It took a global war, with consequent food shortages, to arouse this nation to the possibilities of using soybeans to supplement and substitute for the protein foods that are rationed, scarce, or expensive."[111] She left no doubt that soy proteins are comparable to those of animal origin in terms of chemical composition and nutritional value. Nevertheless, she emphasized the fundamental nature of soy flour as a substitute product, not as one with its own qualities.

It is difficult to say if Americans appreciated the benefits of soy after all, either as a substitute or as a food item in its own right. This is mainly because adequate data is missing. What seems to be telling, however, is that in the late 1930s, just about one percent of all soybean meal was processed into flour for human consumption. Even during the war it was never more than three percent.[112] Apparently, there was a discrepancy between the actual consumption of soybean flour, which remained rather insignificant, and the perception of soybeans in American, particular Midwestern, agriculture and economy. Changing food habits by prescription is a challenging endeavor, even in times of need, as contemporary research has shown. Even meat consumption did not decline during the war. Despite rationing measures, Americans had actually enlarged their annual consumption of meat from 58 to 68 kilogram per capita.[113] "Never before in the long and colorful history of American agriculture can it be said that any grain, cereal or legume—and their various products and by-products—has assumed anywhere nearly [sic] the degree of prominence," wrote the Chicago Board of Trade—which had traded soy since 1936—on the short history of the soybean in the early 1950s.[114] That was aptly put, but the prominence was one related to agriculture and industry, not to soybeans as food. Instead, any effort to establish soybeans or soybean flour as a savory foodstuff in the United States was a rather unsuccessful endeavor.

What saw greater success was sending vast amounts of soybean flour abroad as aid shipments. The flour, together with a product called soybean grits and whole soybeans, were sent abroad under the Lend-Lease policy, which came about in 1941. Long before the war, lessons from the First World War spurred experts in the USDA as well as in other U.S. authorities to monitor the civilian supply of food not only at home but also worldwide.[115] They knew that modern wars were not only about fighting the enemy at the front but also supplying the soldiers with food and helping avoid starvation among desperate and fleeing people. Formal ground for supplying the Allies and neutral countries with fuel, matériel, and food was thus laid through the Lend-Lease Act in March 1941. Aid included warships and warplanes along with other weaponry, but agricultural commodities were also explicitly defined as defense articles. The act gave the U.S. president authority to procure them from but also provide them to any country deemed "vital to the defense of the United States."[116] In addition to Lend-Lease, international planning and coordination was strengthened during the war, which found its best expression in the emergence of UNRRA, the United Nations Relief and Rehabilitation Administration. Among others, the organization was engaged in coordinating the global supply of food, with meats as well as fats forming a significant share among a variety of other commodities in regions that were newly liberated and in the immediate postwar years. After all, it was through either Lend-Lease or UNRAA shipments that large amounts of soybeans and products made of them left the country.

Instrumental in coordinating these shipments was the Combined Food Board (CFB) and its forerunner the Anglo-American Food Committee. The latter was an intergovernmental agency founded in May 1941 with the intention to coordinating food assistance to the British by budgeting food, planning, and actually programming total supplies according to both countries' needs.[117] To raise the committee's relevance, both governments revised and transformed it into the CFB in June 1942. This body had more direct access to the executive branch of the U.S. government and was put under the direct control of the WFA. It was formed "to co-ordinate and obtain a planned and expeditious utilization of the food resources of the United Nations" and was supposed to pay special attention to foodstuffs in short supply, which were defined as sugar, meats, as well as fats and oils.[118] In practice, the CFB made recommendations regarding the international allocation of food and food-related machinery, as well as the distribution of the supply. It did the groundwork for purchase agreements and recommended shifts in worldwide production in light of needs.

During the war, the CFB made detailed recommendations on how to allocate the potentially available foodstuffs among interested parties worldwide, but the actual distribution followed its own path. That was partly due to an extremely tight shipping situation which required ad-hoc decisions and adjustments. Further difficulties were that responsibilities for food distribution on the U.S. side were anything but clear. In November 1943, President Roosevelt devolved authority for shipping food and other relief commodities to the military, which in turn also claimed responsibility for planning and allocation.[119] Even though the WFA, of which the CFB was a part, was supposed to be the major agency dealing with food supplies during the war, a set of civilian and military agencies were involved in foreign food distribution, such as the Department of State, the WPB, the OPA, the War Shipping Administration, the Office of Foreign Agricultural Relations, and the Foreign Economic Administration.[120] Nevertheless, the CFB was the main body behind the planning of governmental allocations and shipments to be sent abroad for support and relief.

The yearly amount of soybeans and associated products sent under this umbrella varied widely, for instance from 11,200 tons of soybean flour and grits in 1942 to 81,500 tons the following year, back to 35,700 tons in 1944 and 19,800 tons in 1945. The same is true for whole soybeans, which reached an absolute peak in 1945, when 166,000 tons of unprocessed beans left the country for overseas support.[121] There were many reasons for the fluctuations, such as the availability of shipping, transportation costs, and general supply of commodities. Aid shipping was last in line for food distribution, as the bulk of all American supplies was generally reserved for the armed forces, followed by American civilians, with only the remaining surplus then directed toward people elsewhere. Whole soybeans were the only vegetable oil-bearing, unprocessed raw material that left the country for Lend-Lease and relief, which was certainly due to Americans' general lack of familiarity with the crop.

Regarding the precise destinations of these shipments, agricultural statistics are less explicit than those for regular exports. We know, for instance, how much the WFA bought of a certain commodity and, in most cases, how much of it was made available for Lend-Lease shipments. Government statistics do not reveal, however, where in the world the food went, and further difficulties in tracing the shipments arise because the British tended to trade their Lend-Lease goods. In any case, soybean meal found an outlet rather in American food supplies to its allies and neutral states than in domestic consumption.

Conclusion

While agriculturalists and other scientists were enthusiastic about soy as a crop for American agriculture from early on, it does not seem that farmers necessarily shared their passion. Rather, soy entered Midwestern farms due to pure necessity, either in the aftermath of the First World War, during the Great Depression, or in response to wartime needs in the course of the Second World War. In the First World War, soybeans were to a small degree planted as an oil crop in some southern states but vanished quickly from

Americans' farms in the immediate postwar years. In the 1920s, American agriculture simultaneously faced overproduction and declining markets, which resulted in depleted soils, crop failure, and poverty among farmers. It was in this situation that scientists and officials in the USDA paid more attention to soy and presented it as a solution to these domestic problems. The beans were not intended to be sold and milled but rather to nourish depleted soils with nitrogen, which then allowed better yields in other crops and thus better incomes for farmers. Although by the late 1920s an increasing number of farmers were growing soybeans, the beans were still far from assuming any significant economic standing.

It was in response to the Great Depression that soy made a bigger entrance into American agriculture, particularly in the Corn Belt. The rise came about as a secondary effect of the first AAA of 1933, a major New Deal program to restore agricultural prosperity by curtailing farm production, reducing export surpluses, and raising prices. Soy's transition into an oil crop and thus a crop of monetary value was also the result of the 1930s, but even more so of developments during the Second World War. Throughout the war, Americans faced shortages of fat, and the soybean oil was used to substitute fats that were in short supply in the production of margarine and shortening. Similar to the first two surges in cultivation in the 1920s and 1930s, it was a time of crisis that drove soybean cultivation and consumption upward. During the war, the United States became the world's largest producer of soybeans. Soybean fields now covered the Midwest, so that for the United States the former Asian alien quickly became a common crop on their fields. This development came about because government institutions enacted subsidy measures and intervened in a controlling manner in the mechanisms of supply and demand. Simultaneously, soy became Americanized. It was adapted to the needs of the American war economy, which was primarily interested in the oil it contained; all other uses were of secondary importance.

In the long run, soybeans may have entered the country's agriculture to a larger degree anyway, but without wartime efforts to supply Americans with enough fat resources, the United States would not have become globally the largest region for growing soybeans by the end of the war, and soybeans may not have become a cash crop for American farmers at this time.

Notes

1 William McArthur, "Ten Years of Soybean Experience," *Wallaces' Farmer* 52, no. 16 (April 22, 1927): 6 and no. 17 (April 29, 1927): 6.

2 Edwin G. Strand, *Soybean Production in War and Peace* (Report, U.S. Department of Agriculture, Bureau of Agricultural Economics, Washington, DC, September 1945), 2.

3 Anonymous, "Dyer's Pork and Beans," *The American Food Journal* (May 1917): 270; Anonymous, "Dyer's Pork and Beans," *The American Food Journal* (September 1917): 505.

4 U.S. Department of Agriculture, *Use Soy-bean Flour to Save Wheat, Meat and Fat,* Office of the Secretary, Circular no. 13 (Washington, DC: USDA, 1918) 1, 4.
5 When founded, the BPI had about 200 employees. The divisions included, among others, the government experimental farm in Arlington, VA. Harold T. Pinkett "Records of the First Century of Interest of the United States Government in Plant Industries," *Agricultural History* 29 (1955): 38–45.
6 Charles V. Piper and William J. Morse, *The Soy Bean: With Special Reference to Its Utilization for Oil, Cake, and other Products*, U.S. Department of Agriculture, Bulletin no. 439 (Washington, DC: 1916). Other early publications include Charles V. Piper and H.T. Nielsen, *Soy Beans* (Washington, DC: Government Printing Office, 1909); Charles V. Piper and William J. Morse, *The Soy Bean: History, Varieties and Field Studies,* Bulletin of the Bureau of Plant Industry no. 197 (Washington, DC: Government Printing Office, 1910); William J. Morse, *Harvesting the Soy Bean Seed*, Washington, DC: USDA, 1917; William Morse, *The Soy Bean: Its Culture and Uses*, USDA, Farmers' Bulletin no. 973 (Washington, DC: Government Printing Office, 1918); William J. Morse and Herbert B. Hendrick, *Illustrated Lecture on Soy Beans* (Washington, DC, 1919); for details on Morse's and Piper's work in the 1910s see Matthew Roth, *Magic Bean: The Rise of Soy in America* (Lawrence, KS: University Press of Kansas, 2018), 41–49.
7 Piper, Morse, *The Soy Bean: With Special Reference,* 7–8.
8 Piper, Morse, *The Soy Bean: With Special Reference,* 1; As early as 1915 Morse published a brochure which pointed in the same direction, namely promoting the use of soy as an oil crop in the Cotton Belt, see William Morse, *Soy Beans in the Cotton Belt* (Washington, DC: Government Printing Office, 1915).
9 Morse, Hendrick, *Illustrated Lecture*, 1–2; Anonymous, "The Soy Bean Industry in the South," *The American Food Journal* (January 1917): 54.
10 Roth, *Magic Bean*, 46–47.
11 U.S. Tariff Commission, *Survey of the American Soya-bean Oil Industry* (Washington DC: Government Printing Office, 1920), 10.
12 Soy is explicitly mentioned as one of the research topics for this trip, David Fairchild and Frank N. Meyer, "South China Explorations: Typescript, July 25, 1916–September 21, 1918": 1, U.S. Department of Agriculture, National Agricultural Library, call Number: aSB108.C6 M48, Internet Archive, accessed August 9, 2021, https://archive.org/details/CAT10662165Meyer-SouthChinaExplorations/CAT31091908. As for tofu being shipped to Morse, see ibid. December 31, 1917, 23.
13 Fairchild and Meyer, "South China Explorations." The journal was kept at BPI and updated every few months, often towards the end of the year. It contains transcripts of letters and additional remarks.
14 L.S. Palen, "The Romance of the Soya Bean," *Asia: Journal of the American Asiatic Society* 19 (January 1919): 73.
15 Fairchild and Meyer, "South China Explorations," September 21, 1918, 12.
16 U.S. Tariff Commission, *Survey*, 11.
17 Roth, *Magic Bean,* 49.
18 R. Douglas Hurt, *American Agriculture: A Brief History* (West Lafayette, IN: Purdue University Press, 2002), 221.
19 Oliver E. Baker, "Agricultural Regions of North America, Part IV: The Corn Belt," *Economic Geography* 3, no. 4 (October 1927): 464. DOI: 10.2307/140759.
20 John C. Hudson, *Making the Corn Belt: A Geographical History of Middle-Western Agriculture* (Bloomington, IN: Indiana University Press, 1994), 150–72.
21 Taylor, *Corn and Hog Surplus*, 92.

22 Jay C. Hackleman, "The Future of the Soybean as a Forage Crop," *Agronomy Journal* 16, no. 3 (1924): 232, https://doi.org/10.2134/agronj1924.00021962001600030016x; Arthur E. Grantham, *Soy Beans*, Delaware College Agricultural Experiment Station, Bulletin no. 96 (Newark, DE, 1912), 15–17.

23 Timothy Johnson, "Nitrogen Nation: The Legacy of World War I and the Politics of Chemical Agriculture in America, 1916–1930," *Agricultural History* 90, no. 2 (2016): 209–29, here 215, 224, https://doi.org/10.3098/ah.2016.090.2.209.

24 Dennis S. Nordin and Roy V. Scott, *From Prairie Farmer to Entrepreneur: The Transformation of Midwestern Agriculture* (Bloomington, IN: Indiana University Press, 2005), 55.

25 Nordin and Scott, *Prairie Farmer*, 67; Paul K. Conkin, *A Revolution Down on the Farm: The Transformation of American Agriculture since 1929* (Lexington, KY: University Press of Kentucky, 2009), 16; Hurt, *American Agriculture*, 230; Deborah K. Fitzgerald, *Every Farm a Factory: The Industrial Ideal in American Agriculture* (New Haven, CT: Yale University Press, 2003), 75–105.

26 Lanny C. Powell, "An Examination of Factors Influencing the Temporal-Spatial Diffusion of Soybean Production in Illinois, 1930–1968" (PhD diss., University of Illinois at Urbana-Champaign, 1971), 46, accessed July 1, 2022, https://www.proquest.com/docview/302464878/citation/D578163662324BECPQ/1.

27 Christine M. Du Bois, "Social Context and Diet: Changing Soy Production and Consumption in the United States," in *The World of Soy*, eds. Christine M. Du Bois, Chee-Beng Tan, and Sidney Mintz, 208–33, here 212 (Chicago, IL: University of Illinois, 2008); Powell, "An Examination," 46.

28 ASA, *Proceedings of the American Soybean Association*, vol. 1 (1928), 9–11, 39–42.

29 ASA, *Proceedings of the American Soybean Association*, vol. 1 (1928), 21.

30 "American Soybean Association, Constitution and By-Laws, [1925]," in American Soybean Association, *Proceedings of the American Soybean Association*, vol. 1 (1928), 15.

31 Figure 4.1 is based on U.S. Department of Agriculture, Crop Reporting Board, *Soybeans, Cowpeas, and Velvetbeans, by States, 1924–1953. Acreage, yield, production, price* (Washington, DC: USDA, 1957), 2.

32 USDA, *Soybeans, Cowpeas, and Velvetbeans*, 2–12.

33 Wolfgang Böhm, "Die Fixierung von elementarem Stickstoff durch die Wurzelknöllchen der Leguminosen: Zur Erinnerung an Hermann Hellriegels epochemachende Entdeckung im Jahre 1886." *Angewandte Botanik* 60 (1986): 1–5; Wolfgang Böhm, "Die Stickstoff-Frage in der Landbauwissenschaft im 19. Jahrhundert," *Zeitschrift für Agrargeschichte und Agrarsoziologie* 34 (1986): 31–54.

34 Hackleman, "The Future of the Soybean," 232; The issue was also raised in Piper and Morse's most famous publication on the soybean, Charles V. Piper and William Morse, *The Soybean* (New York, NY: McGraw-Hill Book Company, 1923), 66–71.

35 Morse, Hendrick, *Illustrated Lecture*, 8.

36 ASA Proceedings 1 (1928), 39.

37 Chicago Board of Trade, *The Story of Soybeans, Soybean Oil, Soybean Meal: Their Uses and Products*, (Chicago, IL: Chicago Board of Trade, 1951), 21–4; Bradley, "Domestic Production," 65–69; Forrestal, *The Kernel and the Bean*, 64.

38 Hackleman, "Future of the Soybean," 230–31; Piper and Morse, *The Soybean*, 1.

39 Robert W. Howell, "Golden Beans from China: Now Our No. 1 Cash Crop," in USDA, *Yearbook of Agriculture* (Washington, DC: 1975), 225–36, here 226.

40 Ladd Haystead and Gilbert C. Fite, *The Agricultural Regions of the United States* (Norman, OK: University of Oklahoma Press, 1955), 140–61.

41 Pinkett, "Records of the First Century," 41; Nelson Klose, *America's Crop Heritage: The History of Foreign Plant Introduction by the Federal Government* (Ames, IA: Iowa State College Press, 1950), 120–24.
42 Piper and Morse, *The Soybean*, 1.
43 Roth, *Magic Bean*, 64–68.
44 This is documented in ASA, *Proceedings of the American Soybean Association*, vol. 1 (1928). The publication provides information about the early meetings, and, in view of a lack of minutes, includes lectures given at earlier gatherings and other material relevant for the organization's short history.
45 *Four Men and the Soy*, NARA RG 33: Records of the Extension Service, 1888-2000, ARC Identifier 7217. The film documented the so-called Soy Day of 1925, which USDA had conducted at Ohio State University. For the classification system for soybeans, see U.S. Department of Agriculture, *Handbook of United States Standards for Soybeans. Effective September 1, 1926* (Washington, DC: Government Printing Office, 1928).
46 Klose, *America's Crop Heritage*, 122–23.
47 U.S. Department of Agriculture, Special Collections at the National Agricultural Library, "Dorsett-Morse Oriental Agricultural Exploration Expedition Collection," Series I: Journals (1928–1931), Introduction, 9, 13.
48 F.A. Wand, "Soil and Soybean Special," *The Staley Journal* (May 1927): 10–11; John F. Stover, *History of the Illinois Central Railroad* (New York, NY: Macmillan, 1975), 307.
49 William Morse, "The Present Outlook of the Soybean Industry in the United States," *American Soybean Association Proceedings* 1 (1928), 167–71.
50 Forrestal, *The Kernel and the Bean*, 60–64.
51 Stover, *History of the Illinois Central*, 306, see also "Thousands Visit Illinois Central Soy Bean Train," *The Daily Independent* [of Murphysboro, IL] (March 30, 1927): 1; similar wording in "Farm aid train here," *The Daily Independent* [of Murphysboro, IL] (March 19, 1927): 1; and "I[llinois] C[entral]: Soybean Special are Here." *Journal Gazette* [of Mattoon, IL] (April 7, 1927): 6.
52 Stover, *History of the Illinois Central*, 306; Angela Jordan, "The Educational Agricultural Trolley, 1911," *University of Illinois Archives Blog* (May 16, 2014), (accessed July 22, 2021, http://archives.library.illinois.edu/blog/the-educational-agricultural-trolley/; Hurt, *American Agriculture*, 257.
53 "Soybean Special to Carry Experts." *The Decatur Review* (March 11, 1927).
54 Hurt, *American Agriculture*, 256; On farms see Norwood A. Kerr, *The Legacy: A Centennial History of the State Agricultural Experiment Stations, 1887–1987* (Columbia, MO: Missouri Agricultural Experiment Station, University of Missouri-Columbia, 1987), 57; On the difficulties of educating farmers or their offspring, see Nordin and Scott, *Prairie Farmer*, 79–81.
55 "Soy bean train visits Decatur," *The Decatur Review* (April 5, 1927): 5. The railroad company provided at least three other experts in addition to Schwietert as the supervisor of the train (ibid.).
56 "Soy Bean Train Visited by Many People of Dixon," *Dixon Evening Telegraph* (April 19, 1927): 6; similar wording in "Farm Aid Train Here March 29," *Dixon Evening Telegraph*, March 19, 1927, 1 and "I[llinois] C[entral]: Soybean Special Here," *Journal Gazette* [of Mattoon, IL] (April 7, 1927): 6.
57 "Illinois Central: A Special Train to Aid Farmers," *The Daily Free Press* [of Carbondale, IL] (March 5, 1927): 1.
58 "[...] that the lowly bean is some day to become king in the corn belt of Illinois," in "Soy Bean Train Visited by Many People of Dixon," *Dixon Evening Telegraph*, April 19, 1927, 6.
59 USDA, *Soybeans, Cowpeas, and Velvetbeans*, 4, 15. In 1924, beans were harvested from only 25 percent of the 1,782,000 acres planted with soybeans. By

1930, this amount rose to a third (3 million acres were planted with soy, of which beans were harvested from about 1 million acres).

60 Forrestal, *The Kernel and the Bean*, 66; Tables 258 (Soybeans: Production in Specified Countries, 1924/5 to 1935/6) and 261 (Soybeans Crushed and Crude Oil Produced, 1925/6 to 1934/5) in U.S. Department of Agriculture, *Agricultural Statistics 1936*, (Washington, DC: Government Printing Office, 1936), 181–82.

61 Nordin and Scott, *Prairie Farmer*, 71.

62 U.S. Department of Agriculture, *Statistics of Fats, Oils, and Oleaginous Raw Materials,* Statistical Bulletin, no. 24 (Washington, DC: Government Printing Office, 1928), 8.

63 It was later renamed National Soybean Processors Association, Roth, *Magic Bean*, 175.

64 Forrestal, *The Kernel and the Bean*, 64.

65 Strand, *Soybean Production,* 5.

66 Strand, *Soybean Production*, 4; Ernest W. Grove, *Soybeans in the United States: Recent Trends and Present Economic Status* (Technical Bulletin No. 619, U.S. Department of Agriculture, Washington, DC: Government Printing Office, June 1938), 2–3.

67 William J. Morse, J.L. Cartter, "Improvements in Soybeans," *Yearbook of Agriculture for the Year 1937,* ed. U.S. Department of Agriculture (Washington, DC: Government Printing Office, 1937), 1159.

68 Strand, *Soybean Production,* 9.

69 "Soybeans are Salvation," *The Staley Journal* (July 1934): 17.

70 Strand, *Soybean Production,* 9.

71 Strand, *Soybean Production,* table 7 [after p. 24]. It is known that soybean oil was preferred in shortening over margarine. For Germany, such difference was difficult to come by, not least because the German term "Margarine" encompasses both products.

72 Grove, *Soybeans in the United States,* p. 13–6.

73 See Chapter 3 in this book. For the wide variety of possible uses for soybeans and byproducts, see Morse, Cartter, "Improvements in Soybeans," 1160.

74 Piper and Morse, *The Soybean*, 129–43; Edward J. Dies, *Soybeans: Gold from the Soil* (New York, NY: The Macmillan Company, 1943), 17; William Lockeretz, "Agricultural Diversification by Crop Introduction: The U.S. Experience with the Soybean," *Food Policy* 13 (1988): 159; Norman A. Turkish, "Commodities: High Finance in Soybeans," *Financial Analysts Journal* 17 (1961): 91–101.

75 Strand, *Soybean Production,* 20; Sybil Woodruff and Helen Klaas, *A Study of Soybean Varieties with Reference to their Use as Food* (USDA Agricultural Experiment Station Urbana, IL, Bulletin 443, 1938); Elizabeth Fuller Whiteman and Ellen Kingsley Keyt, *Soybeans for the Table* (Washington, DC: U.S. Government Printing Office, 1938); John William Lloyd and W.L. Burlison, *Eighteen Varieties of Edible Soybeans* (USDA Agricultural Experiment Station Urbana, IL, Bulletin 453, 1939).

76 Grove, *Soybeans in the United States,* 17, 22; As for scholarly attention, see Roth, *Magic Bean,* 86–117 (;) Ines Prodöhl, "Versatile and Cheap: A Global History of Soy in the first half of the Twentieth Century," *Journal of Global History* 8, no. 3 (2013): 161–63, https://doi.org/10.1017/S1740022813000375; Ines Prodöhl, "'A Miracle Bean:' How Soy Conquered the West, 1909–1950," *Bulletin of the German Historical Institute*, Washington, DC, 46 (Spring 2010): 113.

77 Mark R. Finlay, "Old Efforts at New Uses: A Brief History of Chemurgy and the American Search for Biobased Materials," *Journal of Industrial Ecology,* 7, 3/4 (2003), 33–46, https://doi.org/10.1162/108819803323059389.

78 Finlay, "Old efforts."
79 Mark R. Finlay, "The Industrial Utilization of Farm Products and By-products: The USDA Regional Research Laboratories," *Agricultural History,* 64, no. 2 (1990): 41–52; see also G.E. Hilbert, "Soybean Studies at the Northern Regional Research Laboratory," *Chemurgic Digest,* 7 (February 1948): 11–14.
80 Benson Ford Research Center, accessed March 23, 2022, http://www.thehenryford.org/research/soybeancar.aspx.
81 *Industrial Soya Protein,* ed. The Glidden Company (Chicago, IL [194?]).
82 J.W. Hayward, "Little Soybean," *Chemurgic Digest,* 2, 11 (1944). 155.
83 Grove, *Soybeans in the United States,* 24.
84 Walter W. Wilcox, *The Farmer in the Second World War,* Ames, IA: Iowa State College Press, 1947, 182–83; Chicago Board of Trade, *The Story of Soybeans, Soybean Oil, Soybean Meal: Their Uses and Products* (Chicago, IL: Chicago Board of Trade, 1951), 6; Booklet promoting soybean production among American farmers, The Missouri Soybean and Soil Fertility War Program, Agricultural Extension Service, Missouri College of Agriculture and the Alton Railroad Cooperation [194?].
85 See USDA, National Agricultural Statistics Service, QuickStats, crops, https://quickstats.nass.usda.gov/ (accessed February 23, 2022).
86 *The Fats and Oils Situation* 1 (March 1937): 1; Karl Brandt, "Production and consumption of fats and oils," *Annals of the American Academy of Political and Social Science* 225 (1943): 210–15.
87 In 1942, the Bureau of Agricultural Chemistry and Engineering conducted experiments with fuel made from organic fats and oils on vehicle and aircraft engines, NARA RG 16, General Correspondence 1942, Box 643, Fats-Oils-Waxes; see also Mark R. Finlay, "Old Efforts at New Uses," 33–46.
88 Brandt, *Production and Consumption*, 214; Robert M. Walsh, "Far Eastern Fats and Oils," *Far Eastern Survey,* 11, no 19 (September 21, 1942): 201–2.
89 Finlay, *Growing American Rubber,* 140, estimates that the United States and its Allies were cut off from 95 percent of their rubber supply after the fall of Singapore in February 1942. For needs in rubber in wartime on a global scale, see William G. Clarence-Smith, "The Battle for Rubber in the Second World War: Cooperation and Resistance," in *Global Histories, Imperial Commodities, Local Interactions,* ed. Jonathan Curry-Machado (Basingstoke: Palgrave Macmillan, 2013), 204–23.
90 Harvey A. Levenstein, *Paradox of Plenty: A Social History of Eating in Modern America* (New York, NY: Oxford University Press, 1993), 80–85, 294–5; T. Swann Harding, "Food, Agriculture, and the War," *Social Forces* 21 (1942): 94–100.
91 U.S. Department of Agriculture, Bureau of Agricultural Economics, *The Fats and Oils Situation* 52 (June 1941): 4; U.S. Office of Price Administration, *Quarterly Report* (Washington, DC: Government Printing Office 1942), 178; Meg Jacobs, *Pocketbook Politics: Economic Citizenship in Twentieth-Century America*, (Princeton, NJ: Princeton University Press, 2005), 190.
92 William Winders, *The Politics of Food Supply: U.S. Agricultural Policy in the World Economy* (New Haven: Yale University Press, 2009), 69–74; Wilcox, *The Farmer*, 184, 188.
93 *Soybeans, cowpeas, and velvetbeans, by States, 1924-1953*, USDA Statistical Bulletin, 211 (Washington, DC: U.S. Government Printing Office, 1957), 2; Strand, *Soybean Production*, 2.
94 "Company Annual Report," *The Staley Journal* (March 1944), 4–15, here 12.
95 L. LeMar Stephan, "Peanut Production in Southeastern United States," *Economic Geography* 21, no. 3 (July 1945): 183–91, https://doi.org/10.2307/141295.

96 "Peanut Butter Can Be Used as Cooking Fat." *The Washington Post* (January 20, 1939): 15; "More Peanut Products Assured Civilians." *The Wall Street Journal* (September 2, 1943), 2; "The Peanut: It Wins a Place as a Major Wartime Food." *The Wall Street Journal* (September 27, 1943), 1–6.

97 Jacobs, *Pocketbook Politics*, 179–219, 306–316; Meg Jacobs, "'How About Some Meat?': The Office of Price Administration, Consumption Politics, and State Building from the Bottom Up, 1941–1946," *The Journal of American History* 84, no. 3 (1997): 910–41.

98 The rationing was lifted successively and differed locally; butter and margarine remained part of the rationing system until November 1945. Joachim Bengelsdorf, *Die Landwirtschaft der Vereinigten Staaten von Amerika im Zweiten Weltkrieg* (St. Katharinen: Scripta Mercaturae-Verlag 1997), 124–30, and Levenstein, *Paradox of Plenty*, 95–96.

99 U.S. Office for Emergency Management, *Priorities in Force. War Production Board. An Alphabetical Listing of All Priorities Orders in the M, P, E, and L Series, Together with Miscellaneous Orders and Regulations Which Have Been Issued under the Priorities Power through March 31, 1942,* National government publication, [1942]; see also *Fats and Oils Situation* 60 (February 1942): 7 and 61/62 (April 1942), 5–8; [Auxier, Georg W.], *Industrial Mobilization for War. History of the War Production Board and Predecessor Agencies, 1940–1945* (New York, NY: Greenwood Press, 1969) [Reprint of the edition: Washington, DC: Government printing office, 1947]: 308–11.

100 Claude R. Wickard, USDA, to Donald M. Nelson, WPB (March 16, 1942), NARA RG 16, General Correspondence, 1942, Box 643, Fats-Oils-Waxes.

101 Priority orders M 59 (palm oil), M 60 (coconut oil, babassu oil, palm kernel oil, and other high lauric acid oils), and M 71 (fats and oils) in U.S. War Production Board, *Conservation Index and Substitution Guide: A Cross-reference of End Products with "L Limitation" and "M Conservation" Orders, Showing Substitution Possibilities,* (Washington, DC: National Government Publication, 1943): section 108; Wilcox, *The Farmer*, 195; Geoffrey Jones, *Beauty Imagined: A History of the Global Beauty Industry* (Oxford: Oxford University Press, 2010), 134.

102 Ines Prodöhl, "From Dinner to Dynamite: Fats and Oils in Wartime America," *Global Food History* 2, no. 1 (March 2016): 31–50, https://doi.org/10.1080/20549547.2016.1138366; Susan Strasser, *Satisfaction Guaranteed: The Making of the American Mass Market* (New York, NY: Pantheon Books, 1989), 229–62.

103 Strand, *Soybean Production*, 24.

104 Alvin A. Munn, "Production and Utilization of the Soybean in the United States," *Economic Geography* 26, no. 3 (1950): 223–234, here 224.

105 Strand, *Soybean Production,* 20.

106 *The Story of Soybeans,* 21–4; Walter W. Wilcox, *The Farmer in the Second World War* (Ames, IA: Iowa State College Press, 1947), 194–95; see also Brandt, *Production and Consumption*, 214.

107 H.J. Dutton, "History of the Development of Soy Oil for Edible Uses," *Journal of the American Oil Chemists' Society* 58, no. 3 (March 1981), 154–166, https://doi.org/10.1007/BF02582347; Warren H. Goss, "Processing Oilseeds and Oils in Germany," *Oil & Soap* 23, no. 8 (August 1946): 241–44. https://doi.org/10.1007/BF02696126.

108 Woodruff and Klaas, *A Study of Soybean,* 1938; Fuller Whiteman and Kingsley Keyt, *Soybeans for the Table*; Marion Julia Drown, *Soybeans and Soybean Products as Food* (Washington, DC: U.S. Government Printing Office, 1943); Lloyd and Burlison, *Eighteen Varieties of Edible Soybeans*; Dies, *Soybeans*, 48–53; *The Story of Soybeans*, 27.

109 Jacobs, *Pocketbook Politics*, 179–220, 306–16; Levenstein, *Paradox of Plenty*, 76–85, 292–95.

110 "Company Annual Report," *The Staley Journal* (March 1944), 4–15, here 13; Staley Manufacturing company. *The Miracle of Soy: The Story of a Revolutionary and Important Development in the History of American Foods*, (Decatur, IL: A.E. Staley Manufacturing company, 1944).

111 Demetria M. Taylor, *The Soy Cook Book* (New York, NY: Greenberg, 1944).

112 Strand, *Soybean Production*, 20.

113 Jacobs, *Pocketbook Politics*, 215.

114 *The Story of Soybeans*, 4.

115 S. McKee Rosen, *The Combined Boards of the Second World War: An Experiment in International Administration* (New York, NY: Columbia University Press, 1951), 191–92, dates the government interest in the global supply of food back to the late 1930s.

116 Transcript of the Lend-Lease Act (1941), accessed February 23, 2022, https://www.ourdocuments.gov/doc.php?flash=false&doc=71&page=transcript.

117 McKee Rosen, *Combined Boards*, 197; "Commodities within the Purview of the CFB," leaflet issued March 27, 1946, published in Eric Roll, *The Combined Food Board: A Study in Wartime International Planning* (Stanford, CA: Stanford University Press, 1956), 325.

118 War Cabinet, Combined Boards, Note by the Minister of Production, December 15, 1942, The National Archives CAB 66/32/45–46, accessed July 6, 2022, http://filestore.nationalarchives.gov.uk/pdfs/large/cab-66-32.pdf; see also U.S. Department of Agriculture, War Food Administration, *Report of the Combined Food Board: Progress of the Work from June 9, 1942, to December 31, 1944*, Washington, DC: USDA, 1945.

119 Bengelsdorf, *Die Landwirtschaft*, 281–301.

120 Claud F. Clayton and John D. Black, "Wartime Food Administration–U.S.A," *Annals of the American Academy of Political and Social Science* 225 (January 1943): 96–105, http://www.jstor.org/stable/1023542; McKee Rosen, *Combined Boards*, 223–32; Bengelsdorf, *Die Landwirtschaft*, 281–301.

121 *Agricultural Statistics*, 1943: 524; 1944: 563; 1945: 581; 1946: 709. The final amount for 1945 was higher because statistics for 1945 excluded shipments made for the UNRRA.

Epilogue

The Tofu Fighter

When I started researching the history of the soybean, a good friend gave me a little mascot, which has decorated my desk ever since. It is a Christmas tree decoration in the shape of a fat, pink pig holding a sign saying, "Tofu fighter." There is so much more truth in that little decoration than this book could have ever hoped to address. What has barely been addressed in the book, for instance, is how soybeans have been perceived at various times in history. Other imported commodities became centerpieces of national identity, for example, tea and cotton in Great Britain or coffee and sugar in the United States and Germany. That certainly did not happen with the soybean. Instead, there is much societal dispute around it, while production figures further rise.

In the early 1940s, the United States had about 5.6 million tons of soybeans at its disposal. Americans mainly used them as fodder for boosting meat production and as an oil resource to fight off war-related shortages in fat. Given that the crop had been introduced to the country only a few decades before and that it had not entered agricultural statistics until 1924, this increase is quite remarkable. What seems even more overwhelming, however, is the tremendous growth in worldwide soybean production in the years since. By 1961, world output in soybeans was already at 27 million tons. Of those, China produced only six million tons that served mainly national demand, while the United States accounted for the lion's share with nearly 20 million tons. In the following decades, new actors such as Brazil entered the market, although it took until 1990 for Brazil to also reach an output level of 20 million tons. In the same year, American farmers produced 52 million tons. About 20 years later, in 2011, soybean production in Brazil and the United States converged, and currently, these two countries produce nearly the same amounts: in 2020, the United States produced 113 million tons and Brazil 122 million tons of soybeans. The third region with a significantly high output level is Argentina, and combined, these three countries were jointly responsible for about 82 percent of global soy production, which currently lies at about 350 million tons. Other regions with noteworthy soy production are China, Paraguay, and Canada, but the crop is cultivated in many other places as well.[1]

The foundation for the present soybean production as well as the use of the tremendous amounts available worldwide were laid in the first half of the twentieth century. It was during this earlier period that the crop was commodified in a way it is still used today. Three-fourths of the soy currently produced is fed to animals, first and foremost to poultry and pigs, but also salmon, cattle, and others. Nevertheless, the FAO categorizes the soybean as an oil crop; in fact, it is considered to be "the most important oilcrop" worldwide.[2] Compared to the crop's value for feed and oil, worldwide interest in soy as human food is marginal. Only 2.6 percent of all soybeans is used in the production of tofu, while soybean milk accounts for 2.1 percent.[3]

These numbers illustrate that industrialized meat production is only possible with protein-rich concentrates like soybean meal. Also, margarine, shortening, cosmetics, and many other consumer products are based on the soybean—specifically its oil—and, finally, everything soft or creamy, from chocolate to leather, contains soy-based lecithin. This current use of soy was established and tested by German and American oil millers and farmers in the economically challenging years of the 1920s, 1930s, and 1940s. They turned soy into an industrial crop, meaning it has since been produced by and used in industrial farming, in addition to playing a major role in industrial fields as diverse as foods, chemicals, energy, paper and plywood production, printing, and many more. Thus, the crop's history helps us set the current globality into perspective and see the present soybean production as a continuity and expansion of earlier developments.

At the beginning of the twentieth century, Northeast China was the main supplier of soybeans worldwide. The region was characterized by quasi-colonial structures, as besides China, Russia and Japan also tried to tighten their grip on the region. Thus, soybeans were mainly traded by Japanese trading companies, first and foremost Mitsui. A long-globalized market with rapid means of communication and transportation allowed this company to offer soy as a cheap alternative to vegetable oil resources to oil mills in Europe. The early growth of the soybean industry was influenced more by shortages of oil for manufacturing and its relatively low price than by the need for the protein-rich byproduct of the milling process. Once in Europe, oil mills in Hamburg, Liverpool, Marseille, and Rotterdam processed the beans and channeled the oil into the production of margarine, shortages, and soap, among others. After initial hesitation and some experimentation, farmers in various regions of Europe found that the residue could be fed to pigs and chickens. Last but not least, dairy cows and cattle were fed with it too. And so the beans entered the food sector through the back door, as it were, in the form of sausage, chicken wings, and cutlets.

Earlier attempts to spread soy in Europe, for example in the late nineteenth century by Friedrich Haberlandt in Austria or Li Shizeng in France, were relevant in the context of public health and nutrition. Their goal was to provide a steadily growing population with sufficient and inexpensive food. With soybeans containing significant amounts of two macronutrients, fat and protein, many nutritionists and doctors believed they had found a solution to any food shortage. Yet, soybeans would not enter European markets as a foodstuff. They were difficult to digest and cooking them like other dried beans and peas—that is, soaking them in water and then boiling them—did not improve soybeans. Preparing the beans according to Asian eating habits seemed altogether too strange, and they were thus only eaten in times of need when other foods became scarce.

It was in the Weimar Republic that soybeans entered the secondary food sector on a large scale, and even though they remained almost invisible to consumers, they became the backbone of modern food production. Initially, German oil millers imported the beans to serve the country's high demand for fats, but with soybeans containing comparatively little oil, large amounts of residue found use as fodder. With this dual use, soy became firmly established in the production of margarine and meat. Through technological innovation, German oil millers also found a way to produce the sought-after softener lecithin.

Americans, on the other hand, did initially not suffer shortages of fat but began growing soybeans to help repair depleted soils. It was only in the years to come that American farmers and oil millers combined forces also to produce mainly fat, feed, and some food. This book has identified farmers and oil millers as driving forces behind the commodification of the soybean in the Western world. In addition, the crop's westward movement was invoked by political decisions, and those were driven by war or economic crises. The Russo-Japanese War and the First World War were highly influential for soybeans entering Europe to a larger degree than ever before. In the United States, the agricultural crisis of the 1920s, the Great Depression, and eventually the Second World War were decisive for American farmers beginning to plant and make use of the crop.

During the First World War, almost all the warring parties in Europe and the United States discovered the residue from oil production for human consumption and tried to adapt it to their customs. Soybean cake could no longer be used to make Asian dishes, as those were based on preparing the whole bean; nevertheless, the residue could be processed further into a flour useful for mixing with grain flours in the production of bread or as an alternative to Sunday roast. Soybean flour was not popular among the population because it was not very tasty, difficult to process, and quickly turned rancid. At some places in Germany, whole beans also appeared on the market, which did not make things any easier. In the United States, special recipe books were published that clearly declared soybeans as a substitute product to overcome shortages in fats and meats.

At the war's end, soybeans vanished quickly from European and American tables, but not from their markets. In the interwar period, Germany rose to become the largest importer of whole soybeans worldwide. With the Treaty of Versailles Germany had not only lost its colonies and thus its "place in the sun" but also direct access to tropical raw materials, such as the fruits of the oil and coconut palms. Chinese soybeans were a cheap alternative which also offered German oil millers the idea of being less dependent on other European powers.

Americans kept an eye on the soybean too, as a crop to be grown on American farms, however, not as a commodity imported from Manchuria. The agricultural crisis that hit the country in the wake of the war led to a few Midwestern farmers discovering the soybean as an alternative crop to oats, corn, and wheat. These efforts remained rather small-scale and it was not until after the Great Depression that soybeans gained significantly more prominence in American agriculture than they had had before. In the 1930s, numerous economic and political changes known as the New Deal got off the ground under the presidency of Franklin D. Roosevelt. Agricultural measures introduced in this context did not address the soybean but nevertheless helped it due to restrictions on other crops. Another attempt at renewing the American economy, albeit initiated more by private actors, was chemurgy. The movement was a loose association of industrialists, chemists, and agriculturalists with the shared goal to make the United States less dependent on foreign raw materials. They promoted experiments with plant-based raw materials both to boost domestic agriculture and to guard against future shocks to the world economy. The New Deal and chemurgy were the main stimulators for the expanding soybean cultivation in the United States in the 1930s.

In Germany, too, efforts were made after the Great Depression to make the country more independent of the world market. The initial steps were taken in the Weimar Republic to reduce imports of oilseeds, including soybeans. The approach played into the hands of the National Socialists, who came to power in 1933. They sought autarky to prepare the people for war and the blockades in food and raw material supplies that would accompany it. For several resources, this goal was highly impractical; two crucial ones were fats and meats. Among the *Volk*, the Nazi leadership propagandistically sold the dilemma of dependence on imports of these products as the "fat gap" or "fat and protein gap." As early as 1935, customer lists for fats were introduced to curb consumption. Only three years later, the so-called fat card was issued, which was the first food rationing in the country. This card regulated exactly how much fat or oil a person according to race, age, profession, and sex should receive per week.

Nevertheless, Germany could not stop imports of oilseeds altogether, and, in 1936, the Nazi government boosted the import of soybeans by concluding a trade agreement with the Japanese puppet state of Manchukuo. This and several follow-up agreements stipulated that Manchukuo would supply hundreds of thousands of tons of soybeans annually in exchange for German heavy industrial goods. It was a losing proposition, but one that was maintained until the invasion of the Soviet Union. Simultaneously, officials and experts on nutrition in Nazi Germany tried to bring soybean cultivation closer to the Reich. As cultivation trials failed to yield noteworthy results, their focus shifted to climatically more favorable countries in southeastern Europe. Chemical magnate IG Farben initiated the crop's cultivation in Romania, Bulgaria, and Hungary in the 1940s, but yields fell far short of imports from Asia.

Fats and oils were also in short supply on the other side of the Atlantic, and the measures taken by the U.S. government to get to grips with the problem were similar to those taken in Nazi Germany. With the entry into the war and the fighting in the Pacific, the United States was cut off from tropical oil crop supplies. For this reason, the government promoted soybean production among American farmers. This was done so extensively that by the end of the 1940s Americans were already the world leaders in soybean cultivation.

During the war, the U.S. government channeled the beans primarily into margarine production. Oil mills also produced soybean flour and promoted it to American housewives as a substitute for cooking, frying, and baking. Despite all the advertising, among other means through recipe books, however, families remained skeptical of the flour. The new product was too unknown, quickly turned rancid, and there was little to be done with it. The name soy flour raised expectations of a cereal product, but it was anything but. Only soldiers were supplied with a small amount of soy flour, similar to the German Wehrmacht. It found entry into K rations, pork link sausages, and macaroni for the U.S. Army.[4] It is therefore not surprising that soy flour soon disappeared from American tables after the end of the war. American newspapers cheered that the period of deprivation was over and that it was no longer necessary to consume soy flour. Domestically, the beans were now used just as before the war. In addition, they were shipped in tremendous quantities to help fight off hunger in postwar Asia and Europe.[5] With worldwide economies in recovery, Americans discovered new markets for their beans. At the end of the war, Manchukuo ceased to exist. Politically and economically unsettled, the region was not able to restore its former soybean production, and the foundation of the People's Republic of China in 1949 hindered trade relations with Europe further. U.S. soy producers were eager to fill the gap.

Thanks to the lobbying efforts of the ASA, the governmental subsidy measures initiated during the war continued thereafter and so soybean production rose further.[6] During the Korean War (1950–1953), U.S. government farm policies raised and stabilized soybean prices, again leading to an increase in production. However, ever-increasing soybean production led to the search for new markets and outlets for the surplus. It is in the specific context of the 1950s and beyond that further research is needed to fully understand the global impacts of rising soybean production in the United States.

In the mid-1970s, for example, the USDA wrote in its yearbook:

> By 1973, soybeans had become our No. 1 cash crop, the leading export commodity, the major alternative crop of midwestern and southern farmers, the world's most effective producer of protein per acre, and the hope of starving millions for a better diet.[7]

This quote opens for more questions than the text from which it is taken answers, and these questions reach far beyond American soybean production alone. In fact, by the early 1970s, the soybean was the "No. 1 cash crop" in American agriculture, meaning it was mainly grown to sell and earn money. Only a decade earlier, in 1960, soy still had ranked fourth in value after corn, hay, and wheat. Back then, the crop's production value was at 1.18 billion U.S. dollars while those for corn at 3.9 billion U.S. dollars. In the following decade, soy production rose in quantity and value, so much so that by 1970 it ranked second after corn. At 5.5 billion U.S. dollars in value, corn was significantly higher than soy, which was at 3.2 billion U.S. dollars. What made the USDA nevertheless consider soybeans being the country's no. 1 cash crop was that it left the farm to be sold. Corn was a staple or subsistence crop, grown to meet farmers' own need for feed. Soy, on the other hand, was grown to sell for profit.

In a wider economic sense, only the oil truly left the farm as the meal eventually returned to the farm in the form of livestock feed. By that time almost all soybeans were harvested and then sold, and hardly any farmer kept beans for hay or grazing. American farmers along with oil millers (or crushers, as they were called by then) and margarine producers certainly had an interest in keeping this business turning as much as possible. The ever-rising production numbers provided above testify that these people, and potentially others besides, were quite successful in doing so.

How precisely did they do that? And who were "they"? Who exactly was involved in what anthropologist Christine Du Bois called "the soy industry"? She came up with the term in lack of an alternative to describe the group of actors involved in the soy-related agribusiness, which besides farmers was composed of companies dealing with the production, processing, product formulation, marketing, and distribution of soy and products based on it.[8] Other scholars also made attempts in capturing that industry. By following the biography of Dwayne Andreas and his engagement in big soybean players such as Cargill and ADM, Matthew Roth provided some insight into how the soybean business evolved in the 1950s and 1960s.[9] Still, there is more to explore regarding the composition and formulation of the soy industry in the United States and the implications between domestic agriculture, global business, and international politics.

While soybeans meant money to a variety of businesses, it is less known what the beans meant to their customers, including American farmers who bought back soybean-based fodder. In addition, it is less known what the beans meant for the animals fed with it. With the "world's most effective producer of protein per acre," the author quoted above addressed the worldwide use of soybeans as feed but left open what that meant. The increase in soybean production had a worldwide knock-on effect on global consumption patterns: more concentrated feed meant declining prices for meat, which then led to a rise in the consumption of chicken, pork, and beef.[10] My little pink Tofu fighter comes to mind. Another example is the large breasts of male chickens, or broilers, which have become an all-purpose ingredient in Western diets. To help these chickens to grow such oversized breast muscles, protein-rich concentrates are needed, and, in fact, the lion's share of today's soybean meal is fed to chickens. Today, soybean cake accounts for around 70 percent of the global production of protein meals. Besides poultry, it is used in the production of beef, pork, sheep and goat meat, and fish.

According to a recent study on the current use of soybeans, it seems likely that in the second half of the twentieth century, the growth in soy production was primarily driven by the demand for soy cake for feed, and hence by the growing demand for animal-based products.[11] That would be a departure from earlier periods, when in Europe and the United States the bean's economic value lay in the oil it contained, while a market for the protein-rich byproduct first needed to be found. Nevertheless, the increasing consumption of meat was followed by a rising need for fats as well, as one important use of soy oil is as fat sold to fast-food restaurants for deep-fat frying. Historians have not yet fully understood the correlation between soybeans and changing eating habits worldwide, particularly regarding the increase in meat intake. Less known is also the relation between agricultural policies, public health, and rising soybean production in the twentieth and twenty-first centuries in general.

Finally, there is the "hope of starving millions for a better diet" mentioned in the quote above which raises further questions. The author addresses shipments of soybean-based products to fight off hunger abroad. Likewise, the ASA is proud to have played a significant role in American food aid to the world in the 1950s and 1960s. However, it seems that further research is needed to understand how and why the soybean contributed to relieving worldwide food shortages at these and later times.

Relief shipments were made possible under the Agricultural Trade Development and Assistance Act of 1954, which is also known as Public Law 480 (PL 480). The law authorized the exchange of excess agricultural commodities for foreign currency, and the aid system that evolved on the basis of this law intended to rectify the situation of the domestic grain surplus, first and foremost wheat. In addition, soybean oil was also shipped abroad in large quantities under PL 480. While the soybean industry is proud to have played a significant role in fighting hunger, scholars make the implicit or explicit reproval that PL 480 only helped to grow this industry even larger. Some have shown that the law had "an indirect, but effective influence on the increase in soybean acreage through the disposal of surplus oil," and that the program "helped maintain favorable market prices for soybeans."[12] Another study estimated that in 1959 the program financed four out of every five dollars' worth of wheat exports and nine out of every ten dollars' worth of soybean oil exports.[13]

Again, the overproduction of soybean oil in the second half of the twentieth century points to the fact that the beans had departed from their initial use as a resource of fat. In the first half of the twentieth century, soybean crushers had pushed soy almost completely into secondary food uses. When domestic markets for fats matured after the war, the same companies suddenly needed new outlets for the oil, not the feed. Perhaps PL 480 was just the perfect vehicle to keep production levels rising? In any case, the correlation between American agriculture, business, and international politics, and their national and global implications, still needs further research.

Under the Kennedy administration, PL 480 turned into a program called Food for Peace, in which soybeans also found entry. This time the focus lay on proteins, not oil, and once again historians have not fully understood whether this helped to grow and market even more soybeans or to feed malnourished children in developing countries. There are hardly any studies analyzing the relation between the extent of these shipments and possible soybean (over-)production in the United States, and to what degree this ratio has changed over time. In the early 2000s, shipments of soybean products as part of U.S. food programs did not exceed more than half a million tons. This amount seems small considering the current output of soybean production. Maybe the talk about helping children was bigger than the actual aid?[14]

In more recent years, much has been said about soy in today's societies—for example, about deforestation and its consequences for the climate and the environment, genetically modified soy, the use of soy meal in livestock fattening, and not least about healthy and unhealthy lifestyles. These debates are important because they help us understand how and why humans exploit the planet in the way they do.[15] My book has contributed to them insofar as it has studied how the crop found entry into modern industry and agriculture. I have identified the driving forces behind the emergence of soy on global markets in the first half of the twentieth century. Scholars in the humanities and social scientists should further engage in the debate to understand what and who has driven the global increase in soy production in the decades since.

Notes

1 FAOSTAT, "Crops and Livestock Products," accessed June 30, 2022, https://www.fao.org/faostat/en/#data/QCL.
2 FOA Term portal, accessed June 30, 2022, https://www.fao.org/faoterm/viewentry/en/?entryId=160036.
3 Walter Fraanje, Tara Garnett, "Soy: Food, Feed, and Land Use Change" (Foodsource: Building Blocks). Food Climate Research Network, University of Oxford, 2020.
4 Christine M. Du Bois, "Social Context and Diet: Changing Soy Production and Consumption in the United States," in *The World of Soy,* eds. Christine M. Du Bois, Chee-Beng Tan, and Sidney Mintz, 208–33, here 215 (Chicago: University of Illinois, 2008).
5 Du Bois, "Social Context and Diet," 216.
6 ASA, "Our Timeline," accessed June 30, 2022, https://soygrowers.com/about/timeline/.

7 Robert W. Howell, "Golden Beans from China: Now Our No. 1 Cash Crop," in USDA, *Yearbook of Agriculture,* 225–36, here 225 (Washington, DC: National Government Publication, 1975).

8 Du Bois, "Social Context and Diet," 209.

9 Matthew Roth, *Magic Bean: The Rise of Soy in America* (Lawrence: University Press of Kansas, 2018), 180–99.

10 A rather short attempt at bringing together food, technology, and business in the American culture has been made by Roger Horowitz, *Putting Meat on the American Table: Taste, Technology, Transformation* (Baltimore, MD: Johns Hopkins University Press, 2006).

11 Fraanje, Garnett, "Soy: Food, Feed, and Land Use Change," 8.

12 Lanny C. Powell, "An Examination of Factors Influencing the Temporal-Spatial Diffusion of Soybean Production in Illinois, 1930–1968" (PhD diss., University of Illinois at Urbana–Champaign, 1971), 59, accessed July 1, 2022, https://www.proquest.com/docview/302464878/citation/D578163662324BECPQ/1; Du Bois, "Social Context and Diet," 216.

13 Dan Morgan, *Merchants of Grain* (New York, NY: Viking, 1979), 101–2.

14 Du Bois, "Social Context and Diet," 217.

15 Among others, Pablo Lapegna, *Soybeans and Power: Genetically Modified Crops, Environmental Politics, and Social Movements in Argentina* (New York, NY: Oxford University Press, 2016); Gustavo De L.T. Oliveira and Susanna B. Hecht, eds., *Soy, Globalization, and Environmental Politics in South America* (London; New York, NY: Routledge, 2018); *Raising Resistance*, documentary by Bettina Borgfeld and David Bernet (Germany, Switzerland: Joint Venture, 2011); *Neue Zürcher Zeitung, Folio* 253, August 2012 (special issue "Soya").

Index

Note: Page references in italics denote figures and with "n" endnotes.